The Portrait of a Complete Woman

A guide to woman's personality development

Prof. Avinash Chandra M.S.

PUSTAK MAHAL®
DELHI • MUMBAI • BANGALORE • PATNA • HYDERABAD

J-3/16 , Daryaganj, New Delhi-110002
☎ 23276539, 23272783, 23272784 • *Fax:* 011-23260518
E-mail: info@pustakmahal.com • *Website:* www.pustakmahal.com

Sales Centre

- 10-B, Netaji Subhash Marg, Daryaganj, New Delhi-110002
  ☎ 23268292, 23268293, 23279900 • *Fax:* 011-23280567
  E-mail: rapidexdelhi@indiatimes.com
- **Hind Pustak Bhawan**
  6686, Khari Baoli, Delhi-110006
  ☎ 23944314, 23911979

Branches

Bengaluru: ☎ 080-22234025 • *Telefax:* 080-22240209
E-mail: pustak@airtelmail.in • pustak@sancharnet.in
Mumbai: ☎ 022-22010941, 022-22053387
E-mail: rapidex@bom5.vsnl.net.in
Patna: ☎ 0612-3294193 • *Telefax:* 0612-2302719
E-mail: rapidexptn@rediffmail.com
Hyderabad: *Telefax:* 040-24737290
E-mail: pustakmahalhyd@yahoo.co.in

ISBN 978-81-223-0071-0

Edition: 2011

Printed at : **Unique Colour Cartoon, Delhi**

About the Author

Being in the teaching profession for last 25 years, at one of the most reputed and oldest medical colleges and Hospitals of India, writing came naturally to him. He has taught more than three thousands medical graduates uptil now.

His other areas of interest include psycho sexual medicine, ultimate health state (supreme/ultra health programme for busy executives), self-help personality improvement courses for men and women including special emphasis on masterly human behaviour.

He has authored several hundred articles which have found place in reputed national dailies and magazines in the country.

In recent years he has authored few very well received books for busy executives and working women which have been published by some of the most reputed publishing houses of India. Many national dailies and periodicals have published rave reviews about his work.

The best seller to his credit are:

a. **Nissantan Dampati**

b. **Hey Busy Man: Wait a Minute**

c. **Relaxation:** Complete & Effective

Other Books on the pipeline:

a. **The Relationships:** Marriage, love and sex - Problems & Suggestions

b. **Images & Impressions:** Techniques of Masterly Human behaviour

c. **Life is Beautiful Indeed,** Learn to enjoy it

His current interest goes with the motivational workshops, lectures, seminars for people from different professions on the topics of high priority areas (based on his books), as pilot faculty in the ANDE. He has conducted several inhouse courses in different parts of India for various institutions uptil now.

Dr. Avinash Chandra M.S.
ANDE (Academy of Natural Development & Personal Excellence)
C/o Jeevan Prakash Hospital
Champa Bagh, Nai Sarak, Lashkar,
Gwalior, M.P. India
Ph.: (0751) 320623, 328623 *Fax:* (0751) 323844

Dedication

The first woman Prime Minister of India

Late Smt. Indira Gandhi

who ruled the hearts of Indian masses
through her charming, dynamic
and energetic personality

—Avinash

DELHI PRESS PATRA PRAKASHAN LTD

ALIVE Political-Social Monthly (English) ● **WOMAN'S ERA** Fortnightly for Women (English) ● **SARITA** Family Fortnightly (Hindi) ● **GRIH SHOBHA** Women's Monthly (Hindi, Gujarati, Kannada & Marathi) ● **MUKTA** Social Monthly for Youth (Hindi) ● **CHAMPAK** Colourful Magazine for Young Children (Fortnightly in Hindi, English, Gujarati, Kannada & Marathi) ● **SUMAN SAURABH** Monthly for Adolescents (Hindi) ● **SARAS SALIL** Fortnightly for the masses (Hindi)

Ph : 526311, 525677

Delhi Press Building
E-3 Jhandewala Estate
Rani Jhansi Marg
New-Delhi-110055
●
Grams : DELHIPRESS
Tlx : 31-63053 DEPR IN
Fax : 7525020

I have had the pleasure to go through this voluminous work of Dr. Avinash Chandra Agarwal. Women today are trying to find a new identity for themselves. After liberating themselves from the four corners of the house, they are now vibrant units of the society and each of them tries to put her best face forward.

This book is an attempt to help a woman achieve this and the author has definitely worked hard on the subject. I hope that readers will find it both useful and enjoying.

Sd/-
Paresh Nath
Managing Editor
Delhi Press Group of Magazines

A book that may help today's overworked woman in a stressed out society to deal with herself, her home environment and her work situation could be very useful for not just the working woman or the home-maker, but also for men – who contribute substantially to her environment, both at home and at work. I look forward to reading Dr. Avinash Chandra's "The Portrait of a Complete Woman".

Sd/-

Antara Dev Sen
Senior Editor
Hindustan Times
(Life & Style)

HINDUSTAN

ALOK MEHTA
EXECUTIVE EDITOR (NEWS)

Recently I have seen one Bestselling European book advising women on how to hold on to their blokes. There is no doubt that relationships are built on friendship, companionship and mutual support. Therefore this book "The Portrait of a Complete Woman" will certainly help not only Indian society but world community to understand woman, to give her proper place and respect in family, love with life-partners and other friends.

I am also confident this remarkable book will help Indian woman to be more perfect and successful in life. Western societies are still fighting for the rights of women, but they are not aware that Indian woman had very special and respected place thousands years back. They use to take decisions about family, land and properties. Man is not complete without the woman. I hope this book will inspire millions of Indians to understand inside of a woman.

Sd/-
Alok Mehta
Executive Editor
Dainik Hindustan

SATURDAYTIMES

Here's a man writing about women not from a chauvinist male viewpoint, but from a sympathetic female angle. Makes interesting reading, with its straight talk, practical advice and acceptance, rather than outright rejection of many societal stereotypes.

Sd/-
Vinita D. Nangia
Editor,
Saturday Times
The Times of India

Contents

Preface

THE *woman* is probably the most beautiful creation of God. It is a great thing to be a woman. There is nothing like being a woman because it is she who always hogs the limelight, gets the attention, love and care from others.

The *woman* sometimes as wife, mother, sister, daughter, and, often, as a lover has many roles to play in her lifetime. The list goes on. She becomes sister-in-law, mother-in-law and grandmother as time passes on.

It is very difficult to say with certainty which is the most important role for a lady. But it is true that every role has got different expectations, different responsibilities. People expect you to play the 'perfect role model', they want from you almost a flawless performance. No compromises. Everybody around you expects from you the perfection—the perfect wife, perfect mother, perfect cook, perfect bed partner, ideal colleague or a working woman earning a handsome take-home salary. And, at the top of that, you are supposed to look great, young, attractive and desirable with full feminine charms; always smiling, never to complain for anything.

Roles roll on in front of you, in quick succession. In fact, you have to play many of them simultaneously at any given point of time. This is what people expect from you. That is how the 'society' paints the "portrait of a complete woman". The word 'society' of course represents the persons close to you—your father, brother, husband, colleagues, friends and relatives.

Expectations are high, and obstacles are many, problems are endless. And, surrounded by all this is poor "you". Nobody has got the time to think about you. That, what you feel about yourself, about the expectations and responsibilities placed on you. Tell me. Are you living in this world simply to fulfil everybody's expectations? Or, do you want to relate to this world as per your own thinking, interpretations and feelings, to live a life as per your wishes and choices, feel happy and contented?

In a family, it is the homemaker who is always in the commanding position, a centre-point around which rest everything revolves. It is she around whom the intricated fabrics of a happy and healthy family are woven.

It is beyond doubt that in the coming 21st century the woman will acquire more powers, and will play an important role in both society and the nation at large. So, do not feel yourself handicapped if you are a woman; instead, you should be proud of being born so. Your time has come. It is up to you now, how well you play your cards. This is the thing which is going to decide what you can get in life—whether love, care, happiness, respect and attention; or, the taunts, criticism, brickbats and adverse comments. It all depends upon you.

This book primarily aims at making you a successful, confident and perfect woman to face this world. It attempts to mould you in the role of *today's woman,* the *Complete Woman,* who loves accomplishments and enjoys success. She is in perfect harmony with the different phases of life, and afraid of nothing what may come.

How to Make Best Use of This Book

I am fully convinced of the fact that every woman has got an inherent quality of becoming perfect and successful in her life. There is always vast scope for improvement and betterment in one's personality. But, unfortunately, many ladies don't succeed in life. They don't utilize their full potential and so lead a miserable and self-pitying life. What prevents them from becoming the perfect and complete? What should they do to achieve this distinction?

When you buy this book, make sure you are not doing so for entertainment purpose. Because, you shall be completely disappointed from that point of view, as you will not be finding anything entertaining in it. It is solely written with the purpose to help you improve your behaviour, thinking process, working and interaction with other people, your physical well-being, fitness level, and, of course, enhance your feminine charms. In other words, to make you perfect in the art of dealing with the society and the world at large, and develop a pleasing and magnetic personality as a "Complete Woman" liked by all, denounced by none.

I have no intention to write about the most famous and talked about women of India or of the world. Instead, I wish to talk about you, a grown-up young woman of average middle class family, who is well educated, married or single, maybe working or a simple housewife.

Read this book carefully of whatever age you may be—whether in your twenties or forties, no problem. Age is immaterial because we are all trying to become perfect. This trial has to go endlessly because perfection is an art which is so very difficult to master in one's lifetime. In fact, none of us is perfect. That is why I am saying age is no criterion. You can always try honestly at any age. But, of course, honesty and sincerity is must. Half-hearted or casual approach will certainly lead you towards frustration and disappointment. So, be careful about that.

You will enjoy the things if you go through the book chapterwise, i.e. read a chapter then give a gap of few days. During this gap, you simply allow the thoughts to percolate deeply in your mind. Then, again read the same chapter. Start the next chapter only after a few days' gap. This method will ensure the complete grasp of the ideas and thoughts by your mind.

It is very likely that at places you may not agree with my ideas or suggestions, you may have an altogether contrary view. But, this shall not create any problem between us. You can always move on to the next point leaving behind the point where you differed. After a gap of few days re-read that controversial point, which you have marked with pencil. Chances are that you may not differ this time.

At some places problems may arise because I don't intend to be traditional or conservative in handling of this lively topic. It may sound completely unconventional or rebellious sort. But, believe me, it is not the intention at all to sound rebellious. It all appears so because of our conservative and narrow-minded approach since centuries.

Read this book with open mind and, of course, with the intention to give a proper trial to the ideas and thoughts contained in it, which are innovative, purposeful and scientific, based upon the real facts of life.

So then, **best of luck.** Go ahead.

Introduction

ACCORDING to one theory of the evolution of the mankind, God created **HAWAA** from one rib of **ADAM,** because Adam had complained to the God that he felt lonely at times, and he wanted some company with whom he could play, talk, share his feelings and enjoy. And, the matter of sex came later on when Hawaa had eaten that forbidden fruit (prohibited apple). Anyway, through generations, with the evolution, with the flourishing of various cultures, things have changed while passing through several millennia.

The history of human evolution, through various civilizations like Sindhu valley, Nile river and others, shows that the woman has always played a major role in the development of all these civilizations.

Going by the Hindu mythology (Puranas, Upanishads, Vedas, Ramayana, Mahabharata and many other authentic old and recent books), one thing again stands out clearly that the woman has always played a key role in the family and society.

India has a great cultural heritage and probably the oldest and most developed than any other country of the world. The legendary Indian women like Devi Sita and Radha have played a great role in shaping the psyche of the Indian woman since ages. And, India being a religious country, they (Devi Sita and Radha) were always seen as ideals for an average Indian woman. Apart from them, the Indian history from Vedic period onwards is replete with characters like Yashoda Maa (mother of Lord Krishna), Maa Parwati (wife of Bhagwan Shiva), Maa Laxmi (wife of Lord Vishnu) and so on, which have influenced the psyche of Indian women. In the course of time, they no more remained as human beings but acquired the status of Goddesses whom we worship today.

From the more recent history, Rani Laxmibai for her exemplary courage and patriotism, Maharani Padmini of Mewad for her beauty and high moral values of a married Indian woman, Kasturba Gandhi for her model role of true life partner of Father of the Nation Mahatma Gandhi, and Indira Gandhi for her wisdom, courage, administrative acumen and concerns for India, the way she led the country through

1971 Indo-Pak war, are among the lots who have moulded the Indian woman's psyche considerably.

Very often we quote their examples. And, it's no exaggeration to say that thinking (psyche) of a common Indian woman is impregnated by images of these legendary women of our past. In fact, at all times, present or past, there remain certain legends which are considered as idols by the common masses, and we are no exception to that rule. We are also influenced by role models.

When looking around at the local level, we also come across many women who became successful and got what they aspired for despite the constraints; those who have fought the injustice for the comforts of their family, children; and, those who did not succumb to pressure despite all odds. They may not have acquired the national fame, they may not have reached the headlines of national dailies, they may not have been awarded Nobel Prize or Padamshree. But, even then they are quoted and recognised in the society as persons who have blazed new trails and set new examples. They are respected by their friends, acquaintances, relatives and the society at large.

My idea of a complete woman has got nothing to do with a celebrity status or recognition by the media or government. I don't want to perpetuate that kind of idea at all. Instead, the idea is that you think, aspire, behave and interact in manner so that you are respected, recognised and quoted by your family members, friends and acquaintances, and the society at large. Neither I wish that you copy somebody (read celebrity) because a copy always remains a copy, and will, anyway, be identified as a copy. Society never likes the imitations or copies. They respect and honour the originals. Only the originals, nothing short of that. So, no imitations please.

And why not be original? What you don't have which these celebrities had.You have everything. You have got the brain, heart, eyes, ears, hands, feet and rest other parts like any celebrity. Maybe, the colour of your skin is not that much fair, or your eyes are not blue coloured, or your hair may not be that long to touch your knees, or you may not be as much beautiful as some of them. But does that really make a difference? So, what are you afraid of? What are you waiting for?

1

It is a Great Feeling to be a Woman

SINCE ages the poets, novelists, painters, sculptors and musicians have very tenderly loved their main theme, "the woman". They have also handled it **with great care.** Look at the wall paintings of Ajanta Ellora or lively sculptures of Khajuraho or Konark temples. You will see how beautifully the woman has been depicted in various artistic styles.

We come across many shades of a woman's personality in the masterpieces of renowned Indian and foreign writers, like Rabindra Nath Tagore, Sharat Chandra, Bankim Chandra, Vimal Mitra, Munshi Prem Chand, Shakespeare, Leo Tolstoy, Maxim Gorki and so on.

The Sanskrit poet, Mahakavi Kalidas, the famous Hindi poets like Jai Shankar Prasad, Bihari, Ras Khan—in fact, the list is endless—also have portrayed so vividly and beautifully the various aspects of a woman's personality in their poems.

Have you ever thought why so many artists, painters, poets, and other great literary writers have made the woman their central character? Yes, I agree that they have also included the man, children, nature and society into their work. But, still the woman has remained the central theme for poets and artists.

The answer to the question which I have posed to you is simple: without woman, any art creation appears incomplete and dull. For an art work to appear natural and complete, the inclusion of a feminine character is must. For artists, it must have been impossible to think of something else which could be as fascinating, attractive and magnetic in its presence as a woman. So, the choice ultimately narrowed down to her, and it has continued to remain so since ages.

Look at the beauty of the fact that since the dawn of civilization, the woman has remained the central theme. And, despite her being the central character of many great literary works, paintings and sculptures, the woman could not be described in her fullness, wholeness. Isn't it strange? Every time you see a new painting by an accomplished artist, showing the female as central character, you feel, "Yes, this angle I could not see earlier". Similar is the ease of any good story or novel which gives the impression that it has portrayed a new shade of the woman's personality. This feeling is same for men and women viewers alike.

In fact, the collage of a woman's personality is so vast that it is difficult, very difficult to put it exactly in words or in any known shape. Endless is the range of her characterisation.

Childhood — Teenage

Naturally, every woman after a certain age, that is after the puberty, becomes aware of her special status in the society When you were young, school-going, you used to play with your friends, boys and girls alike, without discrimination. You used to run, did the cycle race, played badminton, hockey

and what not, without bothering for anything. But gradually as you grew up, you were surprised that people around you had started looking at you from a different angle. Their main attention turned on how you look. Your "body-look" and "face-look" have suddenly become more important for them. It did not interest them what you can do with that body—how can you run, jump, cook, study, score marks, or do other things. Instead, they used to say: "How beautiful you look, how shapely have your body become, how attractive your face has become, how charming you look in salwar suit or jeans top!"

All these words—beautiful, charming, shapely, attractive—sounded quite strange and awkward to you. As a matter of fact, you never thought about yourself from that angle at all, till now. This was a complete surprise to you. But slowly, slowly you tried to understand the real meaning of this new vocabulary. It had never occurred to you that it was such a great thing to be a woman. Nevertheless, you liked the situation. You liked the attention and recognition which you got from the people around you, specially the men who came in your contact. Whether at home or bus stand or at market place or in school, you liked the attention. But sometimes this extra attention might have bothered you. It made you very much conscious about your ownself. At other times, it became too much to bear especially when it crossed the limits of decency and decorum.

Among these mixed feelings you ultimately grew and became an adult. But, you never forget those school days, the days of pure fun and play when you used to swing like a bird from one branch to another. Neither you forget "your first period", when in school, during the middle of class, you were scared to death. And, you asked your class teacher that you are not feeling well and wanted to go home. At home, you just embarrassed your mother and started weeping

unconsolably. But, your mother tried to soothe you. Dispeling your scare, she said, "Don't worry my darling, it is all very natural for a girl. Don't worry, you will be alright within three-four days". Then she explained you everything about periods and womanhood. Even after that assurance, it took you more than a week to become normal.

Once in the college, the whole world started opening in front of you. How beautiful the world is! You thought Papa was earning reasonably good; even if not, that also you did not know. Because he never showed it to you that he lacks the resources. He always supported you for all your wild dreams and fantacies despite mama's objections.

Sometimes you wanted to become an architect, sometimes a fashion designer. Interior designing was also there in your mind. But you were not very serious about anything. Then, what you desired was good amount of education along with a degree which would be helpful to find a job. In fact, you had no specific career goal. At times, you thought what was the harm in becoming a beautician. Then, your sister-in-law suggested why shouldn't you try your hands at modelling. Oh God, what a wild thought it was! You a model? You never considered yourself that very beautiful to do the cat walking. Nevertheless, you always thought yourself as reasonably good looking, almost a next-door girl image. You loved this image at that time and you love it today also.

You had many friends. Those were the days—canteen, library, gardens, corridors, classrooms, labs and parking. You never knew that you had developed an affair with that college. You still long to go there. You often tell your hubby and kids: How beautiful my college was! That beautiful road was covered by tall, big trees. That is where you met him, Shubhendu, your first love.

Those were the days. And, you know they will never be your again. Anyway, that is the life.

2

What Shapes Your Personality

AS I have mentioned in my earlier books also, the word *personality* has been derived from the word *personal.* Something which is very closely related to you, specific and exclusive, which can be labelled as yours and only yours, is called the personality. In case of a woman, the word personality is often misused in our society to describe her visual appearance, outer attire only, i.e. her face, hair, dress, body, etc.

For some people, personality implies the way you present yourself. Your poise, the way you talk, walk, smile or laugh. While others relate the word personality to your behaviour, the way you carry yourself in the society.

My colleague, Prof. Poornima Tonpay, MD, (Department of Physiology, GR Medical College, Gwalior, MP, India), says, "Personality of a lady is her signature on the vast canvas of life. It means the way she projects herself, the way she relates with others, the way she thinks, acts, and her total

mental makeup". This is how a member of the fair sex herself defines the personality of a woman.

In strict medical terms, the personality of a person (nee lady) means the way she reacts to different situations and stimuli. Any deviation from normal reasonable and just reaction can be aptly regarded as abnormal. And, when this abnormal reaction appears in repetitive manner, we say that "this person is psychologically disturbed or is suffering from split personality."

So, the word personality is quite deep in its meaning. It just cannot be confined to how you look; what is your physique, thin or fat; how you dress up; what is the colour of your skin and hair; and, so on. Neither it implies the way you move, walk, laugh or smile—your poise. Instead, your personality is *you* in totality, in wholeness—the way you think, your ideas, your thought process; your perception of life; your ambitions, dreams, goals; your interaction with the society; and, the way you carry yourself not on the ramp during the catwalk, but on thoroughfares of life. In fact, it specifically denotes your psychological signature. By psychological signature we mean the way your mind works, i.e. thinks, generates ideas. It is a measure of your IQ, the intelligence quotient, i.e. the level of your intelligence.

The mention of catwalk brings to my mind an evening at a famous hotel in Delhi where I had gone to witness a fashion show along with my brother Sharad, who lives there. The show was organised by a well-known fashion designer (name withheld due to some reasons). It had a hoard of photographers, media persons, and spectators. The models were also famous ones. People were clapping and cheering as the models were catwalking on the ramp.

After the show, I met few of the models out of curiosity. I asked various questions while exchanging pleasantries with them. To my specific question, "What exactly do you feel

before entering the ramp?" They gave varying replies according to their individual experiences. One said, "I look carefully at my make-up and dress." Second said "I become overly conscious about my gait and steps".

The third was simply immune to any feeling while stepping onto the ramp. She said, "What is there to feel about. I have done it umpteen times. I am just blank, completely immune, no reactions, it's all mechanical. I know I am being watched by hoards of people, cameras, and so on. I have become used to it. In fact, I do not consider myself more than a glorified hanger on which organizers have hanged some beautiful clothes. So, I just collect my cheque and vanish away while my colleagues hang on to be noticed by the crowd. These fashion show organizers have reduced the woman to a walking-moving hanger and nothing else."

I was not a bit surprised by her outburst because I had also heard almost the same views about the organizers from some top catwalk models in Bombay.

But we are talking about *what exactly shapes your personality*.

Many factors influence your personality. The list is very long. But certainly, few important ones we can discuss here.

Most pyschologists of the world agree to the fact that "Childhood factors" influence the personality of a lady most. It is a well-known fact that children of a secure home, intact family will have a more positive approach towards life than those who come from a broken family.

"A young girl is influenced most by her mother," says Mrs Shobha Goyal of Meerut, mother of two grown-up daughters, Meenu and Juhi. "That is why I always behave cautiously in front of them. I see to it that we (myself and my husband) never argue or quarrel in their presence. Although they don't

look like me, even then many of my friends charmingly say that they are my mirror image. Soon they (daughters) will be going to their homes. I wish that they should get all the respect and care from their in-laws and husbands. I am really worried."

Mrs Bushra, 41, a resident of Maharani Bagh, New Delhi, wife of a senior business executive, says, "I understand what it means when you are not born in a well-to-do family. I had to start the job quite early in my life because my parents were not able to afford higher education for me. In fact, I always wanted to opt for medical course, but then I had to do a simple B.A. That is why I had decided in the beginning of my married life that if I were blessed with a daughter I would give her the best of education and guidance to become a career woman. And, I would see to it that she pursues her vocation after marriage also, unlike me who resigned job of front line manager in a leading five star hotel chain, soon after marriage."

Though Mrs Bushra sacrificed her ambition of becoming a career woman for the sake of her marriage, another woman, Suchita, was not willing to trade her freedom for the so called happy married life. Says Suchita, "Ours was not an unusual marriage. It was a normal one, settled by our parents. Mukesh and I were working in different companies in Chicago, getting good salaries, beautiful cosy home, two cars and almost everything which a couple can desire to begin with. Two years later Abhilasha was born. I took leave from the company. Naturally, when you work, you also have male friends. During my leave many of them used to visit us at our home. One Sudarshan used to visit me more often after Abhilasha's birth.

"America is an open society, but we Indians are pseudo-liberals. Mukesh used to doubt our relationship. He often told me, 'Look Suchita, I do not like that Sudarshan should visit us at all'. We often used to have fights, sometimes bitter ones. Abhilasha was growing up. She was almost five years when I decided enough is enough. I would quit the

matrimony. And why not, I was also a qualified computer engineer. I would continue to live in the States and earn my livelihood. But I would never allow my daughter to carry the unpleasant childhood memories about her parents. Let her be a single-parent child, but cetainly not a quarrelling parents' child. That would spoil everything.

"Now Abhilasha is growing up into a beautiful woman. She is just fifteen, but people say that she will be a successful professor if she chooses academics. Myself and Sudarshan are still good friends. We did not marry because, to begin with, there was nothing like that between us. Anyway, life is like that. I have no regrets about my decisions. I am happy that I could realise my dream of grooming my child into a good person."

Mother has got greatest influence (Mother factor) on the child, specially a girl child. For, the boy, after a certain age, becomes independent and outdoor type. He likes cycling, football, badminton, judo-karate or such other activities. But a girl child due to her feminine character, generally feels awkward in outdoor activities after a certain age. She feels more comfortable in the secure atmosphere of home, near to her mother. Many a time she identifies herself with her mother, and tries to behave and act like her. She expresses motherly affection for her dolls like a mother's love towards her daughter. This universal hobby of young girls to play as mother to their dolls, and then marry them to boy dolls (Gudda) in a mock marriage is a direct reflection of their motherly tendencies which ultimately become a basic ingredient of their personality, the personality filled with care, tenderness and love.

One of my friends, Ramesh Sharma, 43, used to say that mostly you can judge correctly the broad outlines of a girl's personality by meeting her mother. Specifically, Ramesh put

forth this criterion of judging the female personality for selecting a girl for matrimonial alliance.

Another significant factor which influences the personality of a lady is the "Father factor." Here is an example of how important is the father for a girl. Amita, 15, class 9th student, was talking to her friend Rehana, "I love my father. He is so smart, good looking and young, I want to marry him".

"Oh! no. Come on, Amita. What are you talking? Do you know? Marrying your own father? Don't be silly. Be in your senses. Whosoever will listen you, will laugh at you", said Rehana.

Not a bit ashamed, Amita replied: "You are a fool, darling Rehana. I was just expressing that how much I like him. He is so gentle, well educated, manly and always full of energy. He is a real nice guy. His is a great personality. Well, I know I won't be marrying him, but certainly I would like someone like him to marry me".

Few years back, while delivering my scheduled theory-lecture in medical college, I badly scolded a girl student, although normally I don't scold or treat rough my students. But, on that day probably I had some tiff with my head of department. So, I was in a bad mood. Her fault was a minor one—she was talking to her neighbour. Normally, I overlook such things, but on that day I rebuked her.

Later, in the afternoon, during dissection hour she came to my chamber. She was lean and thin but quite charming—a shy looking girl as if afraid of something. First time I noticed her attentively. She said, "Sir, I am really sorry to have disturbed you in the class. I should not have done that, please forgive me".

I said, "No, no, my child, don't be so much apologetic. You have not done anything serious. I just forget everything once the class is over. Don't worry for anything". To further

normalise her, I asked which city did she belong to; what her father was doing; did she have any problem in the hostel? As she told me, she was from Aligarh. Her father, a professor in Aligarh Muslim University, had expired when she was quite young. Her mother had brought them up while doing her job in a private school. Somehow the girl was managing her fee, and she had applied for educational loan to a nationalised bank. But she was finding it difficult to get the loan sanctioned.

I was really moved by her life story. I was finding it increasingly difficult to look at her. I was feeling very sorry to have scolded such a nice child who deserved all the help and care from teachers.

After that incident she used to visit my chamber and sit there for hours together. Now she was in final year. I often told her that her regular visits to my chamber did not look decent. People might talk otherwise, they might pass adverse comments. Being a girl she should be careful about that.

One day, she came in hurry as if she wanted to tell me something but not able to collect herself. She said, "Do you know sir, I have started looking at you as my father. Probably, it may not have much meaning for you as you have plenty of students. But for me, your affection and love has a lot of meaning. For my whole life I have seen hungry eyes of people, elderly ones also. But with you I feel very comfortable as if I am a small girl sitting with my father.

"You may not understand sir, but I miss my father very much. I don't know what father's love is. Whenever I see a little girl walking with her father holding his fingers, I feel like imagining myself into that little girl. I don't know sir why I was attracted towards you. But for God's sake, don't take away your love and care from me, please sir."

I was sitting there dumb and mute, not even able to raise my head to look at her. Feeling very uncomfortable, I was

unable to say anything. Although I consider myself as a good conversationist, I was speechless at that moment. After few minutes, I said, "Don't worry for anything. Whatever little I can do, I will always do for you, be sure of that. You are a few years elder to my own daughter, but you can always depend upon me and consider me as your father".

After sitting for few more minutes she went away. Later on, I was wondering how much emotionally bankrupt one can become on losing one's father in early age.

That is why one very learned poet of Indian origin had once said, a woman always tries to find her father in her lover or husband.

Apart from the mother and father factors, many other family factors affect the psyche and thinking of a lady. Elder brothers or sisters, uncle, aunty, neighbours, family friends—all have got some effect or the other on her thinking.

Traditions, norms, cultural and social values of the society to a great extent affect the psyche of an individual. For example, dating is still a taboo in small cities, even in the highly educated class. But not so in big metros like Delhi and Mumbai. So the city or place in which you are brought up also affects your psyche. That is why one often hears this comment, "Oh, she is bound to react that way because she is a small-town girl". Or, "she is still to shed her small-town mentality". But, once a person starts living in a big city, it does not take him/her much time to change accordingly, and acquire the new tag on her personality, i.e. big city girl. So, the city where you live influences your personality significantly.

Sometimes due to repeated transfers of your parents you are exposed to the lifestyles and cultures of different cities. It adds to your personality in many ways. You imbibe some of the values, habits and behavioural traits peculiar to these cities.

Apart from your city, the type of schooling makes a great deal of influence on your personality. A good public school, with good track record and rich traditions can contribute greatly to the all-round development of your personality. But exceptions are always there. I have seen many children who had studied in ordinary municipal schools but excelled in their careers/professions. It all depends, nothing can be said with certainty who will excel.

Generally, it is assumed that children studying in renowned public schools and colleges, or wards of famous, high-placed parents would excel in life and career. But, as if to belie the common belief, girls belonging to very ordinary backgrounds, meagre upbringing come out with flying colours. Otherwise, how would you explain the phenomenol success of legendary silver screen goddess Madhubala.

So, the schooling makes a lot of difference in your personality development. But it entirely depends upon the type of teachers, your classmates, and your own attitude towards studies.

In fact, the transition of a girl into the young adult woman is influenced by many direct and indirect factors. Some are apparent while others are not so obvious. We have discussed them here briefly. These will be discussed in detail in the following chapters.

3

Hey Young Lady: Your Time Shall Come

MY idea of writing this book was not to suggest you any dress code or make-up tips. Instead I was interested in sharing with you some of my thoughts which may help you emerge as an upright and balanced person to face confidently the ups and downs of life.

Half of India's population consists of the fair sex. Indian women are engaged in various professions. They are doctors, teachers, nurses, steno-typists, computer operators, telephone operators, and so on. There are thousand and one jobs in which Indian women are engaged. They are excellent workers, performing their duties efficiently. In our two South Asian neighbours, the current Heads of State are women.

Women are no more confined to the four walls of their homes. When out of her home, a woman has to deal with the various people, who come from different strata of society, and belong to different backgrounds (social, educational and religious). She has to interact with all of them,

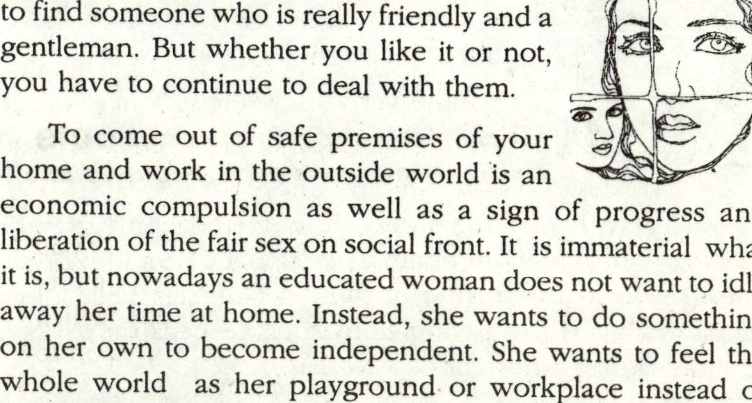

whether as colleagues, friends, clients, customers or just fellow commuters in the bus. Some are difficult and rigid while others are egoistic and snobbish. In fact, it is difficult to find someone who is really friendly and a gentleman. But whether you like it or not, you have to continue to deal with them.

To come out of safe premises of your home and work in the outside world is an economic compulsion as well as a sign of progress and liberation of the fair sex on social front. It is immaterial what it is, but nowadays an educated woman does not want to idle away her time at home. Instead, she wants to do something on her own to become independent. She wants to feel the whole world as her playground or workplace instead of remaining confined to her home, her kitchen. Though this social change is welcome it has resulted in a whole set of new problems for the woman who wants to be successful at any cost. She does not want to be labelled as a failure. She is afraid that people around her will make adverse comments on her failure. They will laugh at her and say, "Didn't I tell you in the beginning to be careful". She is under constant pressure to excel, to pass out with flying colours. That's why every difficulty, every problem she wants to hide from her father or husband. She doesn't want them to rebuke her and say "Sit at home. There is no need to go to office. Do not I earn sufficient enough to feed you? Nothing doing, sit at home".

A woman has to prove herself at both the fronts—her home as well as at her office. And, unfortunately, most of the working ladies in our country (and foreign lands also) don't get sympathising husbands who could understand how difficult it is to discharge dual responsibilities of home and office. It requires a great deal of effort to keep a balance between your home and your workplace. An added problem is that nobody understands your problems. In fact, I consider it foolish to expect somebody, maybe a close one, to share

your problems and give a readymade solution. People are not that much concerned with your problems as you are. You and only you are the best person to solve your problems. No one else is better equipped to handle them as you are.

So, the very first exercise/lesson of the course (Improve your personality) is to **change your perception about yourself.**

It is a fact that 90 to 95 per cent of the ladies are average looking. Remaining are either exceptionally beautiful or are unfortunate in this matter, to whom God has been quite unreasonable (I am saying unreasonable because to look beautiful is the birthright of a woman).

I take it granted that you are an average looking educated woman, pursuing a career.

Generally, women look at themselves with some complex. They compare themselves to the ladies who are more beautiful, more rich and belong to families of higher status. In the process of comparison they push themselves towards unnecessary depression. I understand that comparison is but natural, that it comes to your mind automatically. But tell me what purpose does it serve except depressing you. What is the fun in looking at them who are better equipped than you? Stop looking at them. Instead, start considering yourself as a woman who is exceptional in every sense, consider yourself above average.

First, you have to consider yourself as exceptionally intelligent and talented. Only then rest of the world will consider you so. Until and unless you have a good and positive image of yourself, you just can't expect others to portray a rosy picture of your personality.

There are many reasons why I am saying so. First, according to psychology, you can't see what you don't have in mind. Secondly, you can't achieve your goal or destination unless you dream it. So, you have to dream yourself as a

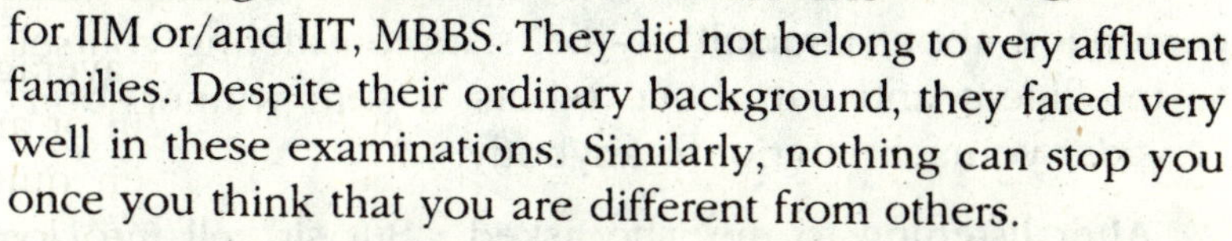

woman cut above others, who is going to win the race of life hands down. You are an ultimate winner'—you must develop this concept in your mind. Never mind what may come, you have all the capabilities to win.

I have seen many ordinary girls, doing exceptionally well in the IAS examination or achieving remarkable success in the CAT for IIM or/and IIT, MBBS. They did not belong to very affluent families. Despite their ordinary background, they fared very well in these examinations. Similarly, nothing can stop you once you think that you are different from others.

This "positive attitude" about oneself is the foundation stone of a successful personality. So far you might have thought only about your shortcomings—that you have a flat nose, or your forehead is too small, or your hairs are not curly and thick, or your chest is flat or too heavy. You might be having a long list of such shortcomings which in your opinion are your real minus points and have made you a nonstarter. As you further grow, i.e. crossing the upper limits of teens, you realise that your family does not have enough financial resources to support your studies and training. Never mind. You have to think positively about yourself. Be of single mind about your ambition or goal. And, start your run despite all your so-called shortcomings.

It is the same old story every time. Every successful woman has got a list of difficulties and odds which she had to overcome to reach the top. That is why I say that you will not be an exception if you are doing so. If you want to become a successful career woman, i.e. business executive, scientist, doctor, IAS, dress designer, interior decorator or architect, then you have to think and imagine yourself into that mould and feel about success in your imagination. **More strongly you feel about success, more decisively you run for your goalpost.** Don't worry if some people laugh at your wild imagination. That is the part and parcel of the game. People

don't take your pursuit for success lying down. They would try to discourage you. Except your close ones who are your real well wishers.

Recently, one of my old students, Archana, 28, MD, visited me in my department. She had just joined as pool officer in medicine department. I was telling her about this theory of "Change your perception about yourself" — i.e. start considering yourself as intelligent and cut above others, a sure winner; don't consider yourself inferior to anybody.

After listening to me, she asked, "But sir, tell me one thing. Is it not like living in a fool's paradise, when you are not realistic and just in your approach, in fact, cut off from the bare truth of life. What purpose is it going to serve if you start thinking yourself as talented and intelligent whereas actually you are not even average? Sir, are you not suggesting us to live in a world of fantacies and making castles in air? Is it not prompting someone to jump from hilltop without the wings?"

Archana was a bit agitated. To calm her down and put my theory in the right perspective, I said, "My idea of change of perception is not to tell you to live away from facts and realities of life. But, I want to **make you aware of your capabilities and your strengths** so that you can think positive about yourself. I am not suggesting you to start imagining yourself something like a super woman. There is no question of any exaggeration, but certainly I am interested that you consider yourself competent enough to act and behave in your usual normal self so that you are able to realise your true potential. One should not be tied down by negative thoughts about oneself".

The negative thoughts about looks, body, skin colour, hair and so on sometimes make you over-conscious resulting into unwarranted failure. So, the idea is to shun any negative

thought about yourself because that may deter you from showing your real performance. You must harbour a new positive attitude about yourself. This new attitude should be based on real facts. If you want to see yourself succeeding in a particular career, cast yourself into that mould. And, get rid of all other negative thoughts with which your mind is always obsessed.

4

Confidence Building: I Can Do It/I Can't Do It

HERE I would like to tell you the story of a young lady whose husband suddenly died of a heart-attack leaving a small happy family completely shattered. They used to live in a small town of Uttar Pradesh, Bulandshahr. They had two sons and two daughters, all under twelve years of age. They were enjoying the life at its fullest, as the husband, Susheel, was a successful criminal lawyer. His wife, Sushma, was content and happy, looking after him and their four children.

One morning after having a cup of tea Susheel complained of chest pain and was taken to nearby doctor. But, before the doctor could do anything, Susheel the young man of 37 years died. The whole world was changed for young Sushma (30) within a second. The young contented housewife was turned into a widow. She was a simple graduate. It was all dark for her. How to run the household? How to earn the bread and butter? Ultimately, she had to take on the role of her husband, i.e. to earn for and support the family.

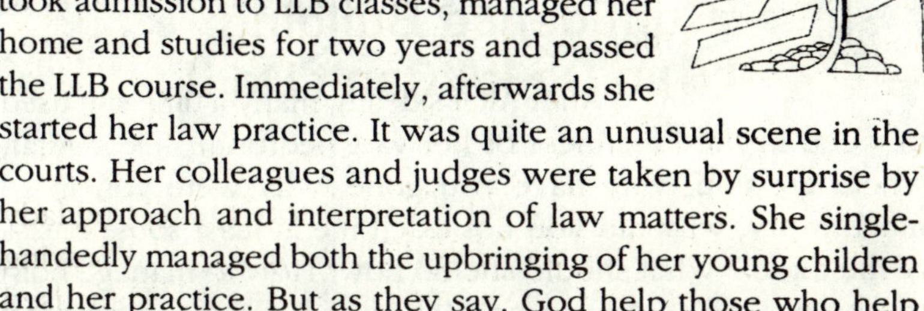

Those were the days of late sixties. Though not living in a large town, she decided to become a lawyer herself to take over the practice of her late husband. She took admission to LLB classes, managed her home and studies for two years and passed the LLB course. Immediately, afterwards she started her law practice. It was quite an unusual scene in the courts. Her colleagues and judges were taken by surprise by her approach and interpretation of law matters. She single-handedly managed both the upbringing of her young children and her practice. But as they say, God help those who help themselves, God helped her.

Whenever you go to Bulandshahr, you can yourself see how successfully she has established herself in law practice and how well settled are her four children. She is a happy contented mother. Often, she remembers her late husband who, she says, has given her the real strength to face the world. (This is a real life story although names have been changed to preserve the true identity.)

Generally, most of the women lose their self-confidence at the time of crisis. They become absent-minded, their mind stops functioning as if they have become paralysed. Nobody, absolutely nobody is immune to this sort of panick reaction. It is all but natural. Those who say, "No, I did not lose my composure even for a short while," are the liars. Yes, liars.

My point here is, that after initial absent-minded stage, one should recover as fast as possible. One must gather the confidence and start planning the future course of action to overcome the crisis.

Take another instance from real life. Life had taken a sudden turn for Mrs Rukhsana Munshi (name changed). Her young husband was a very successful entrepreneur in the clay pottery business. The business was quite good. They along with their three beautiful young daughters were living in a small town, Khurja. They were very well-to-do, enjoying life. On one fateful day, destiny snatched away young Altaf Hussain (name changed) from Rukhsana. She was dumb and mute for weeks together. Not knowing what to do.

After Altaf's death, many a time she used to weep in the loneliness of her vast bedroom: "Dear Altaf, where are you, why have you gone, why were you in so much hurry, why did you not teach me at least some basics of the trade?" What should she do now? How to manage both the home and the business. Her young daughters were all below ten at that time. They used to become very scared on seeing their mother weeping. With their tiny hands they used to wipe her tears, "Mummy, mummy don't weep, everything will be alright, Allah shall help us".

As usual, Rukhsana never took any interest in her husband's business, keeping herself confined to the household affairs. And, suddenly it had all fallen on her shoulders. Now, she had to procure the raw material, select the designs, talk to the prospective buyers, handle the bank account, income tax, sales tax, excise and what not.

After initial setback, Rukhsana was able to manage the business successfully. The buyers were hesitant to begin with, but impressed by her determination and good quality of her items they started buying the pottery from her factory. Soon, she was completely immersed in the business. Her initial helplessness and shakiness was now replaced by confidence and desire to prove herself. Today, to the surprise of everybody, Rukhsana is a leading and probably the most innovative pottery kiln owner of Khurja. So, the lesson is:

You can always succeed, provided you try with your full force. You must be ready to go to any extent to

become successful. You must have the confidence that you will succeed whatever may come.

Confidence is not such a commodity which you can buy. Neither it can be inherited nor acquired as gift or donation from somebody. This exclusive, yet the most cherished quality of human personality has to be cultivated by oneself.

Do not mistake here the word 'confidence' with 'pseudo-confidence'. It is essential that the confidence which you build within yourself should be based on facts and reality. It is easy to say, "I can do it, I will do it". OK, you can do it. But, before attempting the real act, you have done the necessary rehearsal in your mind?

Suppose you are called on to the stage in a function, and asked to give a brief speech on the subject "Woman Power in Today's World". As the exact timing for your speech gets nearer, you may start having the stage phobia. Many disturbing thoughts will come to your mind — "What will happen if suddenly I forget the speech; what shall be the people's reaction on my knowledge; will I be able to face the audience? Oh no, I will not be able to do it. I shall say to Mrs. Pareekh that I will not be able to do it."

You may feel as if you are very thirsty, your palms become wet. Yes, you have heard it that people develop microphone-phobia and now that is becoming true.

When your name is called, somehow you reach the stage. You take out a piece of paper from your notebook and start reading it. Oh, what is this happening? Your whole body is trembling; your throat is becoming dry; you reach for the glass of water placed in front of you as if you are thirsty since ages. You are in a hurry to finish the speech as if you are getting late to catch the train. Your vision is getting blurred, but anyhow you complete your reading. Now, you don't look towards the audience because you are afraid to face their

gaze. Somehow you reach your seat and push yourself in it, taking a deep breath as if you have been running the ten thousand metre race.

You take a deep sigh of relief, "Oh, God it is all over." Thank God. Now you turn your face towards your husband who is sitting next to you, and put a smile on your face as if you don't care for anything. You pretend to look confident but you as well as he know that you are fooling yourself. Anybody could have guessed from your face that you were very tense while reading the speech. However, you ask him, "How was my speech?" He replies, "Superb, you were simply marvellous." Although you know he is just kidding, you exclaim, "really"!

This dismal performance of yours has everything to do with lack of confidence. But they say confidence is not a perfume which you can buy from a counter. One learned speaker, Mr Sunil Goyal, says, "Oratory is an art which you master with experience". In other words, confidence to speak from a podium comes through experience. But then, till the time you gain experience, what to do? Another expert on public speaking, Mr Ramesh Saboo, former National President, Indian Junior Chamber, says, "Confidence building for public speaking or for anything else is a slow process which requires time as well as efforts. It cannot be built overnight, one has to have some patience. First of all, what you require is clarity of thoughts as well as fear shedding".

Mr Saboo further elaborates, "Confidence comes naturally when you are sure of your job, when you are determined to do the job perfectly". His advice is: One should not allow one's mind to be blurred by the fear of failure. For this, you have to train your mind by positive thoughts, like "Why not, I will certainly do it". You should not allow the circumstances and situations to unnecessarily control the course of events. Develop the "positive thought process" about your potential and capabilities.

I remember one plump girl, Rashmi Katiyar, living in my neighbourhood. Belonging to a middle class family having a widowed mother, two brothers, she was determined to become a doctor. Despite financial and emotional handicaps, she continued her studies. She used to attend early morning coaching classes as well as help her mother in household work. Rashmi could not succeed in her first attempt in the medical entrance examination. Not demoralised, she appeared second time in the examination, and ultimately got selected in the MBBS course. Now, Rashmi is studying in second professional.

Actually, confidence is directly related to your determination. It is the burning desire to succeed which sets the ball rolling. Once the basic foundation of confidence building is laid, other things come into picture. In fact, there is no sphere of life where confidence is not required—whether it is simple interview for the job, or negotiating a deal on behalf of your company with the high flying client, or it is bigger than life size problem which makes you emotionally weak, with blurred psyche.

Apart from firm determination, other things, essential for confidence building, are: clarity of thoughts, fear shedding, rehearsal of the forthcoming event in your mind, and complete knowledge of facts and information. You cannot start driving a car from the very first moment, howsoever confident you may be about yourself, till you acquire complete knowledge about it. You have to learn swimming to the perfection before you have the confidence of jumping into the river. Otherwise, you know what can happen—your confidence may remain a one-time affair, you will not have the second chance, by all probabilities.

Here, my learned friend, Mr I.B. Rastogi, Resident Editor of a widely circulated local daily, *Dainik Bhaskar* from Gwalior, differs with me. He says until and unless you take

the risk and experience the failures and accidents, how you are going to learn. According to him, confidence building is, in fact, a learning process in which you are bound to experience failures and frustrations. No one is exception to that rule, no one can have the confidence without going through the whole process of learning. And, when you learn, you have to take the risk and be ready to face the accidents also. There is no short-cut.

I fully endorse Rastogi's viewpoint, but with slight amendment. No doubt, learning process is an essential exercise of the confidence building process where one has to take risks and expose oneself to accidents and disasters. But, I am of the firm belief that risks can be calculated and accidents can be averted with the cautious approach.

Here, I would caution you not to be over-confident. You must be able to differentiate between true confidence and over-confidence. Some people call the latter variety as pseudo-confidence. It does not make any difference whatever term you use — whether pseudo-confidence or over-confidence, things remain the same. And, it will surely lead you towards disaster some day because an over-confident person is far removed from the facts and reality. He is living in a fool's paradise where no one can help him.

In a party at my friend's farm-house, once I met the famous TV News Reader Ms Rupali Dixit (name changed). Few people were invited at this weekend party. She had come there with her husband who was associate professor at Delhi University.

She was sipping orange juice when I approached her. I introduced myself. She responded very politely to my hello, with a smile and nod of head. I initiated the talk: "I watch you with interest. Your accent is flawless, your face does not show any anxiety. In fact, it shows a lot of confidence. From where have you mastered all this? Did you have to undergo a training programme?"

She smiled, saying, "Thank you very much for your pleasant remarks". Then she said, "I belong to a middle class family. My father was a colonel in Indian Army. I have had my education in different schools in India. I never imagined that I would join Doordarshan as a News Reader. After my MA in English, I started teaching in a convent school in Pune, and was planning to do B.Ed. All of a sudden, my marriage was fixed and I came to Delhi with my husband. I used to watch TV like any other woman. One day my husband casually asked me, 'Rupali why don't you try to become a TV announcer'. In early Eighties, I met some officials at Mandi House and expressed my inclination to become an announcer. Soon, they took my screen test and I was assigned to give brief, one-line programme informations.

"Initially, I was very much terrified by lights, TV cameras and all the paraphernalia. In fact, the whole studio setup was not very encouraging. People were busy in their jobs, no one had the time for the new-comers like me. Senior news readers and announcers were too much high-headed. But gradually, I learnt the tricks of trade. Many producers and specially male news readers helped me a lot to gain confidence. After two years, I was assigned to do important jobs like TV reports and commentaries of special events. It was only after four years that I was given my first news reading assignment".

5

It Is Not Easy: Meaning of Career and Success

SOME time back, I asked one of my friends, Dr A.G. Shingwekar, "What is the difference between a celebrity and an ordinary woman?" "Nothing except that one is famous while the other is not, both are women", responded Dr Shingwekar, DCH, MD, associate professor of paediatrics, Gwalior. I further asked him, "What is the difference between a successful woman and an ordinary woman?" This time, his reply echoed his earlier answer: "None except that the former has achieved what she aimed for while the latter is yet to achieve".

Once I was talking to a famous writer-editor and TV personality. The occasion was the releasing ceremony of a book by another renowned writer. I was introduced to her by her editor colleague whom I was friendly with. After two-three meetings, I became quite informal with her. One day, I asked her, "Mrs Pandit, in what way would you describe today's successful woman?"

She said, "What is there to describe about today's successful woman? If she is able to achieve a balance between her home as well as her career, then probably she is successful. But, I feel this is quite difficult to achieve. It is not at all necessary that a successful woman executive will be equally at ease while managing her household chores. Look, in my own case, I am out of my home for more than ten to twelve hours a day. Far away from my residence in a distant colony, I work in my office at Connaught Place till six O'clock in the evening. Then at my home also, I have to devote some time to write reports and articles. That leaves me no time for my husband and children. I am not able to look after the cooking and other household activities, which remain almost neglected.

"I have been brought up in a traditional middle-class family at Indore where my mother, aunty and my sister-in-law (Bhabhi) used to cook food, supervise the cleaning of house and look after almost every need of menfolk at home. But, here in Delhi my job does not permit me at all to look after my family, it really pains me. What to do? I don't know. Sometimes it occurs to me at what cost I am pursuing my career, am I not paying too heavy a price for it? Although I have got a very supportive and understanding life-partner, even then I feel guilty of not doing my duties responsibly at home. Sometimes I become tense on this count—what is the solution? Can you tell me something, you are also a writer and psychologist."

I could not reply instantaneously because I was listening to her attentively and just lost in her problems. She shook me, "Are you listening Dr Agarwal?" "Oh yes, oh yes, I am listening," I responded.

Then, I said, "Look, Mrs Pandit, you are a successful writer and editor by all means. It is not a small achievement. Very few women in our country can boast of the position you command. The recognition which you have got in the literary

circle is almost unparallel and that requires full attention and commitment without which it is not possible to achieve anything in this competitive world. Whatever you have achieved is the result of your undivided attention and skillful management of the career opportunities. If you could not attend to your home and discharge your duties towards your husband and children, you should not be ashamed of that. There is no reason why should you feel guilty about it. Shrug off that feeling from your mind, there is no need for you to feel in that way. Now the world is changing beyond recognition. What you had seen at Indore in your parental house was some twenty-thirty years earlier. Since then, a sea-change has taken place in the social parameters and the role of woman in the social structure. You are living in Delhi since last fifteen-sixteen years. Don't you notice the change in the values and attitudes of people here during this period? It is a part of that sweeping change. Don't worry, you cannot do justice at both the fronts. So, stop feeling guilty."

She sat there for some more time sipping coffee. In a thoughtful mood, she said, "Thank you very much for your kind gesture of listening to my problems and sharing your thoughts with me. Thank you indeed".

I said nothing, except giving a friendly smile which was badly needed by her.

Few years ago, I was assigned the board observer's duty for pre-medical entrance examination, at a Girls' Degree College in my city. There, I met few of the lady professors. One of them who drew my attention most was a tall, slim doe-eyed beauty, Mrs Aparna. She was Assistant Professor for Arts and Painting. She was very shy, almost confined to herself, not a good conversationist to begin with. But, after a few meetings, she opened up. She along with her artist husband had organised many solo shows of her work at famous art galleries of India.

During the brief leisure time at the examinations, I asked her, "How do you manage your career and home so beautifully? How do you manage such long working hours at college and then also find time to paint for your exhibition?"

"Really, you mean that?" She rolled her beautiful big eyes. Then she became a little bit thoughtful and said, "In fact, I don't find it at all difficult to manage the home as well as my career. I enjoy being a mother and wife, and a painter at the same time. Painting gives me immense pleasure. I don't consider it as a career, it is my passion, my life, I am all into it. I love it, my first and only love. It releases every bit of tension and anxiety. It is not at all difficult to divide the time between the painting and home. And, luckily, I have got a wonderful husband too. Anil himself is an India-fame artist who has got respect and consideration for my work. Often, he suggests me colour combinations and landscape designing".

She continued, "I don't think it is at all difficult to pursue your career and manage home simultaneously, provided you have a supportive family and firm determination. Second thing, which I feel necessary is that you must be able to thoroughly enjoy your job/career. You should not consider it as some economic or social compulsion. You should not brood any tension about it. For this you have to observe a very simple principle, and that is, never allow yourself to undergo depression phase. Always fill your heart with all the enthusiasm and positive thinking about the life. That is probably the only way by which you can remain happy and contented while managing your career and home".

I was floored by her deep understanding of the truths of life. I said, "But, Aparna your face does not show that you are so much mature and intelligent, it simply adorns child's innocence". She laughed candidly, "Oh, come on Dr Agarwal. Don't fool me." and she walked into the examination hall to check the students.

Now, I give you the example of another lady, who unlike Aparna, struggled a lot to maintain a balance between her home and career. She was two years senior to me. We became friendly when she was in fourth year and I in second year. Our common interest was painting. Nicknamed Manno, her full name was Manorama Sihare. She was one of the two organizers of the college art exhibition during annual celebrations. Later on, during the internship we parted company as she went to Indore to do her MD in anaesthesia, and I came to Gwalior to become demonstrator in Medical College. We met occasionally whenever I went to Bhopal where she had joined the job as a lecturer. Two years ago, I received a call from her that she was coming to Gwalior to join as professor in the department of anaesthesia. "Could you arrange some place for my stay?" she asked. I said, "First, you come here, then we will decide where you shall be staying, maybe you get a government accommodation".

Along with her husband she came to join her duty, and went back after two days to collect her bag and baggage. Manno stayed in Gwalior for almost two years before she was transferred back to Bhopal. During her posting in Gwalior, she used to stay there from Monday to Friday, and used to spend weekend with her family at Bhopal. Her weekend schedule was very hectic. Going every Friday to Bhopal and then returning by Sunday night train which used to reach Gwalior around three O'clock in the morning, thereafter staying alone in the waiting room till the wee hours of the day, catch an auto-rickshaw to medical college, and then getting ready fast to reach the department at 8.30 sharp. This was really too much for a lovely, tender lady like Manorama. But she never showed any remorse feeling or had cut the sorry figure for the tremendous amount of physical and emotional strain she was going through. She was her usual self—bubbly, smiling and cutting jokes.

She often visited me at my department or home whenever she found time. One Monday evening she came to my home a little disturbed. I and my wife consoled her and asked her what was the matter. She was silently sipping the coffee. After a few minutes of silence, she said, "Sona, my daughter, was running fever yesterday when I came here. She (Sona) was weeping when I was leaving home. My son was also having his half yearly examinations. He was also weeping".

I said to her, "Then you should not have come here, you could have taken few days off. How does it matter? After all, it is your family which matters first. Anyway, I am putting up a call to inquire about their well-being". As soon as the children came on the line, Manno started sobbing, although talking but with a choked voice. She talked for ten minutes or so, but all through she was sobbing and wiping her tears.

It took her more than half an hour to collect herself. Later, in a pensive mood, she said, "Avinash, I want to resign my job. It is too much to bear, it is tearing me apart. Really, I am unable to carry on. My children have become mental wreck. My husband has withdrawn himself, he does not talk to me now. Many a time our maid servant becomes absent, then my husband and children have to clean all the utensils and do the cooking. It is really the height of nonsense. My family is very much disturbed. It cannot continue like this any more".

I said to her, "Look, Manno, it is true that you are paying quite a heavy price for your career. But, all this is a temporary phase which will pass off very soon. Be rest assured that it will pass off very soon. Don't be in panic, have patience, don't permit this to disturb you, this all will end soon". And, to the surprise of many she got transferred in the same academic session itself.

So, a career woman has to adjust a lot, in her office, with the husband, with in-laws, with everybody living in her home. She has to confine her problems to herself. Otherwise, husband or mother-in-law may say, "Sit at home, we don't need your salary to run this home. I am competent enough to feed you and the children, don't go from tomorrow".

But when you take a casual leave, the next day he says, "Hey, what's the matter? Are you not going to office, what is the problem?" He very conveniently forgets what had happened yesterday. So, life is like that, learn to adjust because that is the way things are.

6

They are Cool Like Ice

FEW years back I sent my first Hindi manuscript to a leading publisher in Delhi. After one month, he wrote me back that he had got my script checked up by one of his editors and was returning the script with the editorial comments. The comments were as follows: "The language has got many grammatical mistakes. At places the writer has used unparliamentary (read cheap) language. There are many factual as well as technical mistakes. The whole text needs thorough rewriting, heavy dressing down and complete deleting of many parts in the script. And, the editor is afraid that the book will be drastically reduced in size, hence script is returned in original".

I felt very insulted, almost tossing in my chair, unable to do anything. And, immediately I sat down to write a letter which was like this:

"Dear Publisher, received your letter which was full of insult and humiliation. I have gone through many of your so-called best-seller books and found them substandard and

full of mistakes. It appeared that your writers did not know the ABC of the subject and had copied the text from somewhere. And, yet you have the guts to say that my work is full of grammatical and factual mistakes, and so on. What are the qualifications and credentials of your learned editor, how many publications/titles he has to his credit? Does he, at all, know the technical subject which he is editing. I am sorry to say that you have employed a wrong person who does not have any aptitude for quality work. He cannot differentiate between a gem and an ordinary glass. Lastly, there is no dearth of publishers. There are thousands and one in the trade, and certainly I will find one who will be better than you. You should know the loss is not mine, but yours...."

After getting the letter typed, as per practice, I showed it to my wife. After going through the letter, she said, "I understand that you are very hurt, but I simply want you to withhold this letter for a week, and thereafter if you still feel the same as today, then post it. As the days passed, I thought to myself, why are you so dejected, what wrong he has done? He did not like the script, so he has returned it. Since he was honest, he also sent you the editorial comments. Why do you think that the editor is wrong in his assessment? Has he not done an honest job? Why should he hide the facts from you? He is doing his job to call a spade a spade. Why don't you send it to some other publisher and get it printed, instead of fighting with this one? That will certainly show you in cheap light.

Even before the week ended, I tore off the earlier drafted letter and wrote him a new letter, whose text was like this: "Thank you very much for your kind letter... I was much delighted to go through it simply because it has shown me the mirror wherein I could see my real self. It is very difficult to get the efficient and impartial critics in the world, who can really pinpoint your mistakes. Please convey my sincere

thanks and regards to your learned editor who has taken so much pains to go through the entire manuscript and has marked the specific mistakes. A great job indeed! I have a great desire to see him in person and to learn something about the language and script writing. Whenever next I will come to Delhi, surely I would like to spend some time with him. Thank you once again. With kind personal regards. Sincerely yours, Dr Avinash...

Needless to say, as soon as the publisher got this letter, he rang me (which normally they don't do until and unless you are a celebrity writer) and asked me to send the script for reconsideration, or whenever I went to Delhi to meet him positively along with the script.

It is true that nobody is spared of the negative effect of anger on one's personality. Anger is one of the basic animal instincts. It is really very difficult to control anger and keep mum, or convert the feeling of anger into that of love and politeness.

I vividly remember my childhood days when my mother used to call us all children to the prayer meeting in a small room where we used to sing 'Aarti' and 'Bhajans' (prayers, devotional songs). In English translation, one of the prayers was like this, "Oh God, give me strength to fight my anger, greed and hatred; give me wisdom to forgive and love my enemies; courage to think beyond the materialistic world; senses to be honest, just and sincere to everybody".

This small prayer we all used to sing while living in a small rented house in the sleeping town of Rewa in Madhya Pradesh in the fifties. The real meaning and purpose of this prayer I could never understand during my childhood. And, still I don't claim that I have fully followed it in my life. But, I have found it very useful, comforting and I try to live up to this prayer.

The Father of Nation, Mahatma Gandhi, has given us the lesson of "Ahimsa". Lord Gautam Buddha has taught us centuries ago: "Develop no hatred towards anybody, let nobody shall be able to instigate you, make yourself immune to insult and humiliation".

But what we see in the present-day world is just contrary to all these teachings. Probably, no one is following these words of wisdom. Everybody is following the policy of tit for tat, blood for blood, slap for slap, bullet for bullet. In our own life, we will observe that daily a significant amount of our energy goes waste in planning to retaliate the insult and humiliation meted out to us at some point of time in our lives. There are so many clashes, stabbings and murders taking place in our world that it has virtually become a battlefield for all the negative human instincts, like anger, hatred, greed and enmity. In these circumstances, the enmity then becomes almost like a habit, one after another, a vicious circle, from which it becomes almost impossible to get away.

On physical level, you might have noticed that while settling the scores with our enemies we raise our blood pressure, heart beat and tension to the danger levels, sometimes even jeopardising our lives.

Liking and **disliking** are two basic but important feelings of our psyche. You like somebody because you feel that way. If somebody asks you to explain your liking for a particular person, then you may say it is just like any other feeling, such as pleasure. So, how to describe **liking** in a simple way? It can be explained as a positive feeling, attitude which you develop for a particular person. In other words, you approve, appreciate and feel pleasure in the company of that person. As simple as that.

So, **liking** is a subjective feeling for the qualities of that person, his/her behaviour, thinking, poise and so on. Just opposite of this feeling is **disliking.** You don't like somebody

because you don't approve, appreciate, and feel comfortable with his/her behaviour, way of talking, thinking or other traits of his/her personality. So, **disliking** is also a subjective feeling.

But, why I am discussing all this? What is new about this? Everybody knows what is liking and disliking because that is what they have a personal experience of. Here, if I suggest that you stop disliking anybody, or stop showing your resentment or disapproval any more, then probably I will be kidding. Nobody can do that, not even the saints. It is very natural that when you don't like something or you don't approve of some thought or behaviour, you feel uncomfortable. In such circumstances, your face betrays signs of resentment and disapproval. But, what I wish to tell you is that it is not at all necessary to show your disapproval in a harsh language or in an insulting manner. Who gave you the licence to do that? Being educated and a bit more intelligent does not give you the licence to insult or humiliate anybody. That is the crux of all my above discussion. Disliking for any person or thing you may have. That is your personal matter. But you don't have the right to insult or humiliate somebody. And, in your own case also, you will not like to be humiliated or insulted even if you have committed some blunder.

Second thing, it is much easier to smile than tense up your facial muscles in the expression of anger and hatred. Here, I would like to quote one of the great thinkers and saints of our times, Acharya Vinoba Bhave, "Go to your bed daily with a feeling that you have forgiven those who have insulted or humiliated you during daytime, throw away that enmity and hatred. You will find that you are much relaxed, and it will be much easier for you to get a perfect sleep".

"It is much easier for a woman to stay young and beautiful when she leads a life full of pleasure, happiness and relaxed coexistence with her fellow beings than to undergo a series of facelift and cosmetic surgery operations". This valuable advice is from my learned colleague, Professor Dr I.N. Tiwari, MS, MCH, Ex-Professor and Head of the Department, Burns and Plastic Surgery unit, Maulana Azad Medical College and attached hospitals, New Delhi, and Ex-Medical Superintendent, LNJP Hospital, New Delhi.

Prof. Tiwari says: "Don't let the petty things disturb you. Like, if bus is coming late, or if you don't get a proper seat in the bus or train, or if you have missed your 9.30 local, don't draw transverse wrinkles on your forehead. Don't do that because that may become your permanent habit. Take it easy. That will preserve your youth".

A popular saying is **beauty with brains is a rare combination.** But, our own silver screen goddess Madhuri Dixit seems to be that rare combination. Recently in her candid interview to a Hindi magazine, she was asked about the secret of her enthusiasm, spontaneity and stunning looks? In reply what she said was the mantra for a happy life: "I don't allow myself to be disturbed by the minor or major irritants. I acquire a cool, very cool attitude towards adverse situations and misgivings. I prefer to forget the unpleasant events instead of pondering over them for days together. I don't waste my energy in enmity, hatred or jealousy but prefer to concentrate on my performance. This probably I think is my biggest strength".

However, it is easy said than done. But whosoever is able to follow her words in the true sense is a sureshot winner. Instead of settling scores with your enemies, instead of wasting your energies and mental resources in fighting them, develop the attitude of forgetting, if not forgiving them. That will save you much trouble and tension.

I fully understand that in the process of "self restraint" you may encounter many problems. Like, your heart will say what you are waiting for, reply in no uncertain terms, set

her/him right immediately. But wait, why you want to compete with your enemy in the field of hatred and anger. These traits are pure and pure animal instincts. Why do you want to be taken for a ride? You have not come to this world to waste your time and energy in these useless animal instincts. But, you are required to perform much bigger tasks which otherwise you will not be able to do.

I agree that if you don't retaliate, people may call you a coward, may label you as a non-courageous person. But, don't worry for all that. It may take them some time to understand your true character and nature. Give them this time. But, in the meantime, you must stick to the cardinal principle that, 'I will not allow any humiliation, insult or any comment to disturb me'.

And don't, please don't, endorse my view blindly. But do one thing. Give this one-line principle a thorough trial for a month during which you will do as suggested. Thereafter, notice the change in your life—how much beautiful has it become without extra efforts and money!

7

"I Am Not Beautiful" Syndrome

IT is almost impossible to think about a woman without an essential aspect of her personality—'beauty'. Beauty and woman are two inseparable things. Every woman, of whatever age she may be, is always conscious about her looks. Here, exception is those who are very elderly ones. But this consciousness is more overpowering when you are young.

Whether you agree or not, it is a fact that a significant part of a woman's thought process is directed towards her concern for her looks and body. No, I am not pointing an accusing finger in your direction. Rather, I would say, it is all very natural for a woman to take care of her body and looks. By virtue of being a woman, it is your birth right to look attractive and beautiful. And, why not? If one is beautiful and attractive, it feels good. Good, because it gives you an opportunity to attract other's attention by almost doing nothing. You get preference over others easily wherever you go. That's right. Isn't it?

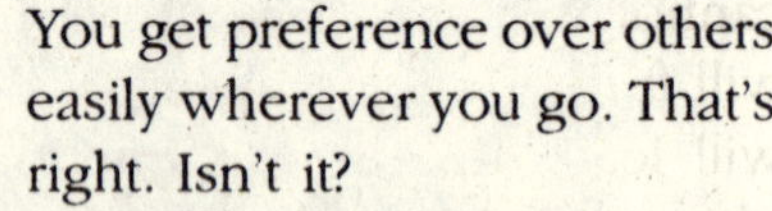

Echoing similar views, says film director Mahesh Bhatt, "A beautiful woman always has an edge. She is liked by everybody. She can always expect a helping hand, in case she needs it. If you have got a beautiful body and matching

looks, you can go places. Lot of opportunities open up before you—you can try your luck in the film world, or opt for ramp modelling, television, advertising, and so on. In other fields also, with your good looks things become much easier. In fact, openings are endless."

"But what the ordinary looking woman should do?" asks Ms Ruby Sengupta, 31, a business management graduate of Calcutta. She has many questions to ask: "If you are not so lucky to have sharp features, fair colour or pink complexion or good height or a balanced body, then what to do? Is it your fault if you do not have charming looks? Why not blame the God for being partial to you? Why the society should be so cruel to the ordinary looking women? Why don't they (society) appreciate in a woman, qualities other than her body features? Why are people so obsessed with the good looking women and just not caring to give a second glance to the ordinary ones".

Well, Ms Sengupta, the trend has been so. None can help if you are born with ordinary looks, or if you are short in height or have dark complexion. No one is to be blamed for that. Neither you nor the society. Yes, of course, you can always blame the God for that. But, of what use is it? What you will get if you curse the God for your not so attractive nose or buck teeth? Certainly, you will not get anything. Things cannot improve on your ordinary looks front. Instead, they will further deteriorate as this constant cursing and nagging will lead you towards inferiority complex, depression and ultimately complete lack of self-confidence. Then life will seem a hell. So, who will be the loser at the end? Of course, you., and only you.

Don't get disheartened with your ordinary looks. Believe me, even in the glamour world, there are thousand and one examples of ordinary looking women who have achieved success despite their so-called ordinary looks. Haven't Shabana Azmi, Jaya Bachchan or Smita Patil succeeded in the glamour

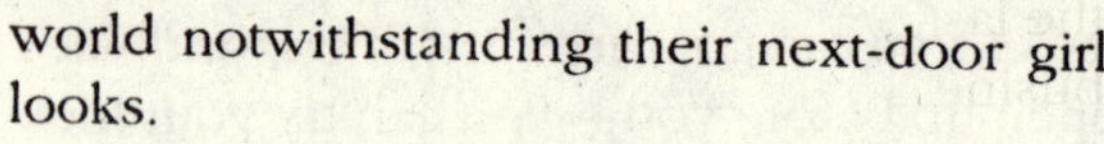

world notwithstanding their next-door girl looks.

In other fields also, like administration, politics or business world, examples are numerous of ordinary looking women reaching the top. Look at our own Kiran Bedi, Magsaysay Award winner, Margaret Alva, Najma Heptulla, Nandini Satpathy, Sushma Swaraj and so on. One can go on adding to the list. I personally know many business women, lady doctors, IAS officers, and women in the corporate world who have proved their mettle and received accolades and appreciations for their job. And, all this was their's, despite their so-called ordinary looks. So, here the lesson is: "Despite being handicapped by the ordinary looks one can become successful in life". Looks can never become a hindrance provided you concentrate on other aspects of your personality and stop bothering about the looks.

If you can develop other qualifications like good education, or acquire some vocational training, or master specific skills, you have good prospects of getting a good start in your life as a career woman. Then, to a large extent you can compensate for your ordinary looks. But, as my friend Dr (Ms) Sangeeta Shukla asked me once, "Is it really possible for a young woman to stop bothering about her looks and concentrate in the direction of career building? How can you expect her to do so? It is just a natural and normal desire of a lady to be admired for her beauty. Isn't it?"

"Well," clarifying my views I replied, "Ms Shukla, I am simply saying, stop bothering, not stop caring. There is a lot of difference between the two. Bothering I mean harbouring depressed or complex feelings. But, as far as caring is concerned, you are always free to take care of your body and looks. In fact, a woman should be very particular about the way she looks. And that is why most of the ladies these days are going to beauty parlours.

"No doubt, a woman can always enhance her looks by getting the services of expert beauticians which are now available aplenty in her neighbourhood. In the last ten-fifteen years, the beauty parlour business has grown tremendously as the average woman has become aware of her looks. In each locality you can easily find one or two parlours. By getting proper hair cut or styling, facial, threading, pedicure and manicure you can certainly improve your looks. There is no doubt about that".

Listening to my views, Ms Shukla was still not completely satisfied. Then, I further said, "There is now a sea-change in the attitude of society. Every woman, whether living in towns or big cities wants to be financially independent. She wants to become a career woman, an individual having the control of her own destiny. And, in this race the looks don't play much role. You need not to be very attractive and glamorous. Even the next-door girl looks will do. To my mind this approach is far better than cursing the God for being not so generous while selecting the mould for you".

8

"Beauty is a Business," Said She

HERE'S how another of my friends underlined the importance of looks for a woman. Anil Somani, B.Tech., MBA (IIM), 46, a young businessman-cum-successful industrialist quizzed me one day, "Well Doctor, by advising young girls and ladies to concentrate on their education and career, and stop worrying about their looks, are not you debarring them from their birth-right, i.e. to look beautiful and to be appreciated for their beauty by the world at large? Look at the magazines, films, TV programmes, beauty pageants, and fashion shows. Arn't all these prove that beauty is a licence for instantaneous success? Simply, you should be aware of how to get entry there, and the world will be at your feet in no time."

Somani paused for a while. Then he asked: "Am I using the wrong expression, 'the world at your feet' or 'instantaneous success'. Overnight you become the celebrity. Your photographs are on the cover of every glossy magazine. Mediapersons run at the break-neck speed to click your photographs the moment you are crowned in Ms India or Ms World beauty pageant. They (the organizers) pretend that they are selecting girls on the

basis of their IQ, education and presence of mind. But, everybody knows they are selected on the basis of their legs, bust and looks. Nobody, I mean really nobody, bothers for your educational background. The only thing which matters is how seductive your smile is, how you look in the evening slit gown or swim-suit or just two-piece bikni. Even the girls try to make fool of themselves by saying that they shall be working for downtrodden and oppressed class of the society once they get selected. But whom they are fooling? Who does not know that they are here to sell their glamour and body, not to work for the poor and backward classes of society. What Ms Sushmita Sen and Ms Aishwarya Rai are doing? They are cashing on their looks and body by joining the films instead of doing anything for the poor. But the show must go on".

Somani seemed quite perturbed. He continued: "Beauty has become a 'commodity,' the woman has become a 'Cheez' (item, thing) to be sold in market like car or carpet. Everybody is earning, whether organizers or magazines, or fashion designers, or cosmetic companies. And, nobody is complaining, not even the victims (poor Ms World competitors). Then, who am I to complain. I shall be a fool to do so. But, I am worried about one thing—where this artificial, much publicised, westernised approach of fashion and glamour will take us? Don't the young girls in the audience of fashion shows and beauty pageants harbour the wish to participate in them someday? Don't the young school or college going girls imitate the Bollywood actresses or ramp queens? Don't the hitherto conservative parents find themselves helpless in permitting their insistent daughters to take part in these competitions? You can find hordes of young modelling aspirants making rounds of the advertising agencies and fashion show organizers. And, look Doctor, you are talking about education, higher degrees, professional colleges and bright careers for them".

I found it a bit difficult to pacify Somani. I tried to convince him: "Anil, things have changed quite fast in our country in the last two decades. Values have changed, morals have changed, so has the society. Then, why do you expect women to remain cut off from the change process. When you and me were young adults, the criteria for beauty was different. Low neckline, semi-clad body, and mini skirts were taboo. All these were considered vulgar and obscene, but no more these days. For bad or worse, the Indian subcontinent is under the influence of western culture due to the onslaught of satellite channels. And, among the most affected is the very image of traditional Indian woman, which was kept guarded carefully till recently. We are now in for a new definition of feminity in the Indian context. So, whether you like it or not, you have to bear with the changed criteria for beauty."

During the course of writing this book, as per my habit, I talked to some well-known women who have become darlings of masses because of their physical assets and stunning looks.

A renowned model and former Miss India (name withheld) met me in Mumbai as I dropped into my photographer friend's studio in one of the suburbs. He was doing a photosession with her for a popular magazine. It was a whole day programme, although tightly planned but atmosphere was relaxed. Earlier also, I had met many beautiful ladies, but here she was. I was unable to take my off eyes from her. Maybe, it was make-up or her stylish dress which made her very charming. After one session was over, they were free for a short tea break. Then, my friend introduced me to her. We exchanged pleasantries. Thereafter, she was again in front of arclights. After one more session, she joined us for lunch. Then, suddenly, she asked me, "Sir, why don't you write on women? You have written two books for men, why not a book for women this time?" (Till then, I had not started writing this book, although I had a plot in my mind.) Jokingly, I counter-questioned her: "Well, would you pose free for my book if I write one for women?" She replied, "Why not, I would love to do that. By the way, what do you want to write about women, have you thought of anything?"

Normally, I don't discuss the plots with anybody, whosoever she or he may be. For, I believe it is the idea or concept which matters most, rest of the work can be done by anybody. That's why I guard the secrecy of my plots. But, revealing my plot, I said: "My next book may be about women titled as "Complete Woman". Before I could tell her what I intend to write, she cut me short, saying, "Sir, can't we meet tomorrow? It is Sunday, and I am free. Would you please drop at my place tomorrow?" Absolutely thrilled, I accepted the offer: "Why not, I will be there at eleven O'clock".

Next day when I visited her Versova flat, she introduced me to her parents, brother and sister. Thereafter, we sat for a chit-chat. Curious to know about her liking for her job, I asked, "How much do you enjoy your modelling assignments? Don't you feel sometimes awkward or being exploited?"

"No sir," she replied quickly, "I feel absolutely comfortable doing them. As I have chosen modelling, I know I have to abide by the rules governing this profession. I have no right to complain. Moreover, I am paid for it. Then, where is the scope for complaining? Secondly, there are hordes of new girls who are willing to do anything to get an entry into the advertising world. If I won't be doing it then somebody else would do it. I am beautiful, I know that. What is the harm in exposing a little bit since you are paid well. It has also given me a sort of celebrity status. I get a lot of exposure in the media. People know me by name. I get instant recognition wherever I go. I really enjoy all this. It is difficult to quit at this stage, or else what will I do. Get married and cook the meals for my husband? That all is so boring and monotonous. I am afraid that I would be able to enjoy that. Right now, I

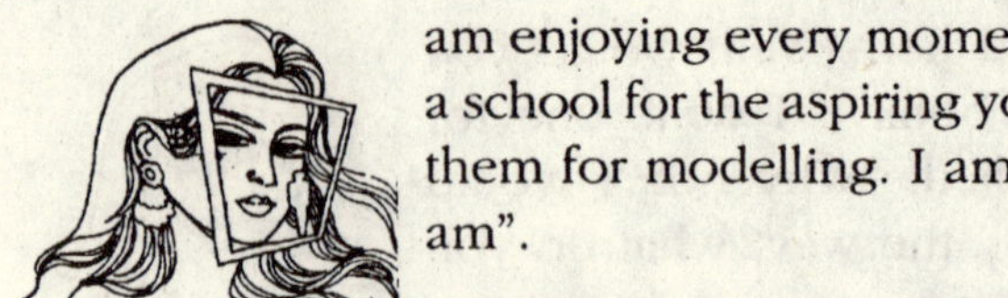

am enjoying every moment. I may also start a school for the aspiring youngsters to groom them for modelling. I am happy the way I am".

After relishing a sumptuous lunch with her family I left the place, wondering whether she fits into my mould of "Complete Woman".

My second encounter was with a film actress, the *numro uno* of Indian filmdom, on the sets of a fild. Shooting was on in a Mumbai studio. It was a whole day shift from morning to evening. The director of the movie was son-in-law of my friend. In between the shots, I was introduced to the heroine of the film, heart-throb of millions, Ms Madhurima Joshi (name changed). The sets were the scene of hectic activity—shifting of cameras and lights, rearranging furniture, etc. Due to my acquaintance with the director I got an opportunity to talk to her in private. Though I was not feeling dumb-struck in the presence of the glamorous heroine, I did have a bit of difficulty in initiating the conversation.

The problem was solved when a boy brought us some orange juice. Breaking my silence, I asked her, "Well, how do you feel when so many pairs of eyes are constantly watching your semi-clad body?" Just after shooting off this question, I realised that I should not have started the talk with such an offending question. Isn't it embarrassing for a girl to respond to such an awkward question?

But, to my pleasant surprise, she smiled, saying, "Sir, I think you are not very serious while asking me this question. But I am very much serious in my reply. Yes, I used to feel very awkward and uncomfortable when I was new in this industry. But, now I have become used to wearing revealing clothes. Not that I have become immune or shameless. Instead, now I consider it a necessary part of my profession. I belong to a very conservative and orthodox middle class Maharashtrian family. No way, my family's views and values permit me to

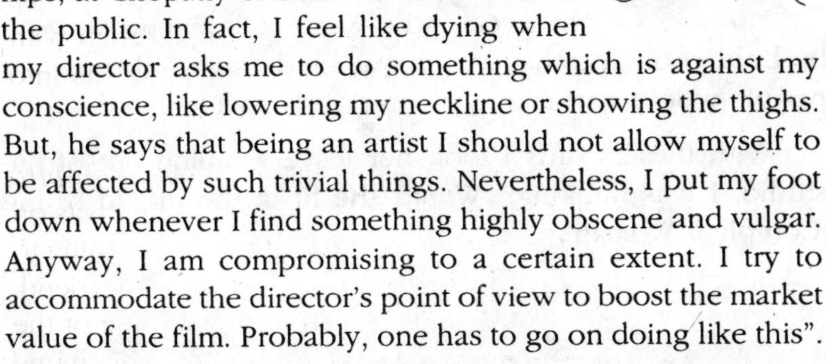

do what I do in the films. But, that's the way things move here. Yes, I do feel uncomfortable when I have to do the vulgar dance movements, like shaking the bust or hips, at Chopatty or India Gate in front of the public. In fact, I feel like dying when my director asks me to do something which is against my conscience, like lowering my neckline or showing the thighs. But, he says that being an artist I should not allow myself to be affected by such trivial things. Nevertheless, I put my foot down whenever I find something highly obscene and vulgar. Anyway, I am compromising to a certain extent. I try to accommodate the director's point of view to boost the market value of the film. Probably, one has to go on doing like this".

She became quiet. Her face which was sporting an infectious smile a short while ago was now expressionless. Then, she left me to give a shot. Joining me about half an hour later, she said, "Many a time I feel that beauty is a burden. If beautiful, you are always considered a damsel or babe. Never you get recognition for your talents. Even if you say something intelligent, you are looked down as if you have committed some mistake. People pass dirty remarks at your back. Sometimes I really feel very much offended when I am treated like a dumb doll, a beautiful thing, an object for everybody's entertainment. It pinches hard. I almost feel like going to some remote village or a small town where I may be treated as a human being, a normal person, instead of a silver screen goddess. At times, I have an unusual feeling of standing on a pedestal at a busy road crossing without my clothes on, and every passerby is looking at me with an animal-like hunger in his eyes."

I was feeling sorry that I had made her distressed. I didn't have the slightest of idea that my casual question would evoke such a depressing response from her, revealing the ugly side of glamour world. To boost her sagging morale, I said, "Young lady, don't feel so much depressed. You can always contribute

to the film world in a more meaningful manner by choosing powerful roles with more scope for your performance. It is good that you still heed to your conscience, and you are able to think sensibly. It is a nice thing. Get rid of your guilt feeling. Instead, be bold enough to have your way, and you would see that people would start taking you seriously as a talented artist".

With these words I took her leave. Coming out of the studio, I was thinking, "Would she fit in the mould of the 'Complete Woman'. —

9

Never Say It Again

(As told by Prof. Dr (Mrs) Saeeda Shinde)

WE had just returned from our evening walk. As usual, my husband, Professor Dr V.A. Shinde, went to the drawing-room and started reading the newspaper. My both daughters were at the sidetable, studying and preparing for their next day's classes in college. I went to kitchen to prepare the dinner. While doing cooking, I was thinking about my husband, "... he is not normal, appears to be a bit worried about departmental affairs, problems of college..." Of course, we share our problems. But, that day he appeared more worried. Often, I feel that my husband takes the things too seriously. He tries to give his hundred per cent to solve the problems, and expects the same from other people. And, here lie all his worries.

After the dinner, daughters were still in the study, but we moved to the bedroom. A little later, he started feeling uncomfortable. He reached for my hand and said, "I am feeling suffocated, as if I am sinking. Oh, this pain in chest is too much to bear, please do something".

I had just changed into my nightclothes and was reading a magazine. I turned my face towards him. It took me no time to understand that he was in great pain and discomfort. He was perspiring, sweat beads were present on his forehead. Being myself in the medical profession, I was able to diagnose immediately what he was suffering from. It was nothing but the acute myocardial infarction.

I shouted for my daughters, and they came running. I asked them to call Doctor Tripathi, who rushed to our house in no time, and we decided to shift my husband to the intensive care unit. At the hospital, it was usual routine. They started every possible treatment, like putting him on oxygen, pain killers, IV drip, ECG, etc. I was witnessing the whole thing as a mute, dumb person, not knowing what was happening. Everybody there consoled me that nothing would happen to him, and control myself. But, I was not able to listen anything as if I had become deaf.

"My whole world had been shattered. What would happen to me and my two little daughters if something untoward happened to him"—these ominous thoughts were just not leaving my mind.

Holding my husband's cold hand in a tight grip, I was thinking what a courageous man he was! Though himself a Maharashtrian (Hindu), he married me, a Muslim. When we married some thirty years ago, the inter-caste marriage, that too from two different religions, was unheard of. But he was there with dreams in his eyes. We passed those tension filled years with so much ease, all due to his confidence and fighting spirit. And now, he was lying in a helpless state fighting for his life. "Oh God, please help him, please save him". I kept praying all through the night. By the grace of God, next morning he gained consciousness. He smiled at me and asked softly, "How was it all the night, could you sleep or not?"

I cannot tell you how I controlled myself at that moment. I wanted to weep loudly, instead I asked quietly, "How are you feeling now? Is it alright now? How is the pain?" He smiled again and closed his eyes as if thanking God for saving his life. After a week's stay in the hospital, doctors advised us to go to the Apollo Hospital, Madras, for the by-pass surgery. But what to do? We had no money. Again, it was a very difficult situation. But God is great, we got immediate sanction of thirty thousand rupees from the government, and with the help of some friends and relatives we were able to go to Madras and got him operated there.

Now, looking back to those horrible days when everything looked grim and lifeless, I would say it was the grace of God which gave me courage to remain confident in the hour of crisis. Otherwise, things might have taken a tragic turn. But, in my heart, I often murmur, "Never say it again. Thank you God, for everything you have done for me and my family".

10

Life is Like That

NOBODY can avoid being attracted towards the opposite sex, especially when one is young. Sometime or the other, this type of situation invariably comes almost in everybody's life, knowingly or unknowingly, that is, intentionally or unintentionally.

Opportunities and chances of male and female interaction have grown tremendously during the past two decades especially in big cities, where girls and women have become more outdoor type while pursuing their education or careers. Secondly, the effect of television, films, glossy magazines, and increased interest in fashion shows have changed considerably the middle class social values.

Few months ago, I was reading the lucid interview of a well-known film actress in a magazine. The interviewer asked the lady, "Well, Ms Nalini Bhatia, there is a rumour circulating in the industry that you are in love with Mr Devanshu Das Gupta (names are changed) who happens to be the hero of your three films.

And, it is also rumoured that you have started asking your producers to complete their films by the year-end as you want to marry your heart-throb by that time. Is it all true, Ms Nalini?"

Nalini's was a matter-of-fact reply: "I have joined this industry notwithstanding the tough opposition of my family. And, today after so much pain and struggle I have made my position here. Secondly, I have put in very hard work and dedication to acquire this place. You know all this is not a single day's work. Do you consider me such a fool who will kick all these achievements for the sake of a man, for a husband? No, I am not that kind of a fool. Yes, I had many friendships in the past, and currently I am having a very warm friendship with my co-star Devanshu, but marriage is out of question. Right now I am too busy in pursuing my career. Marriage with him or with anybody else is not worth quitting my career which I have built up so painstakingly. I don't know why you people think that love is not complete without marriage. Why a couple cannot continue to remain as friends as along as they like, without bothering ever for the nuptial bond?"

I was not at all surprised by the reply of this young starlet. It is all but natural that when you attain a certain position in your career after hard labour and intense struggle, facing cut-throat competition, you don't like at all to give it up for anything, even for the marriage with your dream prince.

Once I was in Calcutta to attend a marriage in my Aunty's family. Her daughter, my cousin, was to be married. My cousin introduced me to one of her friends and colleagues, Ms Neelima Bhattacharya, Assistant General Manager in a private airlines. She was an MBA from a reputed institute and had also done courses in tourism and travel management. In her late twenties, Neelima was fun-loving, bubbly, and kept smiling always. She was drawing around twenty-five thousand rupees or so as salary. Since Neelima was quite frank and free with

all the members of my aunty's family, I did not find it difficult to develop a natural bond with her. And, we became good friends in just one day.

I casually asked her while sipping orange juice, "Well, Neelima, why didn't you marry till now, when all your friends have settled in their life? Didn't you find the right person, or you have something else in your mind?"

Neelima became thoughtful, her face showing a little smile. She said, "Avinash Da, I also have few good male friends. One of them, Amol, is quite handsome and intelligent. We are very close to each other. Well, you may call it love but I treat it as friendship. We are friends for the last four-five years living together under the same roof, but have no intention to marry. In fact, I don't find it at all necessary to convert this beautiful relationship into marriage. What is the use? I love him, he loves me. That is enough, I don't want anything else. I can't sacrifice my freedom for the sake of married life. Then there will be a mother-in-law, a sister-in-law, their tantrums. Then the children, cooking, washing of clothes, and, then all the responsibilities of a typical middle class Indian daughter-in-law. No, all this sends a shiver down my spine. I don't want any such thing to happen to me. I am enjoying my life. I am enjoying the company of my boy-friend, full security of life. Then, why should I go for marriage?"

I tried to caution her: "What would the society say when you live with someone without marriage? Traditions and norms of our society do not approve this at all. Moreover, what will happen in the old age? Who will love you then? Who will then take the responsibility to provide you the security of life?"

Not a bit perturbed, Neelima counter-questioned me: "Avinash Da, tell me how much secure is the middle class housewife today? Does she not fear the divorce or the intrusion of a mistress in her husband's life? Does she get all which is due to her, from her children and husband? Why should she sacrifice her career and freedom in the name of security and traditions"

I did not reply, although I wanted to. I was quite surprised, thinking how fast our society is changing. Instances like Neelima's may not be found in large numbers, but their existence cannot be denied. I changed the topic. I started talking about her job and office. But, deeper in my mind, I was trying to fit her in the mould of my "Complete Woman". Many questions were teasing my mind: "Has Neelima done a wrong thing? Are not the miseries and suffocation gone through by many married women responsible for her attitude. Or, is it her way to declare freedom from the institution of marriage?"

Recently, a well educated beautiful couple visited my wife's clinic. The wife Somya, 32, was an Assistant Professor in a Girls' Degree College while her husband Akhilendu, 38, was an Executive in a steel plant in the nearby Malanpur industrial estate. They had come for the medical termination of pregnancy. It was the fourth time in last ten years that they had come to us for this purpose. My wife Sarita casually asked Somya why didn't she allow her pregnancy to continue and enjoy motherhood? Without a trace of hesitation or any guilt feeling, Somya laughed softly and replied: "But what for? We are happy without children. Why this extra responsibility? We are enjoying our life and our careers. We love each other. We enjoy our sex life. Then, what is the rationale of having children? Doctor, we have decided that we will remain childless throughout our lives. We are more interested in our professional excellence and advancement than increasing the size of our family. And, believe me, we are enjoying the things this way very much. By option, we want to remain childless, and it is a great fun".

That night, at our dinner we (myself and my wife) were talking about Somya and Akhilendu. For us, they were certainly

a breed of working couples who, by choice, wanted to remain childless and had no regrets about that. Justifying their decision, I said, "Sarita, well if Somya gets her husband's full attention and love, and at the same time she is also able to pursue her career then what's wrong? After all, she has got her professorship after great efforts and pain, and she wants to pursue her academic career seriously. Nothing is wrong with that".

Life is full of contradictions. And, it takes all sorts to make this world. Here's the case of Jaya, which is just contrary to that of Somya. After marriage when young Jaya entered her in-laws house in Agra for the first time, she was thrilled by the size of their mansion situated in the heart of city. Beautiful, chirpy and bubbly Jaya was liked by everybody. Her husband Rajkumar was really a prince charming, tall, very fair, almost like a Greek god. He used to roam around her the whole day. She loved it that way, and she bothered least whether he went to his clinic or not.

Jaya's father-in-law, a registered medical practitioner, was earning handsomely in those days—the seventies. Her husband also became an RMP-cum-sex specialist after his intermediate. There was surplus money in the family, and it being a joint family, nobody used to mind Rajkumar's abstaining from his clinic, or enjoying the company of his newly-wed wife. The days were passing smoothly. Then, one day, Jaya noticed that Rajkumar had consumed liquor with his friends. He asked her not to tell about this to anybody, but she showed her annoyance. A week later, he again returned home completely drunk. When she confronted him, he said, "Oh, I am sorry. I was not at all interested. But, you know how it happens in the high society. They insisted very much and then I relented. I am sorry, but I promise you I will not touch it again". But, next morning, Rajkumar forgot what he had promised to Jaya.

After two-three days, he was again knocking at the door in an inebriated state. This time, Jaya lost all her patience and shouted at him. Rajkumar, after listening to her for few minutes, snubbed her, "Look here baby, don't shout like a mad woman. I drink because I can afford it. I don't drink from your father's money, so keep shut and come to bed, I want to make love with you".

This was too much for Jaya to bear. She was furious, and went to her mother-in-law. But, the mother-in-law took this matter very lightly, and said, "Calm down Jaya, calm down. Why are you making so much noise about such a trivial thing. Go to bed and don't create a scene at this hour of night. We will see this matter in the morning." With great mental agony, Jaya came back to her bedroom and tried to sleep. But no way to escape. There he was, wanting to have her. And, the whole night he almost raped her four times. She was unable to stand up in the morning, what to talk of protest. She remained in the bed for the whole day.

Thereafter for three days, Rajkumar remained normal. But, on the fourth day, he again came drunk. And, when he wanted to have sex with Jaya, she refused point blank. But no way, he again raped her as if she was not a wife or life-partner but simply a prostitute. This weekly ritual then became almost a daily affair. She did not know what to do—whether to end the marriage or to continue living such miserable life. It was not even one year complete for her marriage. She wept in front of everybody, her father-in-law, elder brother-in-law, and other relatives, even her own parents, but to no avail. Rajkumar was not changing, not at all. And, to top it all, she was five months pregnant.

She had never imagined that her life would become so miserable. She was having no money in her hand because whatever Rajkumar used to earn was taken care of by his drinks and eating out. Jaya used to weep for hours together. Sometimes she thought of ending her life, but then she thought

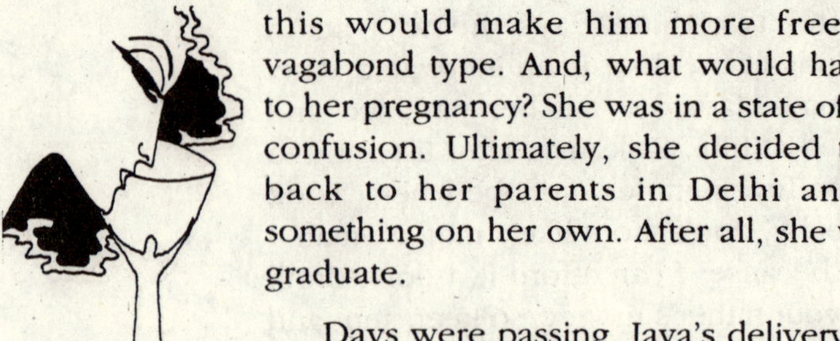

this would make him more free and vagabond type. And, what would happen to her pregnancy? She was in a state of utter confusion. Ultimately, she decided to go back to her parents in Delhi and do something on her own. After all, she was a graduate.

Days were passing, Jaya's delivery time was approaching fast. One day, Rajkumar returned home very late, well past midnight. That night, she was feeling quite exhausted so she fell asleep early. He kept on pressing the call-bell, but she remained slept. Then, he started shouting like a mad man, abusing her in all dirty words. After half an hour or so, Jaya became aware of what was happening. Very much terrified, she went to the front door and opened it. On seeing Jaya, Rajkumar started thrashing her mercilessly. She shouted, pleaded, wept, but to no avail. Jaya's shrieks and wailing in the dead of night brought her mother-in-law down from her room. She somehow pacified her son. Throughout that night Jaya wept unconsolably, and Rajkumar was sleeping and snoring as if enjoying the journey to the seventh heaven.

Feeling physically handicapped since the last month of her pregnancy was going on, Jaya decided to keep her cool till her delivery. Her first child was a baby girl. She lovingly named her Ankita. When Ankita was three months old, Jaya decided to do something of her own, to take the things in her control. She knew it that her husband was not going to mend his ways. He had become a slave to the bottle. Nothing could be done to save him. Only way out was she had to herself become financially independent to save her marriage. Otherwise, she had to quit and go back to Delhi to her parents. With courage and determination she decided to stay back and ameliorate the adverse situation.

Jaya managed herself and started a beauty parlour in the basement of her in-laws' big sprawling mansion. Those days the beauty parlours were an unheard of thing. I am talking

about seventies, i.e. mid seventies. Jaya had talent and desire to succeed. So, within no time her parlour was a success, and she started earning around two-three thousand rupees per day in those late seventies. She tried her best to persuade her husband to mend his ways, help her, so that she could take up more side jobs. But he was a hard nut, his only job was to make life hell for her and to take away whatever money he could grab. Now he had become a complete vagabond, dependent upon her earnings.

Life was passing. Jaya became pregnant again, it was a baby boy this time. But, Rajkumar remained the same irresponsible fellow as before. Rather, his behaviour had gone from bad to worse. Due to excessive liquor intake, he became very weak but more aggressive and violent type. The more she tried to adjust, the more he used to behave beast-like. In this huff and tuff were gone the twelve years of their married life. Then, suddenly one day, Rajkumar fell ill seriously, with bleeding from nose and vomiting blood. He was rushed to the hospital. She nursed him, cared for him for full six months. Nobody came for her help. He had promised that he would go to Delhi with her to take the treatment for alcohol de-addiction. She lived with him in Delhi for three months leaving behind her roaring business of parlour. But, Jaya was happy that now her husband was cured completely. She started feeling that ultimately God had listened to her prayers and had given her the new married life.

But she was highly mistaken. Within a year, Rajkumar was back to his old ways. He again started drinking and all his beast-like behaviour, abusing and beating the children, beating her and calling her dirty names. How long a woman could bear this? Finally, she decided that time had come to say good-bye to her married life. She purchased a separate house in the nearby market and called her aged parents to live with her. She applied for divorce in the court and she got

it. Jaya had thought that after divorce and complete legal separation she would get rid of that beast, which unfortunately was her husband. But, to her utter dismay, the end of sixteen years of "marriage-imprisonment" was nowhere to be seen. Often, he would come at her new house and shout, abuse, weep, dance, drink and do everything to attract the attention of passers-by. He would do his best to malign her reputation in the new locality. But she was determined that she would not relent. She reported the matter to the police. They took him away, but freed him after some days.

What next? Now, with increased vigour and zeal he would try to malign her. But with the passage of time it did not bother her any more. Neighbours and all acquaintances had understood the tantrums of Rajkumar. What else he could do if he did not weep or shout because his regular source of income, the battery of servants and all that facilities and comforts of home were gone. He was bound to weep. But it did not affect Jaya any more. She got admitted both her children in good schools outside Agra. And, now she says, "I am comfortable, at least free from the tension."

When I was told this story by one of my close friends, I chose to meet her to see whether she really fits into the mould of a "Complete Woman" which I am searching so impatiently. And, believe me, I found her very close to the completeness —very cool, intelligent, no extra word, judging before speaking, and to top it all, a hearty laugh, just carefree and confident.

11

Naturally Beautiful

OFTEN I fail to understand that why women use so much makeup and other artificial means to look more attractive. This phenomenon is more pronounced in our marriage parties or other social gatherings. Sometimes, one is surprised to notice that women who use very little makeup in their daily life, come to these parties, wearing heavy and gaudy makeup. The same thing goes for the type of dresses and amount of jewellery they wear on such occasions.

My colleague, Dr (Mrs) Poornima Singh (name changed), a Senior Reader in the medical college surprised me no ends at a marriage party where she had come heavily made up and dressed up. I don't know why, but I had always appreciated her dress-sense and appearance. In the college, I always found her charming even with slightest of makeup. Her natural flair and style was infectious, indeed. Not me, but many of my colleagues were Poornima's admirers for her grace and beauty. But, in that marriage party, strangely, she

chose to wear so much makeup that it was just impossible to look in her direction. On that warm summer night, her layered makeup and heavy silk saree were too much to mix along. Obviously, her efforts to look more attractive and young had just gone waste.

With no intention to embarrass her, one day I casually asked Poornima, "Were you not feeling uncomfortable in the heavy makeup and outfit at that marriage party?" She was a bit uncomfortable and also amused. Probably, she had not expected such a question from a male colleague, and that too about something which is so personal and private. But, since she was quite free with me and secondly being a decent lady, she took it very supportingly. She conceded, "Yes, you are right. I was not very comfortable with that kind of heavy makeup and outfit. But, on that day I thought why to have routine things for such occasions? Why not try something different? But, I failed to draw the line where to stop".

I told her that I had no intention to make her feel awkward. And, just as a friend, I wanted to tell her that she was more beautiful with her natural self, without heavy makeup and other such things.

Generally, in my class there are about thirty to forty girl students, belonging to different backgrounds. Some are from rich families, some belong to highly educated families. And, yet some others are from lower middle class or have business background. But, surprisingly, none of them comes to the class with slightest of makeup although they belong to that age when everybody wants to look attractive and beautiful. Moreover, they also have boys as their classmates. Yet none of them goes for makeup till they pass out from the college. Even after graduation also, whether they join the post-graduate courses or opt for teaching or hospital jobs, they seldom resort to makeup. But once you meet them in college annual functions or in a marriage party of their classmates, they are different creatures altogether, sometimes even difficult to recognise. On such occasions, they are like any other woman, very keen to put on heavy makeup and dress up in the best possible way. God knows what happens to them. Sometimes I wish to talk to them about this sea-change in their personality, appearance-wise, when they visit me in my department or meet otherwise. But, I somehow restrain myself, for all are not as supporting as Mrs Poornima Singh.

In today's fast-paced world, a career woman has many responsibilities to discharge. She has to take care of her tiny-tots or school-going children, look after her ageing mother-in-law, father-in-law and also stand by her busy executive husband in the ups and downs of their life. Not only that. She herself has to attend the office apart from supervising domestic chores, like cooking, cleaning of dishes, house upkeep, washing of clothes and many other routine things. Notwithstanding all these responsibilities, she has to be at her best while doing her job in the office. There, she is supposed to look stunning, young and attractive. But tell me, where is the time for all this? She is always hard pressed for time, looking tense, under constant pressure to make things work, whether at home or in office. In these circumstances how could she do all the makeup, and be meticulous in the selection of her clothes to look ravishingly beautiful?

To look beautiful or preserve one's natural beauty requires a lot of effort. Actually, no one is born beautiful or remains so without proper, systematic care. It is a life-time commitment which a woman makes with herself—taking care of herself inside-outside. She has to take some time off from her busy schedule to understand that to look beautiful and remain so requires a concentrated effort. She has to find ways, within her hectic daily grind and meagre financial means, to enhance her beauty. She must be judicious in selecting the type of makeup and clothes to suit her particular style and requirements. A little extra care would add to the grace and charm of her body, ultimately increasing manifold the magnetism of her sharp features and poised body.

Some women are endowed with the magnetism to make people turn their heads towards them wherever they go. What is so special about these women? What is the secret of their magnetism? How do they compel people to respond and listen to them attentively? Would you call it sex appeal, glamour, or charisma? Or, may we call it allure? But what is allure? Well, it can be explained as the ability to stand apart in a crowd, and make things work for you by your dazzling presence. In other words, it is the quality which gives her courage and self assurance to move and carry herself in her distinctive style; to try new clothes, change hair-do or makeup style with confidence.

Is it very hard to acquire such a quality? What prevents you from doing confidently whatever you want to do? Nothing but fear, the fear of unknown, the fear of failure, the fear of being labelled as foolish and absurd. To some extent your fears may be reasonable. Especially when you go for a drastic change. Like, totally incompatible styling of things which do not suit your face, or body may look awkward. To avoid such an embarrassing situation, you must take care of two-three things.

First, sit comfortably and assess your needs which are directly related to your career, your looks, your face and body texture; in short, to your personality. You may have to experiment, because it builds up your confidence by giving you an opportunity to rectify your mistakes.

Secondly, to overcome the fear of failure, you may get in touch with professional beauticians or makeup men women. Here I would like to give you a word of caution. Though there are lot of such 'experts' available in the colonies and marketplaces, not all of them are trained or skilled workers. Most of them are just experienced assistants of other senior assistants who had started their shops (parlours) a bit earlier. A majority of them are there to make a fast buck without bothering for your genuine requirements. Get in touch with

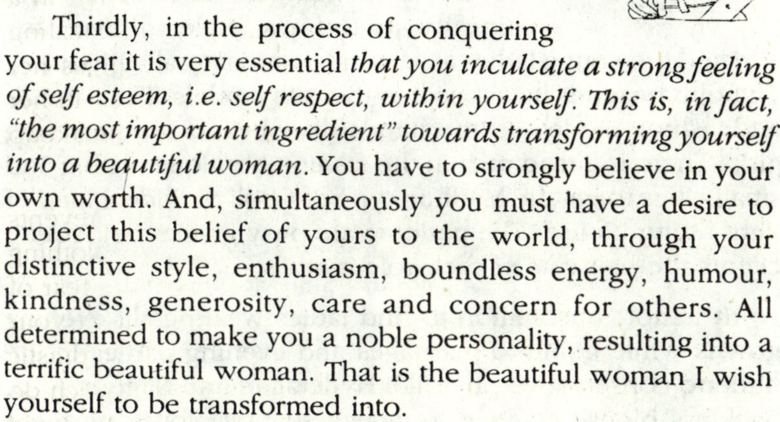

them, assess their capabilities, intelligence and attitude before surrendering yourself into their hands. Some of them, as my experience goes, are of great help and can become your life-long friends. It is better if you take pain to search for the one who is intelligent and is willing to give you a patient hearing. So try them, but always insist on your own personal style.

Thirdly, in the process of conquering your fear it is very essential *that you inculcate a strong feeling of self esteem, i.e. self respect, within yourself. This is, in fact, "the most important ingredient" towards transforming yourself into a beautiful woman*. You have to strongly believe in your own worth. And, simultaneously you must have a desire to project this belief of yours to the world, through your distinctive style, enthusiasm, boundless energy, humour, kindness, generosity, care and concern for others. All determined to make you a noble personality, resulting into a terrific beautiful woman. That is the beautiful woman I wish yourself to be transformed into.

Effort of this book is not to place you on a pedestal from where you could announce that I am beautiful. Instead, it attempts to make you aware of your true potential—that with sincere efforts you could also become a ravishing beauty, a cynosure of all eyes.

The woman's beauty is like a dew drop on the lotus petal. It is like a soothing morning breeze, or the thrilling dance of a peacock in the jungle under cloudy sky, or the singing of black sparrow (Koyal). In fact, it is the most warm thing on earth, probably the epitome of God's creativity. Nothing can match it, not even the soothing cool moonlight. Yet the great writers and poets of our times have tried to focus on the vast canvas of womanhood. They have given numerous similes to describe it. In the process, they have created masterpieces of poetry and fiction. Who can forget Munshi Prem Chand, Sharat Chandra Chattopadhyaya, Bankim Chandra Chatterji, and Nobel laureate Rabindra Nath Tagore.

Notwithstanding India being the land of legendary beauties, like Rani Padmini, Menaka, Urvashi and Chitralekha, the psyche of a common Indian woman today is significantly moulded by films and TV actresses, and models looking from every other page of Indian and western glossy magazines.

The ever changing trends of beauty and femininity in today's society have also affected the young ladies as a normal and natural happening. The film beauties have become the role models. The catwalk and fashion models set the standards of beauty for the young girls. There is a mad rush in the fashion boutiques of big and small cities to get the Madhuri type of Choli or Sridevi kind of tight fitting blouse. The parlours are busy giving their young clients the hair cuts of their role models.

It is not uncommon to find ladies wearing slit evening gowns while going to marriages and evening parties in the hitherto conservative cities like Hyderabad and Nagpur. Also, backless blouse or deep low-neck skimpy blouse no more remains a taboo. Yes, things are changing fast.

An ultra-modern hair style, flamboyant hair-do, bare shoulder gowns, one-strap gown, high slit gowns, deep rounded low-neck blouses may or may not suit you. It may look too cheap and vulgar on your person. People around you may not digest your new look. No doubt, when you show your cleavage and bosom, people are lured towards you. And, why not? When you go all out to exhibit your physical assets then why should menfolk not lick their tongues? If the onlookers give you hungry gazes, they are not to be blamed. And, why should they be?

The skimpy dresses which reveal more than what they cover are best suited for film actresses or fashion models. They may also be appropriate in those social gatherings and parties where people belonging to the fashion and glamour world meet. Wearing such clothes by film actresses and models is just normal and natural because they are earning their

bread and butter on the basis of their physical assets. It is their professional compulsion to look glamorous and wear revealing dresses. For them, it is not at all an uncomfortable situation to move around in a party with deep-neck blouse. The body is their biggest asset, they are here to encash that asset. So, what is unnatural about it? After all, people turn their heads to look at their well kept, well cared beautiful body. And, why not people should turn their heads twice or thrice?

Naturally, they (models or actresses) dress themselves to kill. It is their profession to look attractive and alluring; it is their job to look stunning and promote trendy and mod outfits. Who will, otherwise, come to see their films in theatres or their catwalks in fashion shows? Then who will pay them lakhs and lakhs of rupees for doing just one ad campaign? Why the producers, directors or big companies will put so much at stake? The answer is very simple—it's only because of the craze among the people due to their charming and alluring physical assets.

So what, if some people with old thinking and liking don't like their dresses or makeup. What is wrong with such style or fashion, one may ask. They are simply pursuing their career as any other girl would do. Isn't it normal for a girl to become dress designer or interior designer or doctor? Similarly, they have become actresses and models. So, what is the problem? No, there is no problem. Everybody has got the right to express herself and choose the career of her choice.

But things are not so simple as they appear to be. Simply saying "No problem" would not put them in the right perspective. Actually, the basic requirements of the women engaged in professions like stage shows, fashion modelling, television and film acting, are quite different from those pursuing other careers like business executives, doctors, teachers, etc. Since their (models or actresses) recognition and success entirely depend on their looks and other physical assets, so looking alluring and beautiful is their foremost

requirement. They have to stop bothering about the naturality or artificiality of their clothes and appearance, the code of ethics for social conduct, and their own discomfort while putting on skimpy attires, which many a time surpass all the limits of decency.

In the name of entertainment and under the garb of the so-called liberalisation of the visual and print media, most of the private foreign and Indian TV channels are dishing out such stuff which cannot be termed as civilized or decent as per Indian standards. In the name of high fashion, beauty pageants and catwalks, there is nothing but naked legs and semi-covered boobs all the way.

Whether we agree or not, it is true that almost every young lady of our country has in her mind these fashion models and actresses. They wish to put up such makeup as the actresses do, they try to get that particular dress which such and such heroine has put on to do a dance sequence in that box-office hit.

So, by saying "there is no problem," the problem won't vanish in the thin air. Certainly, there is a problem, and quite serious. That is, the common Indian woman is still not mature enough to differentiate between the artificial world the models and actresses live in, and her own real world where she has to live up to the norms and values of society.

She has to project the true image of the Indian woman. You have to differentiate between the artificial and real. You know, a model has got all the time to look after her face, her skin, her nails, her body shape. She can devote plenty of time in selecting her dresses and their accessories because she has to create an aura of glamour in a make-believe world, where she appears to have descended on earth directly from *devalok* (heavens). Here, you must understand that a makeup which looks quite charming on the heroine in a movie may appear completely absurd on a woman toiling in the office the whole day. The artificial living of modelling and filmdom can never become the cup of tea of an average Indian

housewife or a career woman, howsoever hard she may try to copy it. Yes, she will never succeed in that copying business, but in the process she is bound to lose all her natural charm and beauty.

While going through these pages you may gather an impression that I am against the girls who are engaged in modelling and acting careers. But it's not just like that. No, I am definitely not against them. I have no intention of projecting them in derogatory terms. After all, they are also from our own families, very much our own daughters and sisters. So what, if they have chosen a career of their choice which is more glamorous and highly rewarding in terms of money. But what I am against is their commercial exploitation by the "traders of feminine beauty". The traders being film producers, directors, advertising agency people, the owners and editors of glossy film and other glamour magazines, fashion wear designers and other people in related businesses.

If I start narrating the obscene and ugly incidences of the recent past in the film and advertising world, then this book would be too small to accommodate all of them. But, even then, who can forget that obscene photograph of Mamta Kulkarni covering her bare bosom with her hands, or of that small-time, one-film heroine Trishna being photographed with male hands on her bare bosom, or of Ms Madhu Sapre and Milind Somen appearing in their birthday suits for a shoe company ad.

These are some of the marked out indecent, utterly disgraceful and highly deplorable incidences which I could recall quickly. Of course, there are hundreds more which may be mentioned here. But, I am sure that will spoil your mood. And, secondly, that is not among the issues which we are supposed to highlight in this book. Remember, the book is designed not to denounce the femininity but instead, to uphold its charm, grace and fragrance.

12

The Mystique Language of Beauty: Learn It

EVERY girl, every lady has her own characteristic physical attributes—complexion of skin, height, weight and other such features. Every woman has her own requirements according to her education, career and social status; society and the community she belongs to, city and the country she lives in. Apart from these external factors, her preferences, attitudes and tastes also influence the manner in which she likes to project herself, dress herself, or the way she chooses her wardrobe, her makeup, her accessories like shoes, scarves, gloves, handbag, hat, etc.

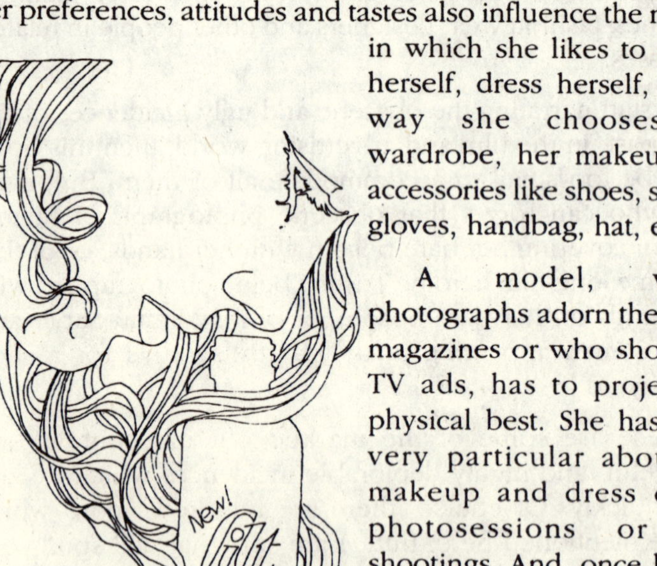

A model, whose photographs adorn the glossy magazines or who shoots for TV ads, has to project her physical best. She has to be very particular about her makeup and dress during photosessions or film shootings. And, once her job is over in a particular photo-session or ad film, no one is bothered to know how she behaves, talks, walks or thinks in her real life. Why is this so? Because, she is considered just as a baby doll, a piece of glamour, whose only job is to look photogenic. And, the matter ends there.

But it is not the case with you. You are being watched constantly. Literally, you are in front of camera all the twenty-four hours —whether in office, or at home or on street or in the market. Wherever you are, you are being judged constantly and evaluated critically. So, your job or requirements are entirely different from that of a model. And, you should understand this difference clearly.

Just open the Oxford dictionary and see what the word "beautiful" means. It says, *"someone delightful to senses". That is, the senses of the onlooker, the beholder. And there goes a saying, 'The beauty lies in the eyes of beholder,' it may or may not be in the person who is considered/called beautiful.*

Albert Einstein, the great scientist once said, "Loveful union of God and nature is the woman".

Great inventor Thomas Alva Edison believed, "The best thing in world is truth, and the most fragrant aspect of that truth is a woman and her inherent qualities"

According to great Indian scientist and Nobel laureate Sir C V Raman, "The woman is the true representation of the magnificent and creative magic of the God. Her creation is the message for purposeful motivation and eternal peace".

Another learned Indian scientist Jagdish Chandra Basu eulogised the woman as: "It is she who nurtures the act of tolerance, love and care for others with her magnetic and alluring presence".

But the wife of a rich Mumbai businessman, who is famous for his collection of vintage cars, feels herself on cloud nine when she loads her body with tonnes of jewellery while going for parties. In her words, "People like my sense of selection for precious stone jewellery and I like to give them surprise

each time I meet them". At any given time the jewellery she puts on is worth more than one crore rupees, as has been stated in one high society, glossy magazine.

But leaving this walking "human jewellery shop" to remain engrossed in her precious belongings, let's now talk about the **mystique language of beauty.**

The nature has desired and designed every woman to be attractive. Every woman wants to improve her personality for getting a good job or an understanding life-partner for leading a happy life. She can certainly achieve all this provided she is determined in her will. For that she has to become a dreamer, the one who can dream her success as an attractive woman, a lady with magnetic appeal, who is sensual. The dream is essential, without which you are not going to make it. All the charms can be yours once you firmly decide to mould yourself into a pleasing personality. Let it be your personal affair, strictly. Don't share it with any one. Once you are determined to become charming and alluring, things would start moving your way. You have to discover your latent qualities and true potentials, and with creative and intelligent application of beauty ideas you can develop a real charming visual appearance.

"Beauty" is the impression which you create about yourself with careful and intelligent planning. You have to discover the ways of putting all your natural assets to work for you. "The life is beautiful indeed"— this fact you can understand only when you know how to project your best image.

Well, there may be many shortcomings, flaws, not so perfect features in your appearance. But, never mind. There are ways to tackle them, to minimise them. And, you will agree with me that there is no adverse situation or problem which cannot be dealt with. You can always go for nose, face or chin uplift, fat reduction and other such things which the modern-day cosmetic surgery offers. Then, thousand and one types of makeup lotions, powders, packs, creams are available which can do wonders with your appearance provided they are used under professional guidance.

For cosmetics' real, wonderful effect you have to simply watch a film heroine without her makeup and other paraphernalia like jewellery and designer dresses. Without beauty aids and trendy clothes, the film heroines are just like you, a next-door girl. Anyway, I feel most of your physical flaws can be minimised or made to look obscure in the heightened presence of your positive points, i.e. perfect features. There is no dearth of such examples. Like, mother of two grownup daughters, Dimple Kapadia, is still going strong despite the fact that the age is on her minus side. Same goes true for the forty-plus Rekha, the darling of many hearts. Why forget the next-door girl type Shabana Azami, or the homely Jaya Bhaduri.

So, the path is not that rough or new. Many ladies before you have treaded that path which leads to success and self accomplishment. There is nothing new. Draw your motivation from the legendary beauties of our times. But you must have a dream of your own; not the dream of joining the filmdom but the dream of becoming a charming woman, who is always at ease with herself and keeps others at ease while interacting with them. Life becomes so full and enjoying for an attractive woman when she feels happy about herself, her family.

A beautiful woman is never too conscious about her makeup, clothes and body. Instead, she is able to devote her time and attention to those around her, and in return she gets the reward of being called as charming and alluring. If her attention remains glued to her ownself only, i.e. on her lipstic or falls of saree or her sandals or other parts of her attire, then where is the time for her to give attention to the people around her, to talk to them. She remains aloof, busy with herself all the time. And, in turn, she receives the comments like, "Oh she is too proud, prudish, snobbish, fidget, drab or snooty".

So, it is for you to decide what you want to become — snooty, or the "Bhuwan Mohini", one who attracts the entire universe by her charming, alluring, graceful presence. And, believe me, every girl (including you) on this earth has got some plus points in her personality which can be further improved or highlighted to attract the people towards her. She can certainly be successful if she knows how best to project her positive features.

There is no school or college in India from where you can learn the art of personality development. Our all the teaching institutions including the professional colleges teach their students various subjects like Physics, Chemistry but not the art of personality development. The curricula of our teaching institutions including professional colleges do not tell how should you present yourself before the people, or why is it important to develop a pleasing personality, or how a lady should acquire the grace, poise and much needed confidence so as to equip herself with the necessary armoury to face the battle of life.

Recently, of course, I have heard about some enterprising ex-models and actresses who have started some finishing or grooming classes in Mumbai and Delhi for the girls interested in modelling as a career. But, still, I did not have an opportunity to visit any of such schools/classes, neither I know any of the teachers personally who conduct these courses. I have no idea what they teach, what is the prospectus or curriculum, what is the satisfaction level of the students? So, it will be unwise on my part to comment on their performance and competence. But, I do hope that these classes and schools would expand both in number and reach in the future.

This book may not be the last word on self improvement, nor may it provide the answer for your each and every query. Yet, it has got the potential of becoming your true guide and friend on whom you can bank upon for sincere and honest advice which is very difficult to get these days.

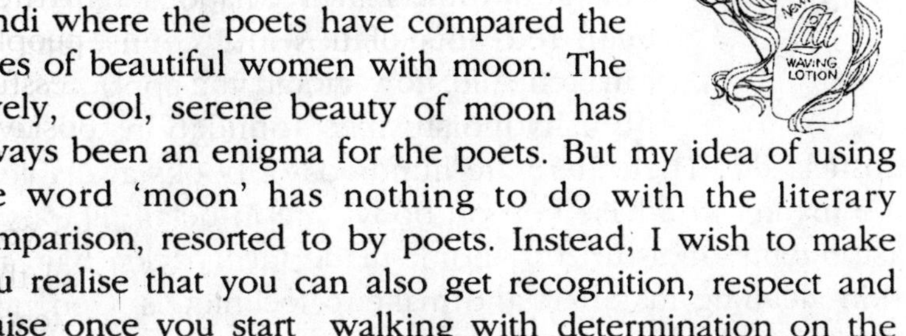

Aim The Moon, Nothing Less But The Moon

There are hundreds of songs and poems in Hindi where the poets have compared the faces of beautiful women with moon. The lovely, cool, serene beauty of moon has always been an enigma for the poets. But my idea of using the word 'moon' has nothing to do with the literary comparison, resorted to by poets. Instead, I wish to make you realise that you can also get recognition, respect and praise once you start walking with determination on the path of enhancing your personal charm and allure.

A director friend of mine told me an interesting incident concerning his leading lady in one of his movies. At an outdoor location, after the packup, he was relaxing with his cup of tea. The leading lady, also sipping tea, joined him. Casually, she said, "Many of my friends say that I look more beautiful and charming in personal life than on screen. I cannot tell you on how many occasions people have told me that I was much more prettier off-screen. Lately, I have also started believing their opinion. I wonder whether the cameraman is doing his job perfectly or not?"

My director friend continued sipping his tea while listening to her. After few moments, he responded, "Yes, your friends are correct in their opinion because you are more full of life, enthusiasm, laughter and zeal in your personal life than on screen. You attract them more in your real life because you are a warm person, down to earth, always smiling. That is why, probably, they like you in your real life more than your screen image."

For Your Looks Only

(A Beautiful Face, the Mirror of Your Heart)

In every woman magazine, fashion and family periodicals, or in the woman pages of Sunday magazines of national dailies you can find lots of tips and counselling on makeup, i.e. how should you apply mascara, blush, moisturizer, foundation, eyeliner, lipstick, etc. Then there are hundreds of books available in the market to advise you on body care in detail, like using astringents, moisturizers, home-made face packs, hair and skin cleaning materials and makeup techniques. Generally, these books are written by experienced makeup experts usually called as beauticians, though few among them are also known as hairstylists. It is quite common to find the makeup men and hairstylists working in the same parlour, or even a single person may be doing both the jobs.

I am not an expert on either the beauty treatment or hairstyling. So, my views on these subjects will be just like those of an average man.

Often, many women believe that whatever they have learnt since their childhood about body care and makeup is sufficient to give their face the required beauty treatment. But, that is seldom true. Yes, it is true that most exotic and beautiful women lived in our country in the bygone era when there were no fashion and beauty magazines, nor the beauty parlours. Probably, believing this fact most religiously, most women do up their face with whatever little is available at their dressing table. And, they remain totally dependent on the home-made traditional beauty care aids available aplenty in the Indian households. I don't consider the use of these beauty aids harmful. On the contrary, I would say that they are far better than what is available in the market in the name of custom-made cosmetics, which are often priced exorbitantly.

No doubt, you should update your knowledge by reading women and fashion magazines. For, they regularly highlight the makeup techniques and the currently available beauty aids, like uses of different cosmetics, new types of hairstyles, beauty treatments for different types of skin, etc. But be careful. Don't allow youself to be swept away by the craze for new things and styles. You should always apply your mind to evaluate the effect of these on your own face before using them. Analyse them thoroughly in your mind, whether they will suit to your type of lifestyle or not. A latest hair-do of a leading lady in a movie may or may not suit you. Simply, because your job requirement is different. Or, that particular hairstyle goes well with a long face, but you have a round face. So, don't go for any new makeup technique blindly.

You can surely go for any amount of makeup or adopt any hairstyle as per your liking or occasion. But, never forget your inner self, who you really are. Never try to be something or someone you are not. Men may usually say that you are exotic and pretty, but don't allow yourself to be carried away by their flattering remarks. They may be right. But you must remain your normal self, keeping your feet firmly on the ground, the ground of reality. Because, what you are, that is your normal self, reflects on your face. I have seen many women start behaving foolishly the moment they hear such flattering comments from the menfolk. But, my simple advice to you is: keep your head on your shoulders, it is going to be a life-time affair, a routine for you, that they (men) will be praising your beauty.

I am personally of the firm view that in no case you should allow yourself to be considered as a lifeless doll, a show-piece, or a clay model (hanger dummy) of a departmental store on which some makeup has been done. Remember, a heavily done up face without its distinctive style and grace is as useless as a rubber doll. Emotionless face, howsoever beautiful, is considered as awkward and

imbecile. A look of intelligence and confidence is a must on your face. Otherwise, you will be called nothing but a 'brainless beauty'. For you to be called as "woman of substance," it is essential that your face must not look like just another face in the crowd. Instead, it should reflect enthusiasm, intelligence, confidence and boundless energy.

So, more than the eyeliner, mascara and lip gloss, it is your strong belief in your inherent qualities that will ultimately provide the much needed glow to your face.

"Sir, what do you think is the most precious piece of jewellery a woman can put on to enhance her charm? Is it a diamond-studded nose ring, ear rings, or necklace?" I asked once my learned colleague Professor (Dr) Y.M. Gupta, Professor and Head, Department of Physics, School of Studies, Jiwaji University, Gwalior. Responding to my question, Dr Gupta said, "Well, friend, I am afraid to say that none of them. In my opinion, the best jewellery is a genuine child-like smile. Nothing can match the glow of an innocent smile, which instantaneously attracts every one around".

A happy and contented life shows on the face because beauty starts from within, and with slight help from outside (makeup) it shall present before the world the total you. To be really charming, take a pride in your personality. You just cannot continue to look pretty if you do not feel contented and happy. Inner happiness and contentment impart your face with a unique glow. Then, you need little makeup to present yourself before the world. At the same time, if you adopt a positive attitude and use your intelligence to increase the beauty of your face then your looks will be really terrific. People will admire you for these qualities instead of taking note of lipstick shades on your face.

For Your Eyes Only

"The mystique is a necessary envelope for making the beauty eternal. It helps in carrying the attraction of a woman for a longer period of time. And, the eyes play an important role in accentuating a woman's beauty." These are the words of my friend, Professor (Dr) G.C. Baijal, Professor and Head, Department of Ophthalmology, GR Medical College and attached J.A. Group of Hospitals, Gwalior.

Eyes constitute the most expressive part of our face. Any facial expression starts from the eyes and is not complete without their involvement. You must have often heard people saying, "Oh, her eyes are very expressive, they (eyes) are always smiling". You can express your feelings and emotions simply through your eyes, without even uttering a single word. In expressing sorrow, amusement, astonishment, admiration, pleasure, in short every feeling, the role of eyes is indispensable.

If you like somebody, and you want to know more about him, then it is not at all necessary for you to say so in words. You can express your feelings simply by a long interested look (stare). That will convey the message. If you have gone to your friend's place to pay your homage to the departed soul of his/her father, your tear-filled eyes are enough to convey your sad feelings. You don't need words for that. Rather, words are useless on such occasions.

We come across many meaningful, hit songs from our old Hindi films whose lyrics have the eyes of woman as their theme. In such songs, the lyricist compares the leading lady's eyes with almost everything beautiful and serene. Like, he says, "Your eyes are the whole world," or "they are like deep lake filled with blue water," or "they give the impression of the eyes of a female deer—Mrignayani," and so on.

Many film stars of yesteryears like late Nargis, Meena Kumari, Madhubala sometimes used to express their intense

feelings of love, sorrow or anger only through their eyes; no dialogues were required. They used to emote so perfectly that in some scenes there was no need at all for the actual dialogue delivery. But you are not an accomplished actress like them. So, you have to learn this art by practice which you can do, all alone, in front of your bathroom mirror.

Naughty eyes on a beautiful face add an extra charm of innocence. But, this expression comes when you really feel very happy and light within yourself. To send the message of admiration and appreciation across a gathering you simply have to blink your eyelids. An expression of amusement is there when you open them wide. Disapproval or condemnation can be seen in your eyes when you blink them along with shaking of your head.

Use your eyes to the best of your advantage—smiling eyes can say millions of words about the happy state of your mind. These can attract anybody. "Love at first sight"—you must have heard this saying thousand times. It's all about attraction of eyes. Mesmerism of the smiling eyes is something which can affect every one. They immediately put the other person at ease, and he feels like responding in the same manner. When you greet someone with smiling eyes, it creates a very positive impression about you in his mind which lays the perfect foundation for a healthy relationship in times to come. The first eye-contact makes all the difference about the impression, good or bad, a person will carry of you. So, greet everybody with smiling eyes.

For any conversation to be effective, the first pre-requisite is that you must have a full eyeview of your audience. You should have a direct eye-contact, i.e. remain face to face all the time during conversation. This rule holds true whether the audience is just four, or forty, or four hundred. Number of the audience is not important. The most important thing is eye-contact. Nothing can substitute it. Even if you are talking to your friend, or lover, or husband, on one-to-one basis, the roving or unstable eyes create a very bad impression. It simply shows that you are not paying full attention, or it may reflect your disinterest even if you are quite interested in the talk. So, your roving gaze creates an impression which you just don't want to convey.

Some women feel hesitant to look directly into the eyes of their lovers or husband out of shyness. Instead, they look towards their hands or feet, because establishing a direct eye-contact with their men makes them nervous. And, their heart starts pulsating vigorously as if it will come out of their ribs. The man who understands your shyness may take it as a plus point of your personality. But, if your man is not familiar with your shyness, he may feel offended.

In India, on the first night *(Suhag Raat)* of a newly-wed couple, the bride mostly keeps her eyes closed when the bridegroom enters the room. She covers her face with the veil of her saree. Only through the side glance or by the sound of footsteps she knows that the bridegroom has entered the room. Even after he sits on the bed, her eyes remain closed. He requests her to lift the veil but she does not. Then he lifts her veil and requests her to open her eyes. But, feeling shy, she keeps her eyes closed despite his repeated requests. And, he loves it that way because a shy woman (wife or lover) is considered pious, pure, virgin, chaste and untouched; this all she can convey with her closed eyes. Who says that closed eyes cannot speak, they can speak as much as the open naughty eyes.

The language which the hypnotic eyes speak can be very romantic and provocative. It is difficult to describe in words. The mesmerising effect your half opened eyes with slightly parted lips could have on your man in the bedroom is more than thousand words spoken by you. No doubt, the eyes have got great expressive power, they act like the mirror of

your heart. It is not easy to hide your emotions.

To make your eyes more attractive you may follow some of the tips and suggestions given here: If you are using spectacles and feeling awkward by their presence on your face then you should get rid of them at the earliest. This you can do with the help of your eye specialist. Today, with the use of advanced surgery and treatment techniques, it is possible to say good-bye to your heavy-looking specs which mar the beauty of your eyes. Because with the specs on, whatever eye makeup you do is of no use. As an alternative to specs, you can use soft contact lenses or go for Eximer laser surgery. Another more better option is to go for (LASIC) laser surgery of the cornea. Many girls are opting for the Eximer or Lasic laser which are easily available in major cities. But there are some de-merits also of these surgery options which one must evaluate and assess before opting for them.

Second thing, most worrying for many women, is the shape and size of their eyes. They think their eyes are too small or too close. Some are worried that their eyes are too deep set. Some carry the impression that they are too big and popping out. In short, they don't like their eyes.

Well, no two women have got identical eyes. The complex which many ladies carry about their eyes throughout their life is many a time not based on reality. But, they feel depressed when they compare their eyes with others, specially the actresses and models. In fact, if you observe, there cannot be a classic mould set for the ravishingly beautiful eyes. The definition of beautiful eyes differs from face to face. So, don't feel demoralised if you don't like your eyes. Any, every eye can be made to look beautiful and attractive with little care and intelligence.

Many ladies use heavy eye makeup to make their eyes look attractive, but the results are sometimes disastrous. In

fact, no amount of mascara, liner or shadows can help you in beautifying your eyes until and unless you know the rules of the game.

You must understand that heavily madeup eyes may look all right in a fashion show or on the screen but not in your daily routine. In fact, very little eye makeup is required on daily basis. Yes, occasions like marriages or evening parties demand extra makeup for your eyes. But, here again, makeup requirements differ from person to person. Sometimes a simple eye-liner may do wonders in making your eyes alluring. If your eyes have dark circles around them or have puffy or swollen appearance then this may be taken better care of by paying attention to your relaxation and health requirements rather than applying heavy makeup.

Of course, to lighten the dark circles around your eyes you should apply some light coloured foundation or concealer before your routine makeup of cream and powder. But, remember one thing: you must not apply a very light coloured foundation or concealer, otherwise you will start looking like an owl. Sound night sleep, proper relaxation and a diet rich in fresh fruits and green vegetable salad will certainly help you to cope up with your dark circles and swollen eyelids.

The secret of most alluring eyes is that they don't look made-up. Instead, they appear natural. But, then, everywoman has got her own sense of beauty. Some use the makeup to hide this or that shortcoming while others use it simply to enhance the effect of what they have naturally. Often I fail to understand why some ladies try to hide their real beautiful eyes behind a heavy makeup and pretend to look like some actresses or models they fancy for. This type of extra effort may be okay for an occasional evening gathering which may be of special importance to you, but it can't be a routine affair.

For daily life, your eye makeup should be in harmony with your lifestyle and personality, Remember, you have to search for that particular look of your eyes which combines well with your charm and works best for your face in totality, not for your eyes alone. The most effective makeup (which may be a simple application of "Kajal" i.e. cake eyeliner) is that which enhances the enthusiasm, confidence and innocence of your eyes.

To give a permanent fresh look to your eyes, wash your eyes with ice-cold water for two to three minutes, 3-4 times a day. And, never forget to wash them after a strenuous eye-job like reading, writing, typing or sitting with your computer for two hours or more. Make a habit of putting two-three drops of rose water (Gulab Jal) in each eye before going to sleep. This will help overcome any infection and the smudging of eyes, and give your sclera a clear white tinge instead of the usual muddy appearance.

Here is a word of advice from my friend, famous eye-surgeon, Dr Harish Chandra Setiya, MS, DOMS. According to him, a thorough eye checkup by a specialist is necessary if you observe a change in vision like inability to read the small print, or difficulty in seeing the distant objects clearly, or if you develop a headache after doing an eye-job even for just fifteen-twenty minutes, or you have double vision or any other abnormality which was not there earlier.

Imparting a desired look to your eyebrows forms an important part of the eye makeup. Some women are not satisfied with the shape and size of their eyebrows. They wish a change in the thickness and length of their eyebrows or the arch they make. Yes, it is true that eyebrows can be made to look different from what they are. But this change should be well thought of and carefully planned after consulting upon a makeup expert. Because, you can't go for a change in your eyebrows every now and then. Whatever change you opt for will be there for years to come. So, it is essential that you think about the change carefully and be clear about how do you want your eyebrows to look like. It is advisable that you should never attempt the desired change on your own. Instead, seek the help of a professional makeup artist. Tell her/him your expectation, draw a line diagram or sketch of the desired shape of eyebrows, discuss it, and then allow her to do the job for you.

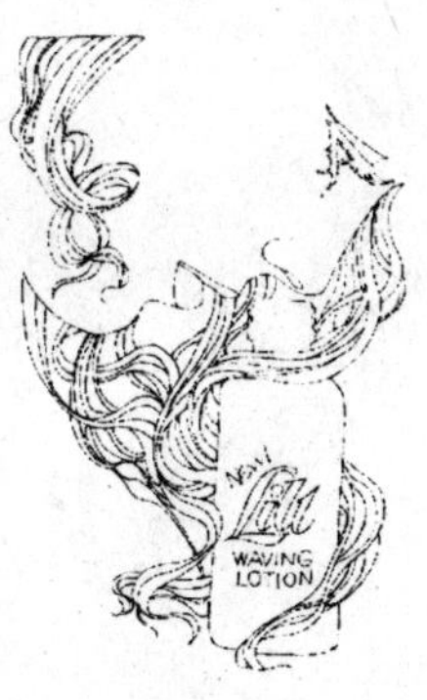

Few months ago, at a party, I met a woman who had her eyebrows completely shaved off and drawn dark black lines at their place, and out of these black lines small thick hair were peeping out. The whole look was so much distracting that it was difficult to look at her face beyond a second.

Another young lady among my acquaintances had shaped her eyebrows in such a sharp-curved arch that they looked totally incompatible on her face. Although on her part she tried to give a new look to them, she ended up giving her face a shocking look.

Instead of opting for drastic changes in your eyebrows' look, what you really require is reshaping through skilful threading by a professional makeup artist. Many light strokes of an eyeliner pencil instead of a bold single can do wonders in imparting a natural look to your eyebrows. Also, do not try to change the colour of your eyebrows by the liner pencil, instead get them dyed by a beauty professional.

The same thing goes for your eyelashes. Thick eyelashes is the dream of every woman, but few have them as a natural gift. Artificial lashes are now in vogue but their proper application must be understood. How to apply them and remove them without damaging your natural eyelashes is a technique which you can master with the help of your makeup expert. Also, you have to learn curling, plucking and dying of the lashes. Application of 'Kajal' (cake eyeliner) at the upper

lid margins add to the allure of the sparkling eyes. Some women apply 'Kajal' on both the upper and lower lids. But, you choose whatever suits your eyes best.

It is Your Lip-time

Tere honth kya hain, Gulabi kamal hain (Oh, your lips are like pink lotus flower); *Anarkali,Tumhare honth bilkul Gulab ki pankhudi ki tarah najuk hain* (Oh dear Anarkali, your lips are as beautiful and tender as the rose petal).

Described above are just two examples of numerous ways in which our poets have eulogised the allure of lady lips. After eyes, your lips are the most expressive part of your face. They are beautiful in every shape and style, and express how happy you feel inside. The happy heart note comes automatically on your lips. If you are not smiling, it has to do a lot with the way you feel about yourself.

I have referred earlier to my colleague Prof and Dr Y.M. Gupta's view that the most precious jewellery a woman can put on, is a child-like smile on her lips which glows her face equal to the glow of thousands of mercury bulbs put together. Another of my friends, Subroto Ghoshal, seemed to echoing Dr Gupta's view when he said, "There is nothing beautiful about a woman who cannot smile". Subroto Ghoshal is former national president, Indian Junior Chamber and Chief staff Trainer, Air India, Mumbai. It seems a woman, who just can't smile, is afraid of disturbing the curd which she has been carrying in her mouth or her dirty-uncanny teeth will show off, or her lipstick will be smeared off. Some people say such a woman has rocks in her jaws. Whatever the description, one thing is certain that one wants to avoid looking at non-smiling, expressionless face. Obviously, it does not interest you at all. Neither you are interested in knowing the reasons which led to the making of such a face.

A woman's face without something put on the lips looks incomplete. The naked lips are all right for some occasions, but not always. A little gloss, or lipshine, or light shade of lipstick can do wonders on your face. And, the most funny and pleasing thing for you would be when people would say, *'Oh Miss Bublee, you look wonderful without any makeup'*.

Here, what I mean is that your lip makeup must blend with your natural appearance. Some women, on the contrary, have the habit of doing very heavy lip makeup. They use very thick layers of lipstick and that too of very dark colours. Some even go to the extent of applying lipsticks of off colours like black berry, Sienna, Fuschia, orange or frosted ones, which give them more artificial and madeup look. In such extreme cases, the highly overdone lips scream for the attention of the onlookers. But, what do they get is a fleeting glance.

In fact, there is no wrong or right way of using the lipstick. It is up to you what do you want to do with your lips. You can put them to best of your advantage. If done-up in a suitable make-up, they can impart you with a look which enhances the basic charm of your face. Lips are never more provocative and inviting than when they are shining with a natural colour lip gloss, i.e. light pink-rose.

Some women do not choose the shades of their lipsticks and gloss as per skin complexion and type of their whole make-up. A very dark colour lipstick will not suit a wheatish or dark complexion, neither it will look good on a very fair coloured lady. Also, the type of foundation and blush has to match with your lip makeup. Otherwise, you will have only your mouth to be looked at in a party.

Another wrong practice followed by many women is that they try to match the shades of their lipsticks with those of their clothes. Like, if they are putting on an orange saree then they will wear an orange colour bindi and lipstick too for the

sake of matching. But, believe me, that looks very odd. Do you know that matching fashion is obsolete. It is a thing of the bygone era. Today, fashion pundits are announcing from the rooftops that a casual, natural look is the order of the day. So, don't go for carefully planned, precisely specified, matched and heavily overdone looks. And, of course, you don't want your lips to enter in the room before you make the actual entry! Do you want your lips to be the only part where onlookers should look and they (lips) remain the only part of your total appearance, they should notice?

You really don't need to change colour of your lipstick everytime when you put a new saree or salwar-kameej or skirt-top. It is natural that you will be putting on clothes of various colours on different days. Yet, it won't be difficult for you to find a suitable, nice shade of lipstick which will match with all of them. And, that shade can be light rose pink in the daytime and little brown pink for the night.

Many a time you might have noticed that a simple lip gloss is all which you require for a particular occasion. You can use highlighter or lighter foundation between your nose and upper lip. This will reflect the light and will make your upper lip protruding. The protruding upper lip gives an innocent and sexy look to your face.

Many women do not like the natural shape of their lips. They think that they would look better if they are able to have more full lips or thin lips or protruding ones. And, as per their own definition of beautiful lips they try to give them the desired shape with the use of lip liners and pencils. Consequently, they even go to the extent of changing the natural shape of their mouth by applying the lip makeup beyond or over their natural lip margins. And, when they take tea or juice, the artificial shape of their lips is transposed onto the cup or glass and the lips are left with their natural shape. And you know what may happen if they happen to

meet their man during the day time, which of course can very much happen, then what about the lips at that time if he insists for a kiss? It is better not to talk about them because they will be half left half gone with passionate kiss which shall be there as part of normal exchange of pleasantries. Or, she will tell him, "Oh, please don't kiss me, my lipstick will be smeared off". So, it is always comfortable to stick to the original shape of your mouth. Don't give in to the temptation to change it.

Still, I believe that you can always enhance the glamour and appeal of your lips without really changing their natural shape. After applying basic powder and foundation on your liplines, you can go beyond them a little bit if your lips are too thin. Or, you can apply makeup just short of the liplines if your lips are thick.

If you are in the habit of chewing your lips as some women do, then resist it as it looks bad and also gives the impression that you are nervous.

In winters, always apply some vaseline on your lips to prevent their becoming dry or pealed off. But, you must not lick them with your tongue as it will make them further dry.

You can always touch up your lipstick two or three times with lip pencils. But, in no case, you should resort to full lip makeup after eating or drinking or after delivering a lecture as on all such occasions your lipstick is going to be smeared off with your lip movement.

What about Rest of Your Face

(The Chin, Cheeks, Ears, Nose, Neck, Forehead)

She has got the chiselled features, she has got very sharp features. Oh, God has made her in leisure time—these are some of the comments which you may hear about some women, but, these are some very occasional faces which you do not encounter as a routine. Yet, there is no classical set of

features which can be called as ideal. Still we are in habit of drawing comparisons and conclusions as per our fancy.

You must understand one thing: though eyes and lips add to the beauty and attraction of your face, yet they cannot look beautiful if set in a clumsy background (face). It is just like a painting which cannot look beautiful if we mishandle the canvas on which it is being made. So, you should not underestimate the overall look of your face. But, then every woman has got her own fancy and sense of ideal facial beauty and allure, in whose mould she tries to fit herself.

Here, I wish to remind you that my idea of discussing the female beauty has nothing to do with the makeup styles and tips. I simply want to make you aware of some basic "physical facts" about your face which you may not know. I consider this discussion essential because most of the articles in the fashion magazines are written by makeup experts (beauticians) not by the people from medical profession. These experts, though well-versed about the role and effect of various cosmetics in beauty care, lack the basic medical knowledge. Since these articles and beauty experts are the usual source of information for an ordinary woman, she is deprived of the basic medical knowledge which is so essential for effective beauty care.

Facts: Skin of Your Face

Any woman who desires to enhance her facial beauty should understand that she can only succeed if she knows about her face inside out. The skin of your face (including neck) is very delicate, and is somewhat different from that of your other body parts. The first difference is, nowhere else in the body, skin is providing direct insertion (attachment) to the underlying muscles. The pale and soft facial muscles are of smooth (involuntry) variety. These are commonly called as muscles of facial expression, and their number varies from 13 to 15 on each side of your face. The facial skin is constantly pulled and stretched with each expression without you being aware of it. Creases and wrinkles develop on your face depending upon the expression you use most often.

There is a term 'amoebic facies' which applies to those who suffer from chronic intestinal amoebiasis. These persons usually suffer from constant indigestion, hyperacidity, dull aching pain and fear of compulsion to go to the toilet. All this get imprinted on their face giving it a typical tense look.

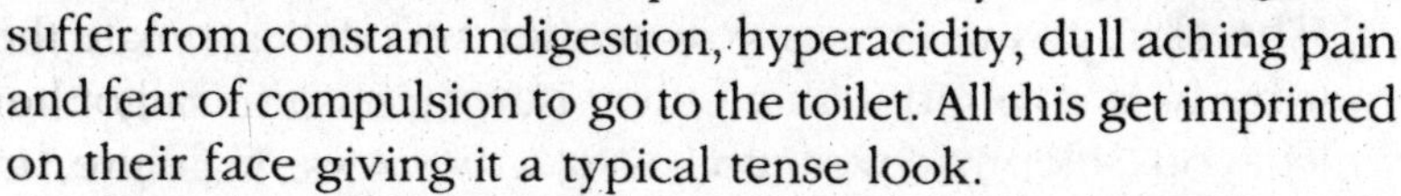

Same thing goes for other type of tensions which may leave a permanent mark on your face such as creases at places like forehead, root of nose, truncated and everted upperlip, pulling of the eyebrows towards the centrepoint. So the point is, if you want to give your face a permanent allure and attraction then try to avoid becoming tense every now and then. This would spoil all your efforts towards looking beautiful.

Sagging of the skin at the chin, under the mendible, side of the neck, side of the eyes, below the eyes, and at the naso-labial fold is the usual sign of ageing. Same goes with the wrinkles and creases. They will be there whether you like it or not. By no means you can avoid them. But, certainly, you can delay their onset. You can prevent their early appearance. You can subdue their effect.

Here, I would suggest, among tips, a well proportionate diet, healthy food habits, proper sleep and relaxation. These are some of the essential things which you must adopt for a healthy skin. After all, skin is a part of your body. Whatever you eat also goes for its nourishment via the blood vessels. One essential thing people often forget about skin care. It is that external help and pampering of skin cannot succeed until and unless it is supported by the internal (systemic) means. No amount of cold creams toners, moisturizers,

cleansers can be of any help until you give proper nourishment to your skin from within. Remember, a lustreless skin, dry leather-like appearance is the result of bad food habits, excessive work and little relaxation. It is impossible to be corrected just by makeup. (You will read more about the health aspect in the *"Body Beautiful"* chapter.)

The skin of the face is very tender and delicate. Rest of your body is covered with clothes. But, face is the only part which you seldom cover, not even in winters; it is always exposed. So, naturally, the skin of face has to bear the brunt of adverse atmospheric effects and changing weather conditions. It has to face the cold breezes, or the ultra violet (UV) rays of the sun without complaining.

Weather extremes tell on your face. In winters, exposure to extremely low temperature and cold winds may lead to dryness, chopping of skin and bursting of the subcutaneous blood vessels resulting into subcutaneous haemorrhages, roughness and breach in the continuity (cracking) of the skin at many places. If your facial skin weathers the extreme winter conditions without proper care and preparation, then remain in no doubt that it would leave permanent scars on your face. The best protection for the tender facial skin is the lavish application of cold creams and body lotions which contain various oils and moisturizers. Simple application of any good body lotion or cold cream helps a lot in the low temperature climates.

Another natural phenomenon having an adverse effect on your facial skin is UV rays of the sun. It is better if you avoid falling sunlight direct on your face which can be best done by using a cap or umbrella. If you are on the sea beach, try to remain under cover of the beach umbrella, and when resting on the beach, cover your face with a small towel. While driving the scooter, use a cap to protect the skin of your face. Sun screen lotions and creams are of great help in

the summers and they should be used as often as required. If your job requires you to remain outdoor for most of the day, then you must understand that even a small exposure to the sun daily during April-September may sometimes result in a permanent damage to your tender facial skin. It may be in the form of premature ageing, wrinkles, darkening of the exposed parts, and cracking of the skin.

Also remember, direct sun is not the only thing which is harmful. The UV rays, in fact, are known to pass through window glasses (85%), car windscreens (70%), and also through your clothings, specially synthetic ones. Daily use of sunscreen lotions and moisturizers is a must to neutralise the adverse effects of UV rays.

Skin Care is a Habit

Beautiful skin cannot be taken for granted. Neither it is an accident if one is beautiful. To preserve one's attractive looks and beauty requires lot of effort and care. It is not that you have to take skin care when there is some damage or problem (acne, spots, black heads, allergies, infections). But you should turn skin care into a habit which you have to follow religiously. And, believe me, it is never too late to start caring about your skin, which will prevent its further damage though it may not ensure the complete reversal of the damage already done. Many people around you may wonder why you need to go to a beauty parlour when you have got a natural beautiful skin. One thing they don't understand is that your skin is so beautiful simply because you look after it regularly. A clean, clear, radiant skin is the foundation of any beauty programme.

Skin care, if started at a young age, is like a life-long insurance which will ensure that your skin remains sparkling, radiant and supple even when you grow old. As in the life insurance, if you take a policy late in the life (when your body is afflicted by various diseases like heart attack, diabetes,

hypertension) the premium paid by you is quite high. This premium would have been considerably low had you taken the policy in your young age. Similar is the case of your skin care. If you have not bothered about the damage borne by your skin in your young age, then naturally efforts required to rectify the damage would be more time-consuming, hard and sincere. But once you get into the habit of it then you will feel pleasure in pursuing your skin care. All this will ultimately prove rewarding in terms of yourself moulding into a charming and confident person.

It goes without saying that tall claims made by the cosmetic manufacturers (including bathing soap) are often blunt lies. Some may promise to give you a complexion similar to Juhi Chawla or Madhuri Dixit, while others may claim to make you as beautiful as Sridevi. But, the fact remains that they are drumming their tunes simply to lure you. Maximum share of price which you pay for any popular cosmetic goes to the packaging and container. Second largest share is taken care of by advertising campaign and the manufacturer overheads. The actual price which you pay for the real product is not more than 15 to 20 per cent in any case. So, what you are paying is actually for the things (packaging and advertising) which are least important to you as a consumer.

A brand name is of no use if the cosmetic inside is ordinary and is available at a much lower cost elsewhere. That is why before selecting the cosmetics and other toileteries at your favourite departmental store, look around for the alternative products available to you at a very low cost, and sometimes at no cost at all. Yes, you have guessed it right, I am talking about the age-old, time tested, traditional home-made products available in plenty in your kitchen and garden.

And, tell me, who knows better about them? You or me? Obviously, you. But, even then, I would like to discuss with you some of them, simply to remind you of their real benefits.

But before that let me talk something else, i.e. skin stressors.

Skin Stressors and Skin Problems

I have talked with you about the bad effects of cold weather, UV rays of sunlight, and mental tension. But, this is just tip of the iceberg. Among other factors affecting your skin adversely are dry air, hordes of chemicals present in soaps and cosmetics, air pollutants like fumes from automobiles and industries, polluted water which you use for washing and cleaning your face. All these affect skin of your face very badly. They alter its normal acid pH state and weaken its immune system.

Use of airconditioners in hot weather or room heaters in winter is also accompanied with their harmful effects. They render the air of your room absolutely dry which affects your skin adversely, making it dry too. This de-moisturizing effect of the dry air can be prevented by keeping an open water-filled bowl on the table or desk, some fresh flowers in a water-filled vase may have the same effect. Or else, you can use a humidifier to make the room air moist and fresh. Some may advise you to use the latest modern gadget, the ionizer, which makes the air fresh and charged with negative ions.

You may not be aware that most of the soaps, bath products, shampoos and cosmetics contain lots of chemicals which have a deleterious effect on your skin. Although manufacturers of these products go all-out in advertising their plus points, seldom they take pains to tell you about the damage they cause to your skin. The damage to your skin may be in the form of premature ageing, dryness, allergies, decreased body defence mechanism, altered acid pH, etc.

The normal healthy skin has got tremendous capacity to bear the onslaught of these damaging products for a long period of time without any visible effects. This is mistakenly taken as 'no bad effect' status of these products. Actually, the harmful effects of these products start appearing only after

their constant use for about 15 to 20 years. Therefore, it is but natural for anyone to conclude that they are harmless. But, that is seldom true. Many costly, so-called beauty soaps, in fact, may cause so much damage to your tender facial skin in the form of dryness that it becomes aged, i.e. wrinkled, quite earlier. Caustic content of soaps, colouring agents, perfumes and other chemicals are directly responsible for damaging your skin. While choosing your soap, make it sure that your choice is based on its positive effects (benefits) rather than the beauty of model advertising ıt. It is better if you go for a mild variety soap, i.e. the one having less or no caustic effect with a cream or glycerine base, and containing natural oils. Well, it may take you some time for deciding the right soap for you, but opt for the one with negligible side-effects.

The same holds true for other cosmetic products like shampoos, cleansers, moisturizers, toners, etc. They are also made of a variety of chemicals. These are nothing but absolutely synthetic products. As a normal procedure they are tested for their safety on animals and then protected trials are conducted on volunteers also. Even then there are cases when they have caused rashes and various types of skin problems in the form of allergies and acnes. Apart from their immediate side-effects, there are many long term side-effects similar to soaps, i.e. lustreless skin, premature ageing, excessive dryness, etc.

Why do you close your eyes and nose as soon as you come across a truck or a tempo emitting black smoke, passing by your side? Simply because you cannot tolerate the smoke. But, can your skin tolerate it which is unable to cover itself? No, it also cannot bear these poisonous fumes, giving rise to acnes and allergies. Apart from these fumes, the suspended dust particles and other air pollutants make your skin infection-prone and lustreless. One million tonne of smoke and gases are produced by automobiles fumes in Delhi per day, according to a recent report prepared by Delhi Traffic Police and the Pollution Control Board, Delhi. In the rainy season, you might have often noticed that your skin is more prone to infections. This is due to the air-borne pollens, fungi, spores which are responsible for this.

If you wash your face with sea water, within few minutes you would notice a layer of salt on your face. This salt you can even rub off on your palm. Similarly, hard water from other sources, like well and boring, affects your skin adversely. It does not clean your skin properly, and leaves some deposits on it. The chlorine in the water also damages the skin. Same goes for other hazardous substances which are present in the contaminated water. As contaminated water is the main cause of various stomach diseases, make sure that water you are using is clean and safe, both at home and outside.

Before discussing specific skin problems I would like to talk to you about the "normal skin profile of your face". This multilayered cellular organ of your body is not merely a plastic covering of you. It is a dynamicaly active organ consisting of two layers—epidermis, superficial layer; and dermis, deep layer. There are many pores which give passage to the hair. On your face the hair growth is quite different than that on your husband's face. In his case, the face sports a beard whereas your face has very small, light coloured, fine and delicate hair which are attached to their bases, hair follicles. By the side of these follicles are present the sebaceous glands which produce an oily substance called sebum. It is the activity of these glands which determine the nature of your skin, whether it is oily, dry, mixed, or normal. The number of these glands ranges from 65 to 100 per square cm. Apart from these glands, sweat glands are also present near the hair root. They produce sweat, and their activity is governed by many factors like climate, emotional state, endocrine balance, autonomic activity — sympathetic and parasympathetic

functioning, etc. The normal skin pH is always towards acidic side, roughly 4 and 5.

Your skin is affected by your overall health status. It is also likely to be affected by the way you counter the environmental stressors. The nutrients which you take in the food go a long way in helping you fight the harmful effects of extreme weather, whether winter or summer. Certain vitamins and minerals are essential to the formation of collagen and elastin fibres present under your skin. When the skin is deprived of essential nutrients, it becomes dry and rough, and may have rashes and eruptions. And, it is prone to early and rapid ageing.

So, remember, your skin care is just not complete without a balanced diet. The menu for such a diet is simple: fresh green leafy vegetables in their raw uncooked form, fresh fruits, particularly citrous variety, fruit juices, milk, yoghurt, eggs, pure ghee, vegetable oils, whole-wheat flour bread, and total abstinence from fried, oily, spicy, over-cooked variety of food. Generally, if you are on a balanced diet then you are not required to take extra supplements of essential nutrients, minerals and vitamins for skin care. They are only required for the special skin conditions like ageing, dryness, roughness, highly wrinkled and lustreless skin.

There can be some benefit by taking evening primrose oil capsule 1500 to 3000 mg per day, vitamin E capsule 200 to 400 mg per day, 50-100 mg vitamin B3 and 25-50 mg of potassium. Vitamins A, C, D in their respective therapeutic doses are also beneficial. But it is essential that you consult a dermatologist or your family physician before taking any medicine. The self medication is very dangerous and completely uncalled for.

"Acne" is a problem specific to the face, affecting particularly teenage girls and young ladies. It can occur to anyone. One out of every five women suffers from it. Whether black, white or wheatish, any type of skin complexion can become afflicted by it. Usually, those having the oily skin are prone to get acnes and pimples. Many people regard it as a nervous disease while others term it as a hormonal problem. There are many experts who claim it to be a disease due to defective dietary habits.

Whatever maybe the causative factors, the fact remains that the acne problem shatters a girl's confidence, and she feels very much depressed about it. If not treated properly, it leaves scars, roughness and uneven shabby-looking patches on the face which are difficult to hide even by heavy makeup.

Acne can be classified in mild to very severe type. In between these two categories come two more types. First type is the simple mild black heads which you may get occasionally on your cheek or chin. In second type, the black heads may be large and difficult to heal quickly. Third is the inflammatory variety which have definite pus collection and they may leave scars. The most severe of all is the fourth type of pus-filled pimples having cavities. These cover the whole face and may also erupt on other parts of the body, like neck.

Acne treatment becomes a bit difficult for the doctor when the patient loses self-confidence due to her ugly look. Somehow or other the patient wants to get rid of acne at the earliest. A harmful tendency of the acne patient is that she develops the bad habit of pinching and scratching her pimples. She does not have patience, and wants to wipe off acnes from her cheeks at the very first opportunity.

Under the effect of 'androgens,' the male hormones, the sebum producing glands of your face become highly activated during the puberty resulting in excessive production of oil. Apart from excess oil, the skin thickness also increases due to overactivity of basal layer of skin cells. Excessive oil and dead skin cells along with blocked ducts play havoc on your face,

creating an ideal situation for acne formation. Anxiety and nervousness are among the important factors responsible for hormonal imbalance.

The "help for acne" starts with proper cleaning habits. You should daily wash your face three-four times with a mild soap to remove excess oil and dead skin cell debris. Do not rub or scrub your face with turkish towel. Always blot dry it with tissue paper. Resist any temptation to break up or scratch the pimples, as this leads to spreading the infection to a wider area. And, chances are that scratching would leave scarmarks on your face. After cleaning the face and making it dry, apply some good acne cream containing 'Retinoic Acid' i.e. topical vitamin A. This shall break down the oil as well as the dead cells. Many good acne creams also contain Benzoyl Peroxide along with vitamin A. This combination is most effective as Benzoyl Peroxide is a potent bacteriocidal. In the most severe form of acne, a small amount of sulphur (1–5 gm), in its pure form, can be mixed with Benzoyl Peroxide and applied on the face till the acne heals.

Zinc, vitamins A, C and B complex are of great help when taken orally in extra doses. For good results, light balanced diet is recommended during treatment. Many a time the inflammatory and infected acne may require local and systemic antibiotic use, but it all depends upon the choice of your physician.

"Skin allergies" are among the common diseases which the so-called modern living has given to mankind. The environmental pollution, increased use of various chemicals in daily-life in the form of soaps, shampoos, detergents, tanning lotions, cosmetics, synthetic clothes, allopathic medicines and the ever-increasing stress— all these have resulted into skin becoming more sensitive to allergic reactions. You may not be aware of another new phenomenon—in the last eight-ten years the wastelands in our country have seen the haphazard growth of 'Gajar Ghas,' a useless weed with small white flowers. This vegetation is known to sensitize human skin and mucus membrane in a very harmful way.

Chemical hair dyes also do not suit many people, giving rise to severe allergic reactions. Certain types of diet also lead to allergic reactions in some people. Remember, your body is particularly more prone to allergic reactions in days just prior to the onset of your periods, during and after the fever especially viral. Many chemicals, present on your body, may cause allergic reaction when exposed to the direct sunlight. Sometimes, in the winter months some chemicals may become allergic which were not so during the other months.

Be cautious that whenever you get any allergic reaction on your face including lips and eyes, immediately take the advice of your family doctor. But before you get proper medical attention, you may wash your face with cold or just ordinary water. Resist the temptation to apply any cream or lotion because you never know it may further worsen the reaction. So it's better to wait for the doctor to diagnose your allergy and prescribe the treatment. Sometimes due to insect bite or the herpes you may get skin sensitization. Here again, don't go for spirit or antiseptic cream, instead pay heed to the physician's advice.

Now, I come to the 'home remedies'. My idea of discussing these remedies is not to dismiss as useless various cosmetic products available in the market. Instead, I wish that you should partake of the immense benefits and unparallel rewards of various home-remedies which are in use since ages in our households even before the entry of cosmetics in our country. In the field of cosmetics production in India, Mr Ibrahim Patanwalla played a pioneering role when he started his unit to produce Afghan Snow in Mumbai in 1909. Before him British, French and Dutch ladies used to bring their cosmetics range from their native lands. But, this all is not more than

hundred years old. A very short history indeed.

In 1954, Max-factor started its production here, followed by Gala of London in 1959. This they had to do because the import of cosmetics was banned by the government. And, in the years to come many more joined the race to create a niche in Indian woman's heart—like Lakme, Ponds, JK Helen Curtis.

Apart from these manufacturers who mostly produced synthetic cosmetics, some other companies also launched their herbal and ayurvedic formulations. Some products were quite effective while others were simply gimmicks. Now, it's very-very difficult or rather impossible for an ordinary consumer to judge whether there is any sense in the tall claims of the cosmetics manufacturers or they are just playing gimmicks.

You often hear many fancy terms like facials, toners, moisturizers, cleansing creams, milk lotions, skin tonics, nourishing creams, vitamin creams, deep cleansing milks, face-packs, night creams, astringents, and so on. It is but natural for you to not having in-depth knowledge of their properties, merits-demerits, side-effects and their constituents. You simply purchase and use them on their face value, not on the basis of their actual action on your tender and soft facial skin.

It may be a bit difficult for you to completely wipe all the cosmetic products off your dressing table. Neither it is advisable. But, it is certainly possible for you to look out for more natural, aptly suitable, and readily available items in your home itself for maintaining and enhancing the glow and suppleness of your facial skin. A long list of such products and their natural ingredients we have inherited from our grandmothers. The simple and practical philosophy behind these natural cosmetics is: "anything in its raw and natural, unprocessed form is more suitable to your skin than the various synthetic products available in the market".

Do you know that as per the recorded history, the first cleansing cream was formulated by the great Greek physician Galen, in second century AD. Galen, in his book, 'Methodus Medendi Vel de Marbis Curandis,' describes the mixture of bees wax, oil and rosewater as a very effective formula for cleansing purposes. You may be surprised to know that his formula was used till recently in the preparation of coldcreams and cleansing creams. Some changes made to Galen's original formula by various cosmetic manufacturers were not to enhance the effectiveness of the product, but to improve its appearance and shelflife.

Now, I would give you some tips about natural, traditional Indian facepacks and cleansers. The cost of these beauty aids is nothing as compared to those artificial ones which you buy from the market. And, most important, they give excellent results without any side-effects.

Have you heard *of Ubatan*. It is a Hindi word used to describe an indigenous facepack. *Ubatan* is quite popular among majority of Indian women who are still not lured by costly, artificial cosmetics. To make it, mix small quantity (50 gm or so, as per requirement) of gram flour *(Besan)* in cold milk along with turmeric powder (just 1–2 gm). Make a thick paste of the mixture and apply it on your face for 15–20 minutes before your morning bath. As it becomes dry, you can remove it by moving your fingers on your face. It will be peeled off easily. Then, have your bath as usual. It acts as a very effective cleanser. Use it for some time, then see your face glowing with a bright tone. For a change, you can also use maize corn flour which also has a good cleansing effect.

Among vegetables, you can use cucumber as a cleanser. Smash a cold, small-size cucumber. Apply it on your face. Keep it intact on your face for ten-fifteen minutes, then wash it off with cold water.

We usually throw away orange peels, but they can be used as face cleansers. Just rub the orange peel against your facial skin so that its juice is smeared on it. After a short while, wash it off with cold water. After continuous use, you will be surprised with its excellent effect in toning up the glow of your face. You can also store orange peels for the off-season use. In that case, soak the dry peels in small amount of milk or rose water and use the resultant mixture as facepack.

Banana pulp also is a very good facepack which can be applied for ten to fifteen minutes before bath. Among other natural facepacks or cleansers are ripe pineapple pulp, raspberry pulp, musk melon (Kharbuja) pulp. They can be used as usual before bath for ten to twenty minutes, depending upon your convenience.

To make an ideal facepack for winters, mix one egg, two teaspoonfuls of rose water and one teaspoonful of bees honey. Make a paste of the mixture and use it just once a week.

Mix few drops of almond oil, juice of one fresh cold lemon, one egg, and ten to fifteen ml of orange juice. Apply the resultant paste on your face and leave it for half an hour. Then take a bath. Your facial skin will get toned up.

Another easy-to-make and very cheap facepack is prepared with "Multani mitti," a yellow greenish coloured, layered clay easily available at general stores. It is mixed with some rose water to make a thick paste, which gives excellent results when used as a facepack daily for ten-fifteen minutes before bath.

To make a soothing facepack for summers, rub sandalwood on a stone. Also keep sprinkling rose-water on the stone every now and then to make a paste. Apply this paste on your face during summer season. It will give you a very-very soothing and cooling sensation. Sandalwood powder can also be added to other mediums to prepare various facepacks.

Another effective facepack for summers can be prepared from mint leaves *(Pudina)*. Crush mint leaves in small quantity of water and apply directly on your face.

You can also make very effective and beneficial facepacks from various pulses like soyabean, masoor, urad, moong, gram dal, etc. Soak overnight any of the above pulses in the required quantity in water, still better if kept soaked for more than twenty-four hours. Smash the soaked pulse in a mixie or on any plain stone to make a paste. Add few drops of almond oil and milk to enhance its beneficial effects. Then, apply it on your face for half an hour. It will soon become dry. You can rub it off with slight pressure of your fingertips. Take your bath as usual.

Here is a formula to prepare a facepack using different oils. Mix warm olive oil, almond oil, Vit. E oil, and evening primrose oil in 10, 2, 1, 1, proportions respectively. Then massage the mixture on your face for 15–20 minutes twice a week in winters. It would keep your skin beautiful and soft for days together.

You can also use steam treatment to make your facial skin beautiful. For this treatment, first cover your face for 5–6 minutes with a towel soaked in hot water. Thereafter cover your face with ice water-soaked towel for the same duration. This would give you a clean, soft, and beautiful skin.

So, these are some of the traditional Indian formulations for keeping your skin glowing and soft for a long time. These are your best protection against the environmental assaults, side-effects arising from liberal use of the synthetic cosmetics and other stressing factors.

13

Body Beautiful

IN India, immediately before the marriage, the would-be bride is looked after specially as far as her looks and body care are concerned. The elderly ladies in the family give various traditional beauty treatments to her face, hands, feet, in fact her whole body, to turn her into a charming *Dulhan,* the bride. This has been going on since ages, and I am sure will continue for ages to come. The special care and beauty treatment of the would-be bride results invariably into a glowing complexion, smooth and soft skin, alleviation of black heads and pimples. And, she is transformed into a real beautiful woman to be loved and appreciated by her husband and in-laws. There is no doubt, if a woman can adopt these advices and methods as a routine in her life then she can have a complexion and beauty as that of a *Dulhan* forever.

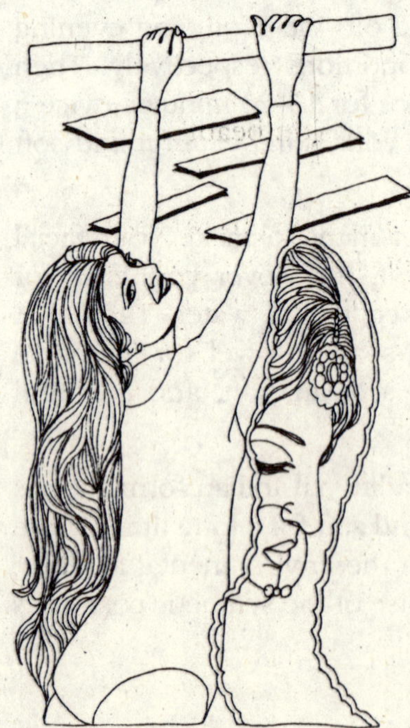

The first and foremost pre-requisite here is **personal hygiene**. No amount of makeup, costly jewellery or dresses is going to make any

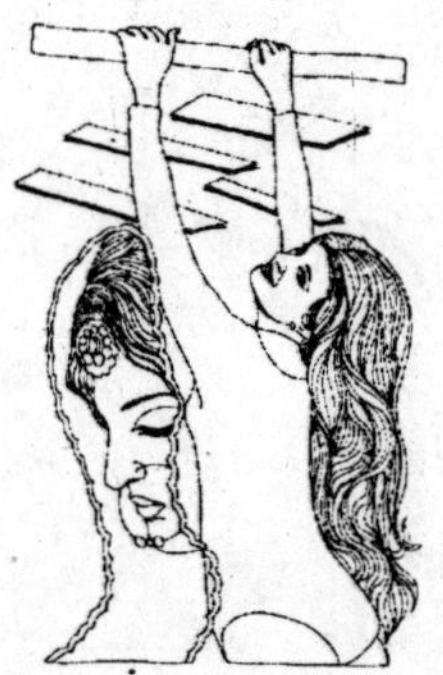

sense, if your body as such is not fit, good and clean.

Let's begin with your **oral hygiene and teeth.** Most of the women are not very particular about their teeth and oral hygiene. They do brush their teeth in the morning, and that is all, they think. But no, things do not end here. Having properly cleaned, bright teeth is very important for your overall health. Because, with unhealthy teeth on your bleeding gums whatever you eat would also infect your body. Moreover, if you have stained, plaqued teeth then naturally you will not like to show them up. But, for this sole reason would you keep your mouth shut all the time? Bleeding gums, dark gums and coated tongue call for immediate attention. Periodontist, orthodontist or simply a dentist is the person whom you should contact for stained and plaqued teeth. Thanks to the advancement in the field of cosmetic dentistry, it is possible now to create a new look for your bucked, chipped, gapped, discoloured teeth.

Don't consider it luxury but it is essential for you to look after your teeth properly. And, for that it is necessary that you have a regular interaction with your dentist at an interval of three to six months, even if you do not have any apparent tooth problem. Remember, brushing your teeth once in morning is certainly not enough to keep your teeth shining like pearls. Make it a habit of brushing your teeth two to three times in a day with a soft round tipped brush. Floss your teeth as often as possible, but at least once a week minimum. Rinse your mouth with water thoroughly each time you drink or eat something. The stains of nicotine, pan masala, tea, coffee, cola, chocolates and of other coloured foodstuffs can be removed by rubbing a mixture of soda bicarbonate and common salt (in equal parts) on your teeth. Or, you can go to your dentist to get them bleached.

Bounding is the procedure which your dentist may use to stop further damage to your gapped, stained or damaged

teeth. He paints, layer after layer, a liquid acrylic on your teeth, thereby creating a new surface on your teeth. This bounding may last for five to six years and can be easily replaced as and when needed.

For overcrowded and bucking teeth you can always go for the metal or invisible plastic retainers or braces available at your dentist's clinic.

For the bad breath, I tell you a fact that most women who have it are not aware of it at all. While leaving bed in the morning, every body without discrimination has got a bad breath. At that time, it is better to avoid coming in contact with anybody before brushing your teeth. But most serious is the problem of bad odour coming from one's mouth during daytime which creates a very bad impression about oneself. Among major causes of bad mouth odour are: lodged food particles between teeth, plaqued teeth, coated tongue, throat infection, digestion of certain foods like raddish, garlic, onion, turnip, etc. Apart from these, local abscess and caries may also cause bad breath. Constipation, indigestion and other medical problems can cause it.

First precaution against bad breath is that you must clean your mouth each time you eat or drink something. Flossing and brushing of your teeth daily is a must. Apart from cleaning your mouth, you can always use mouth freshners in liquid or tablet form. Cardamom, clove, peppermint tablets, aniseed fennel (saunf grains) etc. are very beneficial as mouth freshners. Common tooth pastes are not sufficient to remove the bad odour from your breath. For that many mouth freshners are available in the market. Bad breath bacteria can be taken care by one such potent mouth freshener, marketed as blue coloured solution—listerine. It can kill up to 92 per cent of bad-breath bacteria.

In your personal hygiene, the second most important thing is your clean, pleasant-smelling body. In fact, the skin care

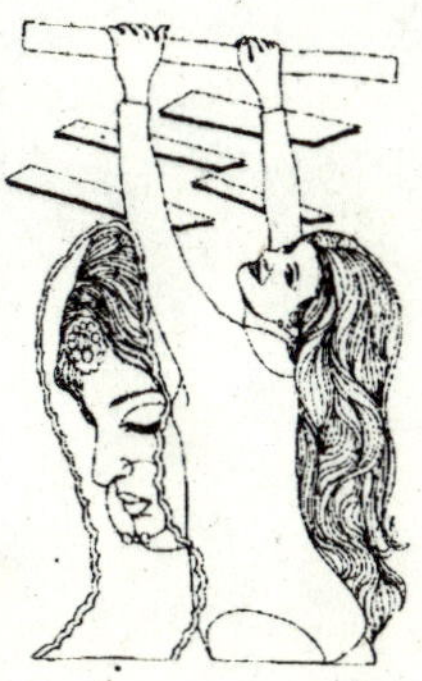

does not end at your chin. Your entire body is covered by twenty-one square feet of skin which is as important as the skin of your face, and needs as much care as your face. Skin is a vital organ which does not need any extra pampering but simple, regular care. Here, comes the significant role of bathing which serves many purposes. And, foremost among them is cleaning the dirt, body odour, dead cells, bacteria, sweat and sebum which accumulate on your body surface when you go about doing your work the whole day.

For skin cleaning, bath with water and soap is the best. Most of the ladies take bath only once in a day, but this is not sufficient from medical point of view. This does not serve the desired purpose. You must take bath at least twice a day—one in the morning, and the other in the evening, or at the bed time. If you are living in a warm climate then you may go for bath thrice also. Because, six to eight hours are enough in summers to make your body dirty and emitting bad odour, notwithstanding the perfumes and deodorants which you might have used lavishly in the morning.

Morning bath and evening bath are two entirely different things. While in the morning you are in hurry, short of time, so an elaborate bathing cannot be advised at this hour. But, even then it is recommended that you should go for oil massage before making it to your shower. Oil massage in winter months is of special significance. A small, palmful of warm olive or mustard or coconut oil can be rubbed all over your body for ten to fifteen minutes. The oil massage you can do yourself or with the help of your mother, sister or maid servant. This oil absorbed in your skin through massage prior to bath will neutralize the bad effects of so-called beauty soaps and also help retain moisutre of your skin.

"Body massage" with massage oils is a great luxury which you must go for as and when you get a chance to have it. Body massage before bath is ideal which you can get either

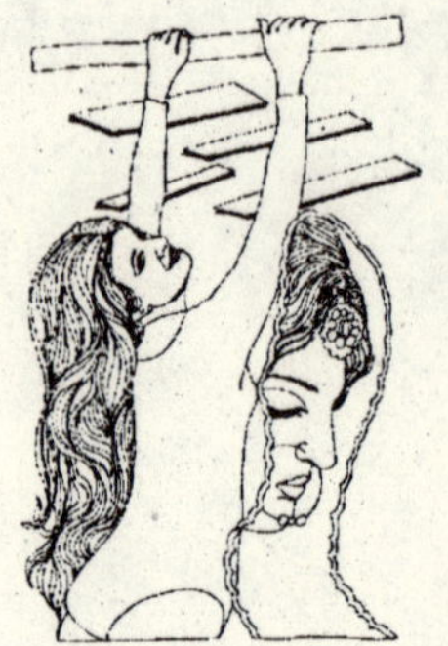

from a professional masseur, or your partner (husband) at your home. In many star hotels, fitness and health clubs have professional masseurs on their rolls who can provide you with this luxury which would cost you anything from one hundred to three hundred rupees per hour sitting.

Actually, if you did not have till now any such experience with a professional masseur, then it would not be possible for you to visualize that how soothing and relaxing such an experience is. The professional masseurs begin massage with your toes and slowly move upwards towards calf, thighs, buttock and so on. The oil used is called as carrier oil like coconut, mustard, or olive oil. You can ask to add in the carrier oil few drops of sandalwood oil, rosemary, wintergreen, jasmine or mongra, any of them you may choose. Second variety of oils is called essential and/or fragrance oils.

After massage from a professional masseur, all your body aches and headache would go away, your nerves and muscles would no more remain tense. Your body will become light and supple like a flower. Stiffness and fatigue will melt away like ice once the fingers of expert masseur will start playing on your body. This transformation of your body is brought about by many changes taking place in it while undergoing the massage—like increased blood and lymphatic circulation, washing away of the excess lactic acid from the muscle tissues, elimination of the oedema or any type of swelling caused by hampering of the venous circulation. Is it not really great?

But be careful, don't go for massage if you are in the family way; or you have allergies, or your skin is very thin and tender, or you have just recovered from an illness, or you are due for your periods in next few days. Wait for things to settle down for normalcy.

You can always go for home-made face masks (masque) as advised in the previous chapter if you feel it good to apply those face masks to the rest of your body. Like, sandalwood paint *(Chandan lape)* in rose water if applied all over the body will enhance the glow of your skin. The same goes for the "multani mitti" pack. Rose flowers in your bath tub will also make it a beautiful experience.

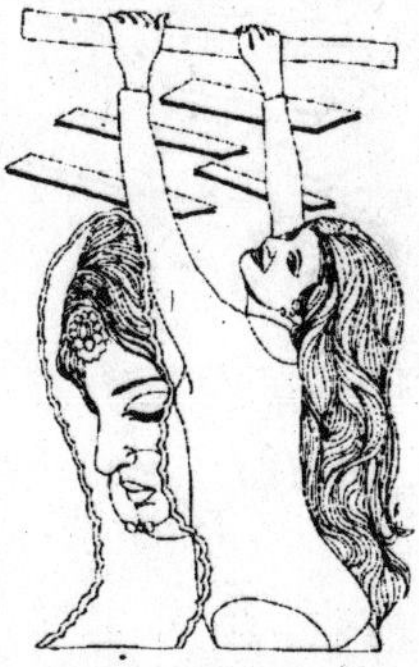

So, the morning bath is more for cleansing purpose and less for refreshing purpose which is naturally there without calling. But the evening bath is more for refreshing the body than for cleaning it. In fact, bath is the cheapest and most effective way of relaxing your body which becomes tired, exhausted and stressed while you undergo your hectic daily routine. And, you would no more require sleeping pills or your soda-scotch.

Here are some tips to give your body a refreshing bath:

1. Choose the time when you are comparatively free, i.e. before dinner or before going to bed, but do not take bath immediately after dinner. You will require at least half an hour to forty minutes for a cosy bath. Allow yourself this luxury of time. No hurry, absolutely no hurry.

2. Arrange for the dim light and light soft music along the bath tub side. You may or may not have telephone in the bathroom depending upon your requirement. Whatever music tape you want to listen to place in the player and make light dim before you enter the tub. Don't touch any electrical switch while taking bath, otherwise an accident may occur.

3. Put the herbal oil or fragrance oil of your choice; it may be jasmine, rose, mongra, kewda; or, any eu de cologn will do. This will be added luxury; it is all yours, enjoy it.

4. You can keep a glass full of iced fresh fruit juice by your side which you can sip whenever you want. It is simply your imagination which can take your pleasure to new heights.

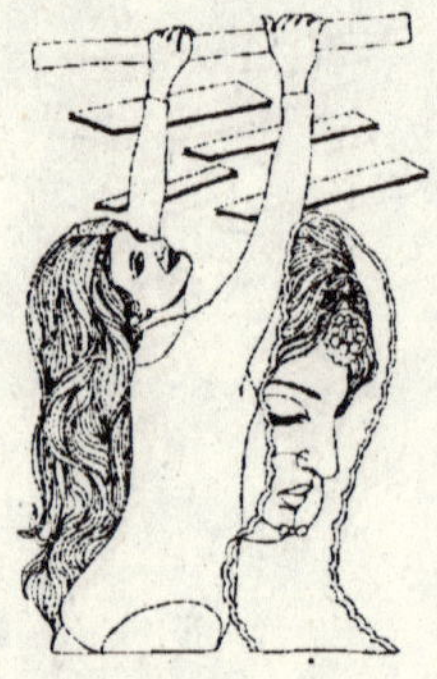

5. Scrub yourself with sea sponge stone or plastic scrubber or scrub brush. You can use pumic stone to remove dead skin of your heels and sole. Remember, there is one essential pre-requisite for a refreshing bath, that is you must feel relaxed all the time. Do not play up your tension switch—tiff with your colleague, tiff with husband, or your money problem. This is your private time and enjoy it. Leave the worries for some other time.

6. The temperature of water you choose depends upon both your liking and the weather conditions. Cold water is best for summers. In winter season, it is better if you choose little lukewarm water, but certainly not the hot water, which may be very bad for your skin and your body as a whole. Bathing in hot water may lead to excessive vaso-dilation, and sebum production is also raised along with increased heart rate and respiration. Very hot water is never soothing or refreshing; on the contrary, it may lead to anxiety and tense state of mind.

   Certainly this sort of relaxing bath is not possible on a daily basis but whenever you get the opportunity, or whenever you feel exhausted or drained out, make it to your bath tub or shower.

Some More Basic Facts about Body Beautiful

How many times you have been attracted to your own bare body while looking in the full-length bathroom mirror? May be umpteen times. That means you love your body, you are proud of it. You think that it is really lovely and attractive, that is why you often fall in love with it. This feeling is very important. It goes a long way in transforming yourself into a pleasing and attractive personality.

In reality, many women don't feel good about their body. They consider themselves either too fat or too thin. Or, they feel that they do not have right bulge at the right place, or

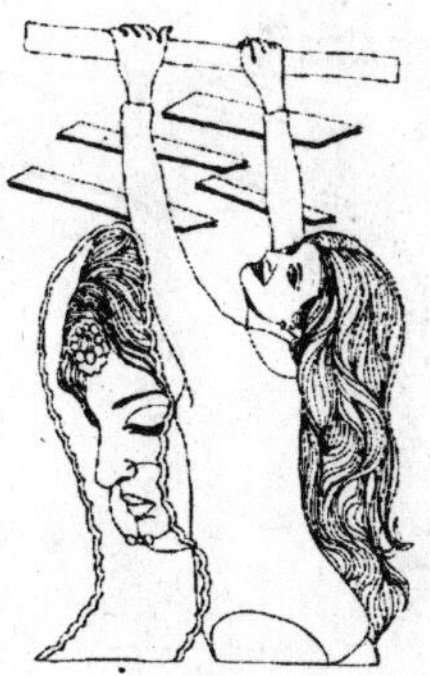

their breasts are too small or sagging, or their hips are too thin. In short, they are just not satisfied with their physical attributes. This negative thinking is the root cause of yourself forming a bad image about your body. The flaws may be there. No doubt, they can be real too, but that does not mean that you stop loving your body. You have to love it, feel good about it, and then you may go for improvement procedures. Be assured that any flaw in your physical attributes, whether major or minor, prominent or obscure, can be minimised, if not totally alleviated.

It is natural for anybody to feel dissatisfied with the way her body looks. This is why, sometimes many otherwise attractive women too feel discontented about minor flaws in their body or looks even if they are almost unnoticeable. It's all due to loss of confidence they suffer from. There is no point suffering in silence, come out with determination to do something for your body flaws about which you strongly feel.

I have talked in detail about "body beautiful" in my other books. I do not consider it proper to repeat those things here. Nevertheless, I would talk here about certain basic requirements with which you must adhere to, to look attractive.

As I have stated earlier how your body looks, the health of its skin, the way it functions—i.e. its total well-being—depends to a large extent on what you eat. The biochemistry of your body is also a reflection of the health of your digestive system. If you go on eating the junk, fried, overcooked, oily, spicy food then you cannot expect your body to preserve its natural beauty for a long time. Your expectations of looking beautiful and remaining so cannot be realised with an unhealthy diet. But then who cares? You may say, "My foot. How can I eat green vegetable salad and fresh fruits? No pizza or cutlets? And, then what about the shami kabab, chicken curry? Oh, I have forgotten the chocolates, so sweet.

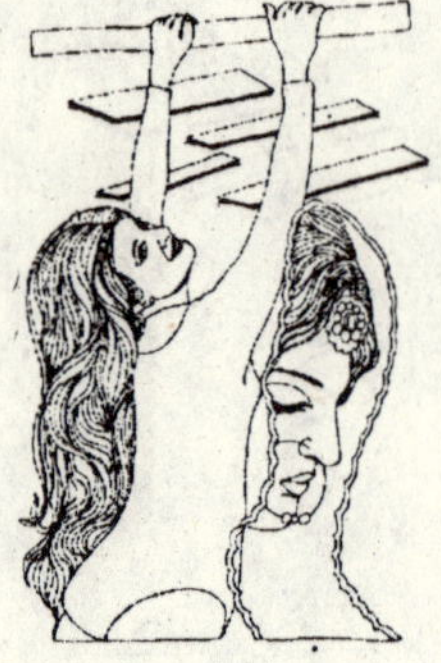

Would you care to pass on a coke to me, please?"

It takes time for you to understand that every beautiful woman in this world if she wants to remain beautiful, adopts a certain pattern in her **dietary habits.** If you go on feeding your body with the junk food you will accelerate the onset of premature wrinkles. Your skin would become sagging, dry and lustreless giving you aged and tired looks. A strict dietary schedule is a must if you want to maintain the hour glass shape of your body and preserve its natural allure with the minimal of makeup. You have to be watchful about what you should or should not eat for the sake of your beauty. No compromises in this regard whatever may be the situation or compulsion, may it be a marriage party, or a family celebration, or repeated offerings of a gentle host. Nothing should make you to say good-bye to your strict diet regime because these are everyday happenings—celebrations, parties, gatherings. Once you make a rule, make sure that you stick to it. Say polite no to the host or friend, but never slip, never bug because once you do so there are chances that you will be doing so again in future.

"The positive way to a beautiful body and good looks surely passes through the careful selection of your food items and your attitude-approach towards the whole biogenic food habits"

Some of the bad food habits and dietary pitfalls are described below:

1. Most of the people select their food on the basis of its look and taste. If you ask them why they eat so, they may simply laugh at you. And, their casual carefree attitude would reflect in the reply: "Well I enjoy my food, I like the pizza or roasted chicken taste. What is new about it? It gives me a great satisfaction, I feel contented. It is a daily routine for me to eat at fast food joints and then

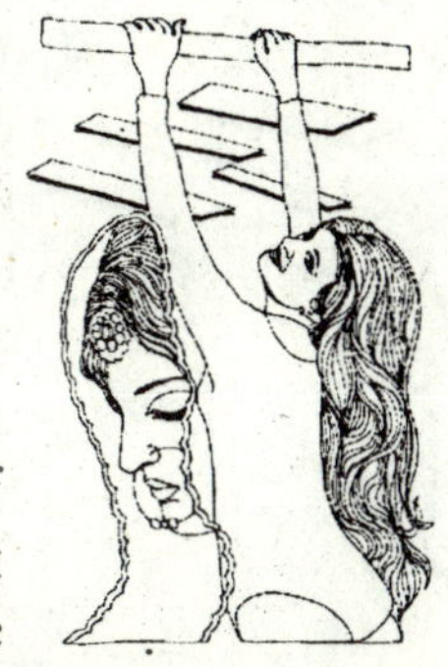

enjoy my favourite ice-cream sometimes two cups in one go. I enjoy that all. So what, if I am a bit overweight, or feel dull and lethargic?"

2. In fact, women, generally, do not at all bother about the nutritive value, static effects, and other important aspects of the food they eat. They are just concerned about the appearance and the tingling-tantalizing effect of the food on their palate. Sometimes, it is impossible for them to resist the temptation for spicy food and snacks, chocolates, coffee, etc. Mega advertising campaigns of junk food manufacturers and fast food joints also lure you willy-nilly towards them. Giving into this temptation leads to many adverse effects, like indigestion, depletion of essential nutrients of your body tissues, storage of toxins and waste products of metabolism, and ultimately ill-health.

3. You have to decide which way you want to go? Whether you want your body to be energetic, supple, swift, with healthy glowing skin, or look dull with a lustreless skin, sleepy, inflicted with diseases, maybe overweight also. If you choose the former option then you must at once get rid of your habit of relishing pre-cooked, highly processed, tinned, overcooked food mixed with chemicals like preservatives, colours, scents, etc. Also to be shunned are food products prepared with white sugar and refined flour. No coke or coffee or frequent bites of cookies or pastries in between your regular meals. Right now start developing the taste for healthy, natural food which are in fact so good to taste that they will become your favourite in no time.

4. Have a strong will-power. Well, you may say, "I have tried but could not keep it up. I know that they are not good for my body, but what I should do for my heart which jumps out of my ribs the moment I look at them".

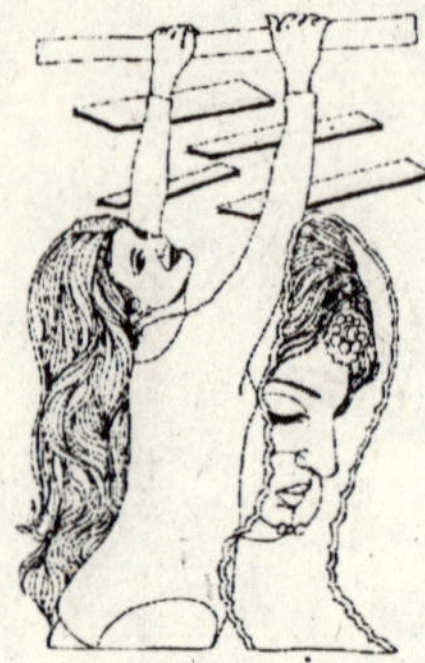

Well, this is no answer. You have to slowly change your food preferences. No sudden or drastic methods are advisable because they are not possible, even if possible in a gush of impulse, then they are not permanent. So, go for slow but steady change, spanning over a period of month or months. Time is immaterial, take your own time. Get rid of that dreadful craving for so-called tasty colourful junk food, it shall be good for you.

5. The strength of a multistorey building basically depends upon the quality of materials used in its construction and in what ratio. Same is true for your body also. Ready-to-eat spicy foods available in the market are often fried in the repeatedly recycled oil. Over-use of a cooking medium, like oil, drastically changes its basic character, turning it into very harmful for human consumption.

   Various hydrogenated oils and nickel compounds are added to chocolates, apart from white sugar, which are very harmful for human body. These cookies, pastries, chocolates give large amount of undesirable source of calories which are stored in the body as fat at wrong places. It is better you eliminate this sort of mouth watering foods from your sight with immediate effect. You may not be knowing how the white crystal sugar is produced. In its manufacture through a chemical process all the beneficial ingredients of the raw brown sugar are destroyed. It is my advice to you that instead of white sugar you start developing a liking for molasses (gur) and jaggery, which are very good and close to the nature.

   The so-called refined cooking oils are, in fact, very harmful because of the chemical process they go through while being refined. Hordes of chemicals are used to make them odourless and colourless which completely destroy their natural beneficial properties. Instead of them, you should go for pure ghee-butter, or raw unrefined mustard oil for

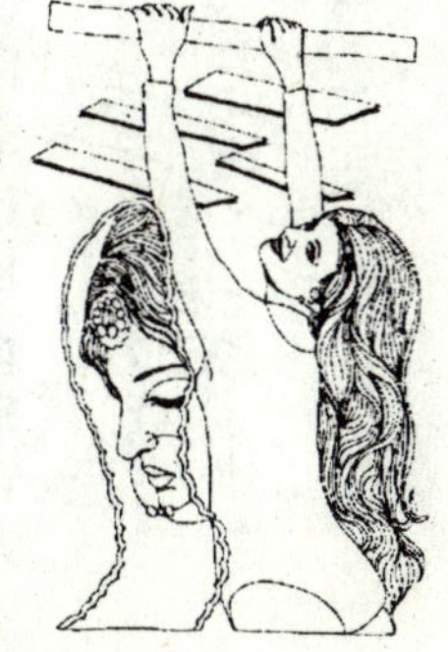

the cooking purposes. But be careful that you have to use minimum of cooking medium which is just sufficient for cooking.

Claudia Schiffer, petite and vivacious international super model, was once asked what she eats to keep herself fit? She replied, "I have fruits, tea and orange juice for breakfast; diced chicken breast, boiled egg and green salad for lunch; tomato juice as afternoon snack, sometimes herbal tea and black grapes; and dinner for me is steamed vegetables along with lot of salad. I do not smoke or drink".

Another international model famous for her sparkling smile, Cindy Crawford says, "My breakfast includes banana, cereals and glass of skimmed milk; salad for lunch; sushi, brown rice and vegetables for dinner. And sometimes I enjoy icecream also".

How does all this sound to you? Impressed a little? Or, it is just okay with you?

What you eat and what you not, goes a long way to shape and influence your mood, nature, thinking, enthusiasm and attitude apart from your figure and looks. In our ancient scriptures like **Vedas** and **Upanishads** the learned scholars have categorised food items as per their effects in two types. First type is *'Satwik'* and the second *'Tamsik'*. Satwik food (like Biogenic food) is easy to digest and gives full satisfaction to heart, mind and tongue. It does not excite the body or brain, nor it make them dull and lethargic. Such food fills the body with energy, gives happy and contented feeling—no evil thoughts, no accumulation of harmful toxic waste in the body. This type of food includes roots and bulbs *(Kand-mool)*, green fresh leafy vegetables; cow's milk and butter, ghee, yoghurt, paneer made from it; whole grain pulses, cereals, beans—sprouted; fresh juicy and pulp fruits, butter milk *(mattha, chach)*, and many other natural foods.

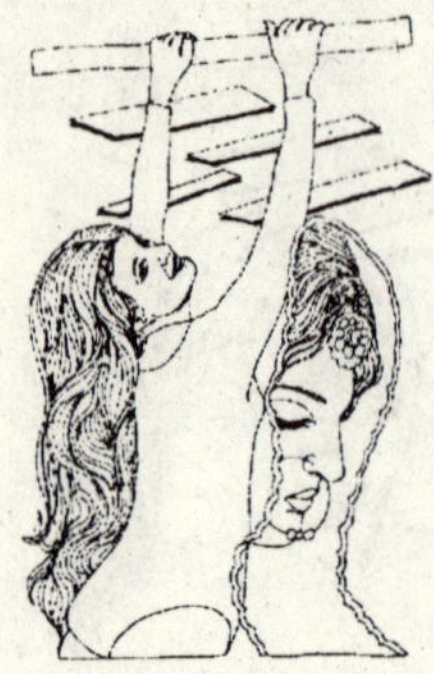

On the contrary, Tamsik food (Bioacidic food) makes the abdomen heavy; causes abdominal discomfort, indigestion and constipation; makes the body dull and lethargic, giving rise to evil thoughts, and produces toxins in the body. Such food includes all the non-vegeterian food like fish, meat, coffee-tea, alcohol, tobacco, cola and other synthetic soft drinks, preserved, stored, processed food items, deep-fried spicy food very tantalising to the palate.

Now, how to go about changing your food habits. Slowly replace, one by one, your Tamsik food items with Satwik ones. For example, when you stop coffee and tea, go for chilled fresh fruit juice or vegetable juice; when you stop munching chocolates and potato chips, go for dry fruits or fresh fruits, whatever is handy.

After a week or so when you would have developed the taste for these things, then you can switch over to changing your lunch which may be a plateful of green salad kept in fridge for cooling, along with fresh fruits. Eat as much as you like. Finish your lunch with a bowl of fresh yoghurt or a glass of butter milk *(Mattha)*. When you are at home, off from your office, then you may add a bowl of sprouted pulses, cereals or beans. Have them with boiled potatoes and sliced tomatoes with a pinch of salt-pepper and lemon juice—a very tasty dish indeed.

Sprouted pulses or beans are very easy to prepare. Take about four to six ounces of your favourite beans or pulses, as per your requirement. Pour them in a plastic jar filled with water. Don't put the lid, instead put a cotton cloth to cover the jar mouth. Change the water every eight hours three to four times, then hang the soaked beans in a wet cotton cloth for next one to three days. When they sprout out then is the time to eat them. They can be stored in fridge for two-three days to be consumed later on.

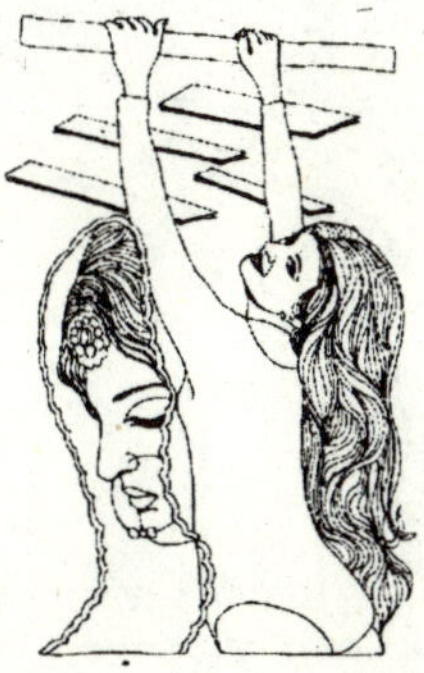

Your dinner may consist of whole cereal bread, steamed vegetables, yoghurt, fresh fruits, green salad, vegetable juice, fruit juice, butter milk, sambar-idly, vada-dosa, noodles, chowmin, brown rice, half boiled egg, and so on. Dinner may be finished with herbal tea or lime-honey tea, or a glass of milk.

You are always free to change your menu as per your taste and fancy. I assure you that there is no dearth of variety in the "health food category". They are available in endless varieties because mother nature has enormous creativity. Believe me, you will love them as they are very tasty and good looking too. Go for them, you will never be sorry for that. On the contrary, chances are that you will feel very thankful to God who has guided you to decide for the Satwik (Biogenic) variety of foods.

Role of exercise for giving your body a perfect and shapely figure cannot be over-emphasised. It is a well-known fact that for a high grade physical fitness you have to adopt a daily excercise routine with all the will-power and determination at your command.

It is a disturbing fact that ninety per cent of educated ladies living in the cities in our country lead a sedentary lifestyle. Either they do not exercise at all, or they are not serious about it. They adopt a very casual approach towards it, leading to their becoming overweight after crossing thirty years. Not only this. Even before reaching thirty years, about thirty to forty per cent fall into the overweight category after their first child-birth.

Some of you may be having a deep-seated wrong impression that physical fitness is not an essential thing. It is meant for those who are jobless, uneducated or useless type of people. For, you might have seen your elder brother or uncle being scolded by your father as good for nothing fellows as they used to pass their whole day in gym or in sports field. They could not study much and ultimately landed a clerical

job. That is why you hate these 'sport nuts' or 'fitness freaks', because they do not fit anywhere in your philosophy of life. They have much brown (i.e. muscles) but less grey matter (come on, this is what intelligent people are proud of).

But things are not like that as you see them. You have to eat food, breathe air and have sunlight to sustain your life and progress in your chosen field. They are essentials, so is the playful exercise. You cannot expect your body to be fit without a regular exercise programme. Beautiful body's biggest secret lies in your understanding that a vigorous physical fitness schedule is one of the essentials of life, equally important as water and nourishment. The body acquires its top-gear potential with this endeavour. If you do exercise regularly, then within six months to one year *there occur in your body many biochemical, physiological and psychological changes which can be well measured by various laboratory methods. But even without scientific evaluation you can feel them that they have taken place.*

Now I discuss these changes, one by one, for your benefit.

First, the "psychological changes". **The positive feeling of total well-being develops.** Exercise is not a simple instrument of achieving physical fitness through which your body becomes strong and healthy, or you shed off some extra kilos from your belly and hips. But, it certainly brings a total change in your attitude about the way you live, you perceive your body. You develop an extra interest about the things happening around you, and you try to relate yourself to them.

It has been long observed during various studies conducted on depressed people that when they are subjected to playful activities like physical exercises, apart from the disease-specific treatment, they show remarkable improvement in their mental well-being. Depression, a common sequel of the present anxiety age, affects many of us quite unknowingly, and before we know what is happening, things aggravate alarmingly and may go out of hand. In depression, regular playful aerobic exercises like cycling, rebounding, under an expert supervision, can show better results than the conventional treatment schedule.

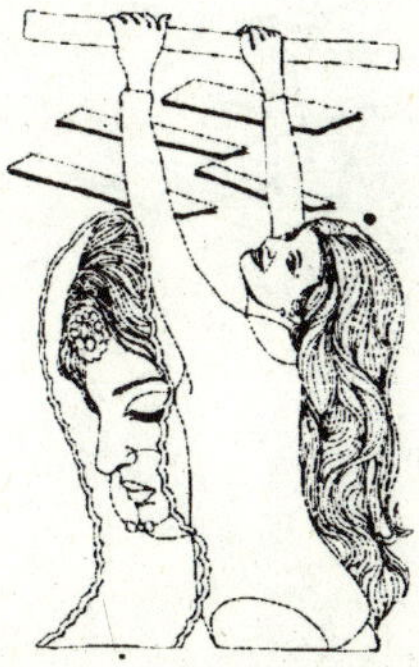

Many physical fitness experts are of the view that the way you perceive your body has a lot to do with the image you have about yourself and your potential. If you consider yourself a strong person then chances are that you will feel capable of handling heavy physical and mental workload. And, you will also be sure of your capability to tackle any adverse situation which may arise by chance. Once you build a positive image of yourself, you are better equipped to handle the stressful conditions which you might have been avoiding earlier. This makes you emotionally more stable, confident, with enhanced will-power to face the day-to-day problems independently.

Physical fitness goes a long way in exalting your self-image and making you confident. Probably looking to these benefits, almost all big corporate houses have started sending their executives to the evening health clubs or fitness centres to improve their physical fitness.

Want to Lose Weight?

Some twenty years ago, in late seventies or early eighties, it was impossible to see any lady or girl in shorts or track suit running on Delhi roads in the morning hours. But, now you can see hundreds of them in colourful track suits running along or jogging on the roads and in the lawns of India Gate or Lodhi Gardens. It has become a common sight. The fitness fever has caught the psyche of average Indian woman to such an extent that they do not mind leaving their cosy warm beds in the wee hours even during winter months of December and January. So intense is the desire to look fit and smart.

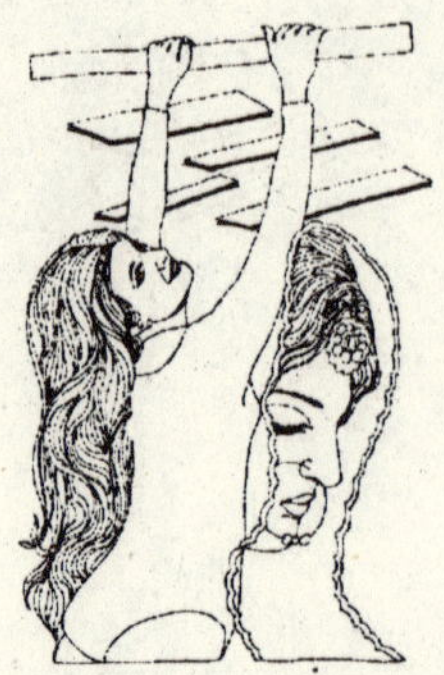

Actually, it is none of their fault. These days so much importance is given to the proper body weight and proportionate body that they have no option but to conform to the physical fitness standards. They can allow themselves to be called as either fat and dull or fit and smart. Choice is theirs.

The rapidly growing awareness about the body looks has resulted into mushrooming of the fitness and weight-loss centres in Delhi. It is a big business now which has caught the eye of the many calculative, manipulative people. Every Tom, Dick and Harry is now a fitness expert and is playing his or her tune at the highest pitch. They are out to make big money out of this health business, that too very fast because they do not know when they might have to close their shop. They are using each and every gimmick like German or American machine or techniques to lure the prospective customers. We Indians are basically foolhardy as we do not apply our mind when we see something foreign or imported in the name of a new technique. We just go crazy about it. Here, I would caution you to beware of such quacks who prescribe slimming tablets or powders which are in fact very-very dangerous to your health. The slimming tablets etc. may destroy your natural appetite. A person given these tablets does not feel like eating anything, leading to a state of dehydration and acute weakness.

Many slimming centres come out with magic weight-loss methods—"no medicine, no diet restriction, no exercise and lose ten to twenty kg of weight in ten to twenty sessions!" Or, some attract the prospective clients by proclaiming lose the weight while watching your favourite TV programme by using the electronic fat dissolver/melter. There are dozens of so-called highly advanced fat-loss centres using so-called latest techniques. And, each one of them has its own flute to play. No doubt, that they are minting money. But, seldom their techniques prove permanently beneficial to the customers without any dangerous side-effects.

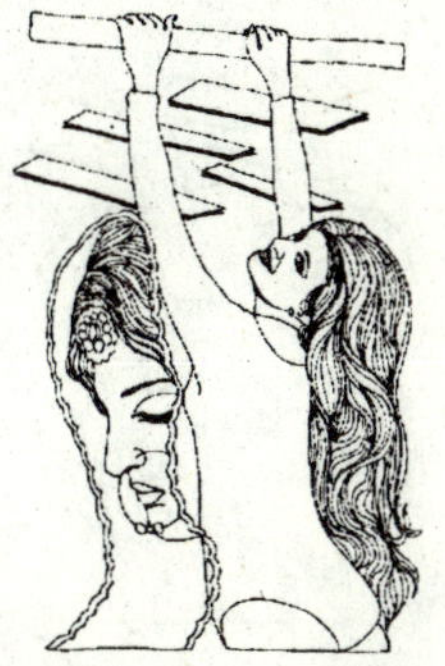

One thing you must note is that no fat-loss programme can ever be successful without incorporating the natural and time-tested fundamental principles of the body mechanism. And, first of them is "playful physical exercise".

Obesity is never a disease until and unless it is there due to some congenital or acquired hormonal imbalance as happens in cases of thyroid or adrenal cortex malfunctioning, which are called myxeodema and cushings syndrome, respectively. Obesity does have a genetic preponderance, i.e. the children of fat parents by all likelihood will be obese until and unless they (children) are extra cautious about it. So, the family history does play a role in promoting obesity.

Some diseases also lend a helping hand in making one obese. For example, diabetes is notorious for promoting the overweight situation. When you are on treatment with cortico-steroids for various ailments like bronchial asthma, irido-cyclitis, skin allergies and eczema you are bound to become over-weight. This is because of the water retention properties of the cortico-steroids. Same is true for the oral contraceptive pills. Those ladies who are using progesteron-estrogen combination to check their family growth are bound to become overweight because of sodium and water retention side effects of contraceptive pills.

Any girl or woman, who has ten per cent more weight than her normal weight as per her age and height is considered obese. Apart from the aged and lazy looks which an obese woman wears, obesity also makes her prone to a horde of diseases like hypertension, heart problem, diabetes mallitus, indigestion-constipation, piles and so on. If you are fat, your level of performance is markedly reduced, and you feel breathlessness while negotiating a few stairs or walking fast even for just ten metres. Also, you often get sleepy and dull while at work creating a very bad impression about you.

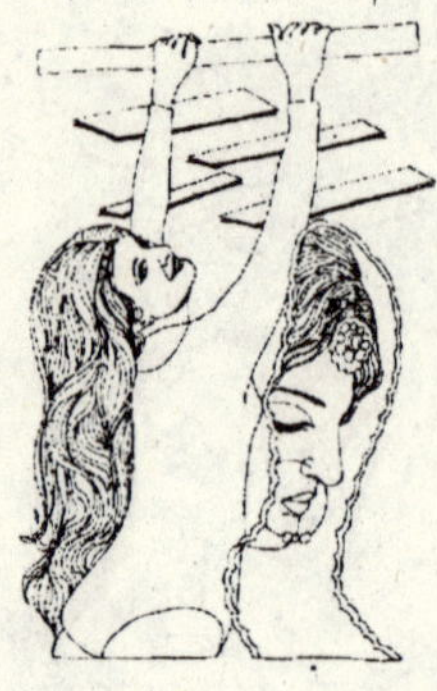

With broad hips and protruding tummy, whatever way you dress up or do the make-up, you will not look smart and beautiful. If you are careful, you can very well observe humiliation and insult in the eyes of onlookers for whom your fat figure may become a laughing stock. People leading a sedentary lifestyle tend to eat more than those who are moderately active, and, in turn, become overweight. On the other hand, those who are athletes or indulge in vigorous physical activity on daily basis, eat more food than those who are moderately active yet surprisingly they remain thin. Because, sportsmen even if they eat sumptuous meals, burn their calories in vigorous physical activity.

Case history—*I remember one of my patients in early eighties, Ms Reeta Singh, 25. Newly married wife of a police officer, she used to visit us for weight problem. She was 5' 4" with a weight of 90 kg. Though her diet was very simple—just two breads and some cooked vegetables in lunch and dinner along with morning and evening cups of tea, yet she had not reduced at all. We knew that she was not lying about her diet. But, this is a fact that overweight people with sedentary habits do not eat much and still they are not able to reduce despite cutting off the calories.*

After Ms Reeta Singh's third visit to our clinic we (my wife and myself) told her to start playing badminton and table-tennis. But, even these sports didn't help her much as far as weight-loss was concerned. Then we asked her to go for brisk walking and running in the morning hours. She started that also but was not happy with the results although she had lost 5 kg in two months. Quite baffled over her body's non-response to various weight-loss therapies, we enquired about her exercise schedule. She used to have twenty minutes sessions in the morning and evening. Then we advised her to go for at least forty-five to sixty minutes exercise session each morning and that too on a daily basis.

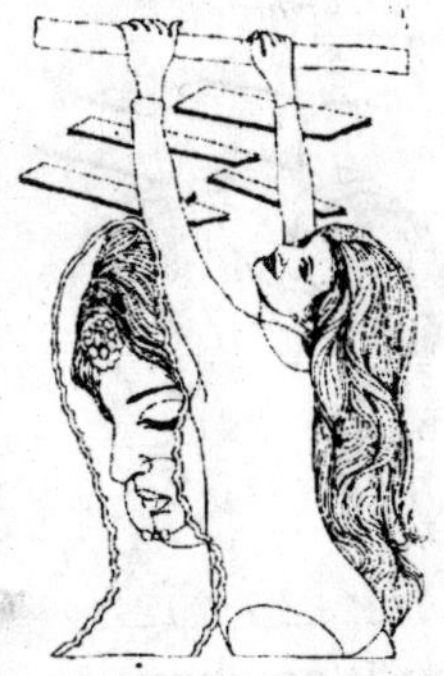

"Why such a long exercising session," she wanted to know. I explained her: "In the first half hour of your physical work-out the glucose and glycogen (both carbohydrates) stored in the muscles and liver are sufficient to meet the total energy requirement of your exercising body. It is only when you go on exercising beyond thirty minutes, the fat stored in your body is called for energy supply to sustain the exercise. So, you have to go for an exercise session lasting beyond thirty minutes. Only then can you expect the burning of excess fat in your body. The "fat burning," in fact, plays a very insignificant direct role in your fat-loss programme. But it plays an important role in increasing the metabolic activity of your whole body as well as the thermogenesis (heat production) leading to better and more effective calorie burning activity even while you are not exercising, i.e. resting".

So, now you know about both the direct and indirect benefits of physical exercise accruing to obese persons. Many people fear that they will have to eat more if they exercise vigorously and this will surely lead to weight-gain instead of weight-loss. But, the fact is that vigorous exercising has a long-term suppressive effect on your appetite, which you can very well feel after doing regular exercise for a year. And then, over-eating is out of question because you have control over your cravings and temptations. All this results in yourself becoming smart, beautiful and confident—you are full of energy and vitality.

The most startling benefits of regular workouts are there for everyone to see, like healthier glowing skin with lesser number of wrinkles and pimples, your more balanced and composed behaviour with lesser number of outbursts and tantrums, enhanced levels of energy and stamina, and remarkable improvement in your sleep pattern, i.e. if you were earlier using sleeping pills, you may not need them any more, thanks to your regular exercise. You can also say good-

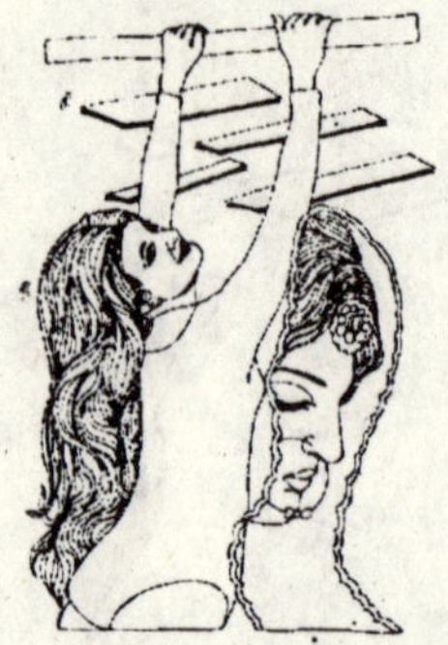

bye to many of the drugs which you take for diabetes, hypertension, asthma or migraine.

All these benefits are there because regular physical workouts bring about very significant changes in your body. You may not believe, but it is a fact that you can avoid many diseases like upset stomach and other digestion problems, headache, fatigue, sudden changes in your glucose levels even if you are diabetic, most of the allergies and even the heart-attack. In short, your body is completely insulated against most of the diseases if you are a regular exerciser.

The "Catecholamines" (adrenaline and like products) build-up due to sympathetic over-activity which itself is there due to stress and strain, impregnates the heart and brain. It (catecholamines) affects their normal functioning or rather does not allow them to function normally. And with defective brain and heart how can you feel normal? The remedy lies in the vigorous exercise which effectively removes the adrenaline and other waste products from your body.

Exercise can even rejuvenate your body if you are in the plus-forty age category. It has been observed that when old people are put on a slow and graded exercise programme, they start looking half of their age with increased stamina and vitality.

If you have a family history of heart attack then there is nothing like exercise for you. Daily cycling, running, or a jogging session is a must for you. Exercise lowers your blood pressure. It lowers the low density lipoproteins (LDL) and increases the high density lipoproteins (HDL), which are good for the heart. The graded exercise programme is like a nectar for those who are IHD (Ischemic heart diseases) prone.

With this, I conclude the 'Body Beautiful' chapter with the hope that you would enjoy the time and effort spent on acquiring the supreme state of health, vitality and total well-

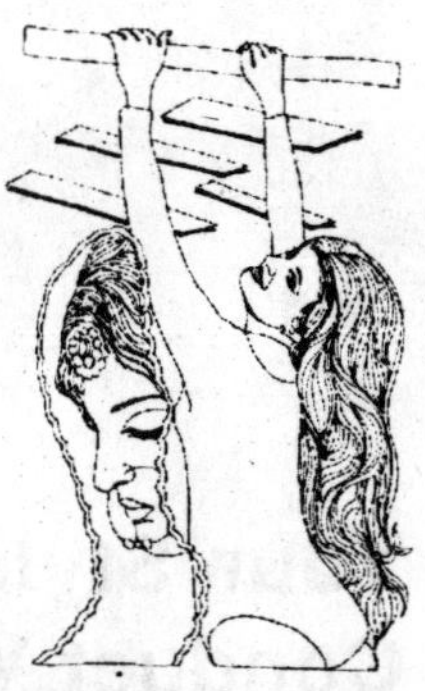

being. Unfortunately, the modern-day medicine, i.e. allopathy, does not have much to offer to those who want to pursue a plan for looking healthy and energetic. Otherwise, it (modern medicine) is very good in diagnosis and treatment of various ailments. Due to unprecedented progress the allopathy has recorded in the fields of diagnosis and treatment, it can offer wonderful help to those who are sick. But it has none to offer to the non-sick individuals. This irony of state of affairs pushes us towards a developing field of 'supreme health,' the ultimate health programme. This would really help those who wish to combat evils of this modern age—anxiety, stress and strain, and realise the full potential of a healthy body in both their work and enjoyment.

Your Style: The Way You Carry and Conduct Yourself in the Society

The poise, grace, elegance, charm, allure and natural attraction, when put together, highlight the personal style of a beautiful woman, the Complete Woman.

The way you stand, walk, sit, converse creates a style of your own.

The way you put on your dress on various occasions is a reflection of your style.

The manner in which you conduct yourself in parties, functions, meetings and other social gatherings tells the class you belong to.

The etiquette you show at dinner table, board meetings and in office, invariably leave an impression of your style.

By a rough estimate 14 to 15 per cent of the woman population, in the age group of 20 to 50 years, belong to working women category. All reasonably educated and knowledgeable, these women are engaged in various jobs, in any big or medium class city. And, we know how the life moves in big cities. Take, for example, Mumbai (Bombay). This megapolis, including all its suburbs, has a large population of working women, about two and half lakh, who go to offices and other establishments. Not only this. There are another about eight to ten lakh women in this city who, though equally educated and qualified, are not engaged in any career activity. They lead the simple life of a housewife.

Everyone of them moves in her own small circle of friends, acquaintances, relatives and colleagues from whom they try to get recognition, appreciation and approvals for their personality and behaviour. Few succeed, ultimately.

What factors decide the success and failure you encounter in your personality presentation? Certainly not the God or luck. Surprisingly, much of your success in showcasing your personality depends on how you carry yourself. The flattering comments, like, "Oh, she is very-very graceful in her presence," or "Oh, she is very elegant in her behaviour" are very soothing to the heart and mind alike. Of course, you can also elicit such comments from people around you, but this depends, I repeat, a lot on how you present yourself to the society.

14

Your Dress Sense

TODAY'S woman expresses herself in many ways. And, one of them is her dress and related accessories. We have already talked in some detail about the makeup sense, and the "body beautiful" which must have given you a basic framework to work upon to enhance your allure. But mind you, a beautiful body and an attractive face requires a definite support from your dressing style. To enhance the attraction of your personality, a perfect dress styling is a must.

A dress chosen and worn, befitting an occasion, adds naturally to your allure. Your presence may become talk of a gathering or a party if you appear in a suitable and charming dress. No doubt, your wardrobe may be full of costly dresses and accessories, some of them specially designed for you. But, they will not make any sense unless you know how to make them do wonders to your appearance—yourself looking dazzling. It all depends on how you apply your mind to dress yourself.

To select suitable and attractive dresses for our film actresses, there are costume/dress designers. Then, there is a director and many other people who are readily available for advice and help. But to help you in making a right choice for your clothes, there are no experts, though you can turn to your family members and close friends for sincere and genuine advice. Still you may not feel free to seek their advice every now and then because they may not be that much keen or interested as you wish them to be.

Secondly, it may sometimes hurt your self-esteem to ask their opinion on your dress. That all depends upon your relationship with them—how cordial and deep it is. However, I would still suggest that never hesitate to seek the opinion of your close friend or of your husband or sister, while trying a new dress design, or when you are buying a new salwar-kameez or saree. But still, your own dress sense should prevail —what would you put on and what should you avoid.

India is a very beautiful country as far as the women dresses go. These are probably most colourful and varied in style than anywhere else in the world. Just have a look at them: gorgeous silk sarees from the South or golden jarie sarees of Banaras, beautiful cotton sarees of Bengal for summer wear, and then Chanderi and Maheshwar sarees of central India. And, don't forget the Punjabi salwar-kameez suit, add to that the Muslim kurta-salwar suit. The list is endless.

Traditional Indian dresses are so beautiful and attractive that it is difficult to resist the temptation to wear them. Traditional dresses of eastern states like Assam and Meghalaya, made of indigenously woven woollen cloth, and woollens from Laddakh and Kashmir are so attractive and colourful that one immediately buys them. Even in today's craze of jeans-top wears, Ghaghra-chunrie, or Ghaghra-choli of Rajasthan is still a much sought-after dress for special occasions like marriage, etc.

And, the typical **Indian woman has all the confidence to carry these traditional dresses gracefully.** She feels very much at ease and comfortable in these attires. She is naturally poised to adorn herself marvellously in most of them. It is an open secret that most celebrated Indian dress-designers design their products according to traditional Indian styles and forms. Well, they do experiment with colours and fabric but without disturbing the basic tradition. Some daring type also style their outfits in shocking colours and combinations, but still they remain within limits because they fear rejection.

Interestingly, our country has also imbibed the western dress(ing) style quite naturally. Much to the surprise and discomfort of elderly persons in our families, the younger generation has taken to the western dresses as fish takes to water. Jeans with shirt top, shorts with blouse top, trousers with shirts, skirts-blouse are among the commonly seen dresses of our girls and ladies in the cities. They no more hesitate to wear these non-Indian dresses in their day-to-day life. But, still some hesitation has been observed among women in smaller towns and yet-to-open-up traditional Indian families in big cities.

No doubt, our society is now changing very fast as far as the ladies dresses go. The views are much more liberal—no more frowned looks from the elders when a young college-going grand-daughter puts on jeans and shirt for a change. Well, that was not the case some fifteen-twenty years ago. In last two decades, the closed conservative Indian society has opened up quite dramatically. But despite all this openness, we Indians are too traditional and conservative to accept slit evening gowns or low-neck party gowns. Although we are very much delighted to watch the fashion models doing catwalk on the ramp, Indian ladies have yet to overcome their hesitation in wearing the modelling dresses in their day-to-day life. Well, occasionally they may go for them, but

hesitatingly. And then, they would be highly conscious about their new dress—all the time trying to adjust it, pull it, crossing the legs, and so on.

Remember, a dress in which you cannot feel normal and at ease, is no dress at all. So, it is very important that when you choose a dress for a particular occasion, you should be very clear about what is right and what is wrong for you. Do not be (mis) guided by anything else except your very own sense of propriety—whether the dress chosen is befitting the occasion and is appropriate for you to wear. This is Lesson No. 1 of your dress code.

Many women who spend lot of money on their wardrobe, do the shopping with the idea—costlier the dress better would it be. Since money is no problem for them, they can choose a rupees fifty thousand embroidered silk suit for that exclusive look (please note the price). Or, they would go for that shocking green salwar-kurta outfit to show their real assets! Seldom they are able to achieve exclusiveness and charm which they badly desire. Anyway, with their money they certainly help that intelligent dress designer in earning her bread and butter (thick layer of it). These neo-rich wives of not so young yuppies and puppies never forget to mention the price tag of their dress and its designer's name to their friends at a party. If by chance no one asks for this vital information about their so-called exclusive dress, they become restless, squirm on their plush sofas. They are naturally very much disturbed that nobody is concerned about their new designer's outfit for which they have paid a hefty sum. In such situations, anyone can read the pain and annoyance on their face.

With or without a designer's label, whatever the outfit, while choosing it apply your common sense, i.e. what suits your personality, what suits the occasion and whether you feel comfortable in your chosen dress. If you are under the impression that the price tag of an outfit makes all the

difference, then I must tell you that most often they (price tags) are highly inflated, even to the tune of ten to twenty times. This is because the celebrity dress designers have to earn high profits in accordance with their exalted status. And, secondly, they also know your psychology that you will not look again towards a dress unless it is exorbitantly priced.

I have seen many young ladies who purchase low-priced dresses. But once they wear them, these dresses look more attractive than the costly designer ones. Many a time, I have marvelled at the graceful cotton Punjabi suits looking so beautiful on many of my students. Money makes no difference. What counts most is the way you style your dress. It makes all the difference. So, never think that with a small budget you cannot plan a graceful, always ready-to-provide-you type of wardrobe, for every occasion. I would again say that it all depends how carefully you plan your things.

Though clothes cannot define a character, they certainly tell a lot about the person, her taste and liking. A right dress always takes you places and gets you all the attention and respect you deserve. You must be discerning while choosing your clothes. First thing, you should be clear about your requirements. If you are a career girl then you need different outfits for different occasions—like dresses you wear to your office, or the ones you require for your business dinners and tours, and yet another type for your official engagements and meetings, and so on.

But the story does not end here, for your wardrobe does not have to cater to your office requirements only. You have also to plan your dresses when you are with your husband at home, or spending a quiet evening with him at the pool side or sipping evening tea, sitting in your balcony, or making dinner in the kitchen. You also need to wear proper clothes on Sundays, when you are doing the weekly home cleaning or doing physical workouts with your loved ones in your garden. Not to be left behind are marriage functions and parties when every woman wants to turn out in her best attire. The proper dress for you will be that outfit which does not make you odd-looking for the visitors, nor should it lessen your feminine charm.

It is a common observation that many otherwise attractively dressed ladies, once back home from their office, casually hang themselves on a crumpled, worn off, shabby looking house-coat. To top that, they have a dirty apron and peticoat to give them company. Now, if a visitor is at their door then how odd it all looks. And, secondly, how do you expect that poor creature (who else, your husband) to smile lovingly in your direction. So, if you are a career woman then it is essential for you to plan your wardrobe for all the purposes—be at office, home, kitchen, bedroom, dinner at home or outside, picnic and so on.

Remember, a dress which is appropriate for the office shall hardly get the approval for the social evening. Similarly, a dress, fit for the two-some pool-side dinner, is just not proper for the shopping purposes. A change is must and just. Otherwise, you may suffer in terms of your charm and elegance. You must not think that planning a wardrobe for all occasions would cost you a fortune. Instead, it simply calls for a dress-sense which is always there in an intelligent woman like you.

Here versatility is the key word. You have to understand that style does not mean a fixed pattern of dressing, or choosing an outfit of a particular type or colour. You should train your mental frame to quickly respond to your preferences and choices. And, without a second thought you should be able to pick up clothes of your choice from an exhaustive selection. Here, I recall one of my friends, Ms Aprajeeta Kashyap, a short (a little bit thin), and very fair complexioned lady. She was my classmate in MBBS course at Jabalpur. The

way she used to experiment with her dresses was really amazing in those days of early seventies. Though a great lover of saree and blouse combination, she was equally at ease in salwar-kameez, or in shirt-trousers when on picnic. Every outfit suited her personality, or so it appeared. And, I repeat, she was quite carefree and comfortable wearing all her dresses, never conscious of her changed style. This probably gave her the confidence necessary to carry her personality with poise and decency. And, this is what is required, apart from befitting clothes, to carry one's personality with ease.

Style is the image you want to project to the society. In other words, it is your class and taste which you express through your clothes, hairstyle and the accessories. No one is born with style. You have to develop it through your observation and imagination and through your sense of judgement. Just think of any glamorous Indian film actress, try to recollect her early days in the filmdom. For example, Rekha. Don't you remember her overall personality as reflected in her first few releases? There is a world of difference in that Rekha who had just made her debut in films and Rekha of today. Let me put it in her own words: "I was a fat, dark coloured raw south Indian belle who knew nothing about the makeup and dressing style. And how I was supposed to know all that at that young age of fifteen. Yes, I was thrown into the film industry at that tender age. It was with the experience and my power of observation that I learnt the art of makeup and dressing-up".

Here's another instance. Rati Agnihotri, another glamorous film actress of yore, once confided to an interviewer that "whenever I look back at my make-up and dresses in my early movies, I feel miserable because it was all awful as I had no idea, at all, how to apply proper makeup and choose my dresses appropriately. It was only after gaining experience

over a period of time that I could master the art of styling myself attractively for the camera".

The key word here is that you learn by experience and a keen desire to improve your appearance. Developing your style includes experiments, trials and errors. No matter what fashion statement do you want to make, you should inculcate enthusiasm in yourself and hold on to it to guide your way towards that perfection which is called allure of a beautifully dressed lady.

Now, how to go about shopping. **Shopping for dresses** should be a planned affair, not a haphazard one. You may be a bit surprised if I tell you that with all power and arguments at my command I always resist to accompany my wife on her shopping sprees. But she derives immense pleasure if she somehow is able to carry me (yes, carry me) along with her for her marathon shopping rounds. Marathon I am saying, because they consume so much time that it is beyond my capacity to tolerate. I get thoroughly bored, but I dare not say a word so as not to unnecessarily spoil her happy mood. Yes, you require a happy, cheerful mood when you go for dress shopping. Better, if you take along your close friend, male, female, anyone, with whom you are comfortable enough. Have at least three to four hours in your hand, depending upon the number of items you want to buy.

I don't intend to tell you what you should go for. But as a constant companion on my wife's shopping sprees and also accompanying several times my sisters-in-law, cousins and female friends on their shopping, I have gathered some **basics for the woman dressing,** which essentially form the elements of style. Surely, I would like to tell you about them from my (male) point of view.

I consider *Quality* first among the basics. It is a thing which you should never compromise on. Today, markets are flooded with a wide array of clothes and readymade garments

manufactured by thousands of companies. Some are of very good quality while others are not. Yet, each of them is on display. Now the choice is entirely yours, which item would you like to go for. Here, my advice is even if you have to pay a bit higher amount for better quality cloth, go for it because its texture and colour will remain stable even after many washes; whereas the cheap variety may go haywire within a few washes. Here, by cheap, I do not mean in terms of money, but quality wise.

A cheap dress or sweater or coat will lose its shape much faster than a quality product. And, remember, quality is not always reflected in the designer's label or the price tag. Apart from good quality of the fabric, another important feature of a durable dress is the quality of its workmanship. No problem, if you cannot buy highly-priced quality clothes in the season itself. You can always wait for the sales; and, secondly, if you are not very keen on a designer's label then you can have almost the same quality stuff from a less sought-after showroom.

Whether to go for synthetic or natural fabric (cotton, silk, woollen), it all depends on the item you intend to buy and your preferences. But, let me tell you that there is nothing like natural clothes, and "naturals" are more costlier than synthetic clothes. So, if your pocket allows, go for the pure natural ones, and, I am sure, you will not regret your decision.

Second basic element of woman dressing is **Simplicity. Your journey to simplicity should encompass the attributes of elegance, grace and dignity of the womanhood.** Never should you allow your choice to be governed by fashion magazines, periodicals, films or television advertisements. If a fashion czar from Paris is shouting from the rooftops that this season all will be yellow or pale, or your own Vallya or Beri is saying that it is time for heavy embroidered outfits, think twice before going for the gaudy

or overdone variety of dresses. By simplicity I do not mean plain attire or a dress which is unattractive. What I mean here is that your dress should not become a dominating feature of your personality, completely hiding or obscuring your true identity. This is what happens if you wear something extra-ordinarily gaudy or daring.

A pretty face with little makeup can very confidently carry a well-cut evening gown. For an added attraction just a beaded necklace may be there at your neck. But here, if you put on heavy diamond earrings, diamond broch, bracelets, bangles, furs, hats and/or scarves then it will simply show you in poor colour. Is it necessary that you load your entire jewellery or accessories in one single party? No, not at all. Resist that temptation. Sometimes, a single piece of jewellery creates a marvellous, wonderful effect, leaving even a combination of ornaments into pale. This is because that single jewellery piece tells your simplicity while many of them loudly announce your lack of taste and imagination.

Sophistication is third basic element in the clothings and accessories. It is governed by your desire to present yourself in a decent and serene manner. A blooming rose attracts every-body by its looks and fragrance. A cool morning breeze at seaside does not have to invite anybody, whosoever comes in its contact just gets carried away by it. Same goes for white rabbit whose little pink eyes tell many tales of innocence. Almost similar is the situation as far as sophistication of a lady goes.

Sophistication is a language which is spoken by that tribe of women who are intelligent, confident and have high degree of self-esteem. This word has been derived from "Sophia" meaning wisdom, skill, divine. It gives a fashionable air to worldly wisdom. Some women have a wrong notion of this word. They think that it means something tender, fragile or weak. Actually, 'sophistication' means the way an educated,

well balanced and self-assured woman expresses her femininity. And, you know, the most apt medium she chooses is her dress-sense. She expresses herself most beautifully in the way she uses her skills and mind to give her an attractive visual appearance.

Here, two names come to my mind to whom the title of most sophisticated woman can be very easily given. They are Waheeda Rehman and Sharmila Tagore. Both are silver screen goddesses of yesteryears. Nevertheless, they are still remembered for their subtle yet decent and attractive dresses and accessories which they adorned in their films. Their selection of clothes, colours, cuts and styles had a hidden grace and pleasantness. Their dress-sense never shocked or horrified their fans who always appreciated their beauty and serenity. This is quite contrary to many of the new generation heroines who by wearing weird dresses astonish their viewers.

The **mystery and mystique of elegance** is not at all governed by the expensive dresses, nor dictated by the editors of fashion magazines nor by the elite foreign fashion houses. In fact, they are all business people who use every trick of trade to attract the buyers, to boost their sales. They use every possible means of communication—whether print, visual or the live shows—to mould your dress preferences in a way which serves their business interests. So never allow your psyche to be clouded by their high-pitched campaigns. Make your own decision, keeping in mind your career and job requirements, your lifestyle, your social circle and family. You have to decide on what item to purchase, how to stock your wardrobe with useful dresses, and so on. Here, you must take care that your selection should be neither too old-fashioned nor so much trendy that people around you are shocked.

Most women have a **fantasy of a perfect wardrobe**. That, for them, is the one in which they can find everything

they fancy for—hundreds of sarees, blouses, trousers, shirts, shawls, expensive cardigans, sweaters, and so on. In fact, there is no limit to their fantasy. Even if they get all the things they go on fantasising, new cravings crop up—there are shoes to match; they would like to stock all types of big and small beautiful leather purses, bangles, slacks, stockings. Maybe, some of you consider your wardrobe incomplete without a laced sheath white dress for a hot summer lunch with your date.

But here, I tell you that no woman, howsoever rich she may be, could have a limitless wardrobe, because every now and then the fashion is changing, and that too very fast. And, to spend money on your wardrobe without giving a serious thought to your requirements is simply a wastage. It serves no purpose, though it may satisfy your craving for variety. But, this satisfaction would be shortlived. Soon, with the evolution of new trends, you would again be craving to diversify your clothes selection. To me, it is a psychic mania, not dress sense or fashion consciousness. The keyword here is a *small* but *perfect* wardrobe, stocked imaginatively to serve your needs on all occasions. Replace your dresses and accessories whenever they are worn off or they become loose in the texture and feel.

Shopping for clothes and accessories is an enjoyment for almost all the members of the fair sex. They enjoy it immensely. But, there is also a negative aspect of this enjoyment. Most women, when visiting a departmental store, do not have the slightest of idea of what exactly they want to purchase. Many a time they are taken for a ride by the smart salesgirls. Or, sometimes overwhelmed by their casual and haphazard buying spree, they end up with a cesspool of useless and reckless purchases. This ultimately makes them a guilty and frustrated owner of a wardrobe which is bulging with clothes of all sorts. Still, one often finds them lamenting, "I do not have

anything to wear for tonight's party". Isn't this a sorry state of affairs of their own making?

Clothes that call for attention, that make you to be noticed, can be yours if you develop the habit of visiting boutiques in lanes and bylanes of your town. For keeping abreast with the current trends you can also refer to the fashion columns of the magazines and newspapers. They carry information on latest national and international fashion trends.

It is well said that all you need is a little bit of style, a creative imagination, a discerning eye, some time to spare, and, most importantly, a burning desire for the emergence of that ultimate look of a stunning beauty. A simple statement in cream pastels or serene white may be a good idea for a summer outing. Be at ease when you adorn an easy-going light coloured shirt and denim trousers, because many a time casual rustic clothes go well provided the mood and occasion is matching.

A 'back to basics' trend often gives you a style, a breather from the uptown tailoring, showing up a soft and languid approach through a soft spectrum of colours—light blue, red or green. Remember, simplification or styling results in clothes that are simple, rustic, comfortable and functional too, suitable for outdoor working schedule and tours. Believe me, nothing is more modern than a wardrobe of relaxed and uncomplicated items in natural shades and designs. A casual culture is the order of the day at weekends and for outdoors, specially in summers,

What suits you is the right fashion for you—this approach should form the basis of your opting for a trend. You know, style and comfort was also the message of a fashion show organised some time ago by 'Pride of India'. The show presented the works of five well-known Indian designers, consisting of suits, lehanga-choli, ghaghra-choli, and of course

sarees. Vibrant and dazzling colours in bold lines highlighted the designers' versatility and their penchant for designing with a difference. While witnessing this all along with my sister-in-law, Kavita, resident of Vasant Kunj, New Delhi, I was most impressed by the 'After Ten' collection. The designer duo presented their collection of skilfully crafted night shirts, shorts, pyjamas, robs for both men and women, in cotton and satin. They succeeded in creating a look that was unique and distinctive yet stylish and comfortable. Well-cut silhouettes and other flowing designs in chiffon silk, crepe and georgette were really eye-catching.

Till few years ago, dress designing was not considered a respectable profession. A career in dress designing was not just suitable for the intelligent and genius students. They were supposed to opt for medicine or engineering, if not business management. But, now equipping oneself with a fashion technology diploma/degree is a much sought-after career option among youngsters all over the country. Numerous institutes of fashion technology have come up in our country in last one decade or so. The best among them is Indian Institute of Fashion Technology (IIFT) with three thousand students on its rolls. Another best is NIFT, National Institute of Fashion Technology. Yes, technology, because today fashion and its designing has all become technical. There are many more schools, near to the status of the best which I am not mentioning due to lack of space.

Most of fashion institutes organize their annual shows in which their students present their skills. Many of these presentations are practical, innovative and very attractive. I visited one of these shows for Summer Collections'97 along with my daughter Shwetambri. Sitting among one thousand-plus gathering I was totally mesmerised by the growth of our fashion industry. It was a revelation for me that Indian fashion industry has come of age, and is all set to rule the world by

its innovative craftsmanship. One after the other, top Indian beauties walked over the ramp presenting soft, sensuous and feminine outfits in subtle statements.

The students had done ornamentation on colourful dresses in chiffons with mirror, shells and beads. Patchwork experiments on printed ghaghra-cholis and traditional Indian dresses resulted in a beautiful blend of traditional and modern fashion. Embroidered designs with their leaf motifs and gorgeous floral sprays were as beautiful and delicate as rose petals with dew drops.

Has the Indian fashion industry ultimately succeeded in getting due recognition from the fashion conscious all over world? There is no denying the fact that fashion world outside India is infinitely large and more complex than what it may appear on a casual glance. In India also the fashion industry has registered tremendous growth in the last two decades or so. Now, it is heading for globalisation. High quality garments exported from India have carved out a niche of a loyal and eager clientele in the fashion-conscious West.

A spin-off benefit of globalisation of our fashion industry is that the Indian woman too has become aware of the world trends. This exchange has given rise to a combination of east and west, in the evolving patterns of our day-to-day dresses. The Indian fashion industry has now become truly international. The big fashion houses do not merely sell clothes, rather they mould or present a lifestyle.

The Indian woman along with our designers has been quick to adapt western designs and patterns in her dresses. Consequently, the image of the quintessential Indian woman is changing very fast. Gone are the days when she would be lost in nine yards of plain looking saree, whether at home, office, in social gatherings or a beach party. Surprisingly, the shy Indian woman has quietly initiated a change in attitudes in our conservative, patriarchal society, heralding a new lifestyle in our cities. She is a new confident woman, hogging the limelight. This has given her a new status both in home and at office, while quenching her urge to excel in every walk of life.

So, with the liberated woman at the helm of affairs, it is not at all surprising that the western outfits have gained an acceptance in our homes, specially those who are upwardly mobile. The chic and sexy look seems to be the order of the day. But, sounding discordant, Rohit Bal, a reputed name in the fashion world, says, "Indian woman has neither figure nor attitude for western clothes." Differing with Bal, Jatin Kochchar, another famous name in the fashion world, believes that our women should definitely have the option to choose. As with any trend, only the time will give the right answer to the question: what impact the western fashion has on the society at large, whether it becomes part of the culture or not? But here, one thing is sure that this preference and liking for western dress code is going to stay. First, because it is a change which has taken more than two decades to happen; and, secondly, it is a need-based change rather than just a craze.

The liberalization of our economy, rather the globalization of Indian business scene, has made the hitherto conservative Indian woman to adopt the new culture of corporate business suits, skirt-blouse, trousers, palazios and other such western dresses, which are better suited to her hectic lifestyle than our own ethnic-traditional wear. Whether driving the car, or moving up and down the flight of stairs at her workplace, or queuing up at the ATM machines and reservation counters, or searching her seat in the plane—all the time the new Indian woman is required to look trendy, smart, and well dressed. And, carefully chosen, properly fitting, western outfits give her the desired look of a modern woman without much effort.

Is it the changed attitude of ours, rather the *change* itself which has given Indian woman the much sought after label of smart woman? Or, is it the moulding of our psyche by the omnipresent western media dominating the open skies which has made us admire our women as smart and wonderful in western dresses? Whatever the case may be, but for God's sake do not consider me as pro-western because I am pure and pure Indian down to the every core of my heart. And, I like my woman most when she adorns the traditional Indian dresses, specially saree. Despite the overpowering influence of western fashion, our women at hotel reception counters, banks and airlines offices and other such places still wear only traditional Indian dresses, particularly saree, and at some places salwar-kameeze also. The frontline female staff in many reputed concerns has been instructed to go for traditional dresses. Probably, no other country takes as much pride in her traditional, aesthetic apparels as India. Any tourist visiting India becomes mesmerised by the colours of this country—vibrant, multihued, soft sometimes and amazingly eye-catching at others—yellow, blue, green and red, all in their best shades. All these colours when combine on our traditional outfits enhance the beauty of our women.

To outsiders, it may seem quite surprising that we so much love our traditional dresses. It's all because at the depth of hearts we all love our country, the great India. We love everything which is Indian. We feel a definite pride when our women appear marvellous in traditional Indian dresses. But, for a change we do love western outfits, because we are broadminded people. And, we would like to imbibe the best of every culture in the world as has been our tradition since ages.

15

In Style, Naturally! (Secrets of Charm, Grace and Poise)

IT is now almost three decades since I first saw her. She was in final year MBBS and myself in third year. Even though so many years have gone by, I am yet to come across another lady like her, so poised and graceful in her body movements. Hers was the most perfect figure. To top that, she knew very well how to carry that figure. Yes, carry herself. And, it's not true of all women even if they are endowed with a beautiful figure.

You may have seen many women who just drag themselves, while others somehow push their bodies. And, few others just do not know where their left leg is going and where their right leg is. Or, when they sit, they slump in their seats in such a leisurely way as if they won't be required to get up again. They spread themselves on the sofa or chair as if it is double bed or lounge chair. Or, when they stand, their protruding tummies make them appear carrying a full-term pregnancy.

Dr Rajeshwary Aieyar, about whom I am talking, had made the whole college her fan. Wherever she used to go she was always watched by numerous pairs of eyes. But she seemed quite oblivious of all the glances and glares. She used to do almost everything naturally. Not a single act of hers betrayed artificiality. Her long hair tucked in a thick plait used to swing like a black snake on her shapely back, as if chiselled by a sculptor. The grace of her measured steps seemed to get enhanced manifold whenever she wore cotton sarees. It was a treat for the eyes to watch her at anytime of the day.

I could not get introduced to Rajeshwary formally. I was junior to her, and she was a much sought-after beauty of our institution. That's why I was a bit hesitant in initiating a talk with her. During my internship I had an opportunity to start a casual conversation with her during our posting in the medicine ward. After self-introduction with a shy and meek hello, I said, "Madam, may I talk to you?" She lifted her dreamy eyelids and shifted her gaze from the case-sheet of a patient to my direction.

Actually, I had not planned what I would say, and when she looked straight at me, I became very nervous. Somehow, I uttered: "Madam, you look so good and beautiful that ...." and the words trailed off my mouth. I could not speak anything more. She smiled, and said softly, "I know that." She paused for a while and then said, "But why did not you complete your sentence?" By this time I was able to gather some confidence. I laughed, and said, "From where have you learnt your beautiful way of walking?" She laughed and said, "Learnt the walking? Well I learnt it from my mother when I was one year old. Come on young doctor, you have given me enough pleasure, let me give you a treat."

I was, naturally, enjoying Rajeshwary's company. But she also seemed quite happy with our conversation. Thereafter, we both went to the college canteen and had a lunch of

coffee and *dosa*. And, you know, that day the whole lot of students (of course, male ones) became astonishingly jealous of me because I had the chance to share a table with Rajeshwary, the queen of hearts of Jabalpur Medical College. I do not know where she is now. But, I feel indebted to her, for she had taught me the first lesson of natural feminine grace and poise.

One thing you must be aware of is that **artificiality** has no role at all in realising your long cherished goal of becoming a "most sought-after woman" (MSW). Remember, artificiality mars your real, natural attraction. Nobody likes artificial looks which in any case are not going to last longer. And, it's also true that nobody would tell you how to use your natural assets to the best of your advantage. You have to learn very early in your life to develop your own individual charm. Never you should attempt to fashion yourself on someone else's looks or style.

Here are a few *don'ts* for you: no awkward body movements to distort your body, no affected mannerism to spoil your natural grace, and no exaggerated make-up. Instead, you should project yourself as a confident person, ready to face any situation with grace and elegance.

It is not so easy to develop grace and elegance. You cannot buy them from the market, like your favourite cosmetics. Grace and elegance, actually, are the direct menifestation of a cool mind. A woman cannot be graceful until and unless she is at ease with herself. With coolness, grace comes naturally. The lady whose feminine charms and mannerism enliven the whole surroundings is as appealing to women as she is to men. She is quite populai in the parties and much sought-after in the job market. She is the next-door girl who is welcome both at home and on the ramp. And this is because she has learnt the secret of putting her potentialities to the best of her advantage. **She is just not a model but a total personality, the Complete Woman.**

Some of you may be harbouring a notion that this grace and charm story is not your cup of tea. Rather, it is something for actresses and models who have to attract thousands of fans by their perfect mannerisms. You may also feel that this charm and elegance business is too much for you to bother— How is it possible to keep caring about yourself all the time, always remaining conscious that you have to look charming and graceful? All this constant exercise puts too much pressure on a woman's mind and takes a toll of her personality. Here, I agree that a lady cannot be her normal self when her mind is always gripped by an overpowering obsession of looking poised and elegant.

Like you, I also consider that the journey on the path of becoming a most sought-after woman (MSW) is not easy, to begin with. For, in this journey, you may have to get rid of your bad habits and indecent mannerisms. And, you have to learn the new ways of charm and grace. Learning as such, you know, is a difficult process initially. But once you are able to overcome initial difficulties, rewards are bountiful. The new habits and behavioural traits may look artificial to you in the beginning. But, sooner when you succeed in inculcating them, you feel quite natural in your behaviour. And, when all these become part and parcel of your mannerism, you look naturally charming and elegant. It all becomes so effortless that all the awkwardness goes away. But, it takes time. You have to imbibe all the advices by heart. You have to be patient if results are not forthcoming quickly.

Every educated grown-up Indian woman cherishes a dream of becoming attractive and charming. There is nothing wrong with this dream, rather it is her birth right to look beautiful. So, do not feel shy if you also nurture such a dream. And, the most important thing is by improving your personality you will increase the opportunities of making yourself happy

and living life to its full. Once you make up your mind that you will transform yourself into a lovely, fascinating and elegant woman, success is bound to be yours whichever way you plan to move.

It is your personal style, i.e. individualistic approach, that will make you charming. You have to proceed intelligently to project yourself in a most pleasing and elegant manner. The better you do it, more attractive you look. Here, you can follow some of the models who are not so beautiful naturally, still they succeed in charming the masses. You know in modelling, visual attraction is on sale. Strangely, in this profession, many women with exceedingly pretty faces do not reach the top whereas those with less perfect and classical features achieve tremendous success. Here, the secret is that the women of latter category know how to enhance their positive features and present (project) them to the best of their advantage.

Now, I would like to give you a word of caution. If you happen to be the wife of a business tycoon or daughter of a big man then don't confuse this *projecting* with anything else, not the least with your spouse's or father's wealth. By loading tonnes of jewellery or diamonds, you will not add to your charm and elegance. Instead, they will distract people from your natural beauty. So, be quite clear in your mind that projecting yourself has nothing to do with the designer's wears and diamonds. Rather, it is *presentation of your personality in totality* tools of which are very simple and basic. Let's discuss them one by one.

Postures (Body Movement, Gestures)

The way you walk, sit, get up and stand add to your attraction or distract people from you. Proper body coordination is needed for rhythmic graceful movement. And any figure is attractive when it is carried gracefully. On the contrary, if not carried gracefully, even the beauty of a perfect

figure may get distorted by the improper body movements. I have seen many overweight ladies who despite their obesity move so gracefully that you are bound to marvel at their ability to get along smoothly.

For graceful movement, it is essential that you should not show any hurry or uneasiness while in a public place or at a place where you are being watched. You should always take well balanced, measured steps, with your high-heel or medium-heel sandal. Even when you are required to hurry up (until and unless they are life-threatening situations), take your own time to adjust yourself; do not become panicky—no anxiety, no nervousness, be in control of yourself. It will show you in a good picture. But mind you, I don't want you to behave like a lazy, dull creature who takes aeons to come down a few stairs. Rather, my advice to you is that except those moments when it is really a matter of life and death, always show yourself in total command of the situation, taking your time to move gracefully. Here, the keyword is *coolness of mind*.

Try to find out and adopt the correct positions of your body which are perfect and graceful in your different body movements. Slumping shoulder, caving in of the chest or protruding belly while in standing posture mars your grace. Avoid these shortcomings.

Among all the living creatures only humans have been endowed with a completely erect, upright posture in their normal working condition. In his erect posture, the human primate is singular, if not unique, in having the trunk and lower limbs straightened to such an extent that the centre of gravity of any segment of the body is substantially above the joints upon which its weight impinges. Even the head is almost, if not wholly, balanced upon the cervical spinal column.

A 'vertical' line from the centre of gravity of the whole body (a point about a centimetre behind the sacral

promontory) falls in front of the ankle joint. Have you ever observed that the standing position is often changed to relieve the stress of the ligaments and muscles, although such a posture, if maintained for long periods, requires little muscular activity. The line of gravity is related to the curvatures of spine in such a way that they are, on the whole, exaggerated by the gravity. To facilitate walking, this centre of gravity shifts constantly, necessitating the balancing movements like swinging of the arms (upper limbs), lifting of one foot forward while the other one is firmly placed backward on the ground.

Every human being can acquire normal, easy, rhythmic walking movements (locomotion) provided he/she is not suffering from any deformity or painful joint conditions. But, to look graceful while walking, standing, or sitting you have to do efforts consciously. Well here, I must explain that *graceful* or *attractive* does not mean artificial. Your designer's clothes cannot add charm to a protruding belly or caved in chest. You look aged and out of proportion notwithstanding your efforts to hide it. You can look naturally attractive only through a carefully cultivated habit which becomes your "normal" feature in the course of time. You must understand that the poised human body is one that nature has meant it to look like—beautiful and graceful.

There are many disadvantages of a faulty body posture. Apart from destroying your natural grace and charm, it also affects your body adversely. For example, it can lead to indigestion due to compression of the abdominal visceras, poor circulation of blood and congestion of lungs, headache, and so on. A wrong body posture can also lead to dampening of your spirits and depression. You may also feel fatigued and exhausted easily. The combined effect of all these is lack of confidence, enthusiasm, vitality and interest in your day-to-day life. Without any valid reasons, you may feel dejected, frustrated and bored. And, all this reflects through your face

and behaviour. In this modern age of fast track competition, who would like to look dejected or exhausted? Certainly not you. And, believe me, very little is required to change all this depressing scenario—an upright mental attitude. Most important thing is that you have to feel all the time that only an upright, erect posture can give your body a confident, perfect look, and that is what you have to present to the world.

In my human anatomy classes, I teach about the correct anatomical position of the body. I often feel that it should also be taught to the non-medical students. For, it gives you an idea how the nature has designed your body. And, among other things you also learn what is the line of weight transmission in different positions of the body, i.e. sitting, standing and bending; what is the centre of gravity; and, how important it is for a woman to know the correct body alignments.

Do you know what does it mean to stand in the correct anatomical position. The basic requirements of such a body posture are: standing erect; feet firmly on the ground—no gap in between them; looking straight—eyes horizontally parallel to the ground; arms resting by the side of the body with the palms facing forward—no flexion at elbow; and, knees straight—no flexion. When you stand in this position, your line of body weight transmission passes from top of head (vertex) - tip of the ear - lobule of the ear - tip of shoulder (acromian process) - vertebral column - pelvis - head of femur - greater tronchanter - knee joint - shin of tebia - ankle joint - melleoli - heel bone (calcanium). Then, it is spread up in feet through the outer margin of feet and front of foot-toes.

I understand that all this is becoming too much theoretical for you, a fun-loving creature. But, all this is necessary to make you understand the correct body posture. You must be aware of the basic body framework, and how it functions.

But, I promise that I will not go into finer details and limit myself only to the basics.

Your feet constitute a very useful and important part of your body. With them you carry out routine activities like walking, running, standing. And, they also sustain your body weight. Many girls look very poised when standing, but the moment they start walking, their limbs seem to swing out in every possible direction, hands dangle wildly from everywhere. On the other hand, many girls acquire such a stiff posture while walking that it appears as if a robot is in motion instead of a living creature. Or, some walk like a log, while others' movement resembles that of a jumping jack.

Walking is such a natural activity that you yourself are quite oblivious of your walking posture. Or, you don't consider paying any attention to it. But, beware, you are being constantly watched by others while walking. Your walking posture, in fact, tells a lot about you. A graceful natural walk, like a swan floating in a lake or a female deer moving in a forest, attracts everybody. Though walking is as effortless as breathing, it adds to your charm if it is graceful. Well, then what are the **essential components of graceful walking?** To master them, read on carefully.

- Many ladies walk unattractively because they are in hurry, always. The just do not know what actually graceful walking is all about. As I have told you earlier, for your walking to be graceful, you should always take your time to walk in measured, steps, not too long strides. If you have put on high heels, spare some time at your home to practise walking in high heels before you go out wearing them because affectedly short steps may destroy your walking grace.
- Keep your eyes straight as far as possible, chin high, arms close to your body, and palms facing inwards. If you are carrying your handbag, hold it in your hand or better

hang it on your shoulder. If other items are also there like water bottle, umbrella, briefcase or some carry bag then try to put them altogether in a shoulder bag so that you are not too much bothered about them.

- Let your weight roll from your heel through the front foot and to your toes. The knees should be flexed and relaxed, not fixed and stiff. I have heard that earlier in the training of air hostesses they were made to walk while balancing a book kept on their heads. The idea was to train them in graceful way of walking. But instead of graceful, balanced walking, it often led to the trainees walking in an affected way. Though walking with a book on head may correct and control the undesirable head movements, it certainly cannot produce a graceful walking.

- Some young ladies, in an attempt to make their walk attractive, do put on tight fitting trousers or shorts, and then walk in a cross-legged manner to give extra swing to their hips. They feel that this extra swing will make their walk attractive. But, the result is quite contrary—that is, extraordinarily swinging hips in tight-fitting clothes look very distracting. In fact, your legs should swing from your hips, not the vice-versa. Keep your feet parallel and close while walking, no scissors gait like.

- While selecting shoes, you must ensure that apart from being good looking and attractive, they should be of good quality and comfortable. By good quality I mean shoes made of seasoned leather; shining but soft; and, their sole firm yet delicate. Before going to party in your new pair of shoes, give a fair trial to them at your home for a day or two. Otherwise, if by chance they start troubling you in the midst of party, what would you do? Maybe, one of your shoes starts asking your name—that is, starts biting you, or its buckle comes out, or the heel wood gives way due to poor craftsmanship. So trial of your shoes is necessary before you wear them to your office or to attend an important social event.

- If you know in advance that you will be required to walk on uneven surfaces or on hilly tracks or roads then do not venture out in the spiky high heels because they can be really uncomfortable. It may happen on such occasions when you are with your family on a picnic to a hill-resort or a historic monument. In such situations, better if you select canvas shoes for you. Oh no, do not make faces now. You would surely have a second opinion on canvas shoes when you go and see in the market a vast variety of soft colour and attractive canvas shoes. They will immediately catch your fancy. They are available with or without laces—choice is yours.

- Also available in the market are a wide array of sandals, slippers *(chappals)*, slip-ons or casuals. What you opt for would ultimately depend on your mood and taste apart from the occasion. There cannot be a fixed rule or guideline for your selection, but a basic rule is that if you are putting on the western clothes then go for the shoes. And, if you are in a saree or salwar suit then opt for either sandals or *chappals* as per your liking.

- Do not put on the shoes without proper fitting socks, preferably of pure cotton; the cotton mixed variety would also do. Keep an extra pair of socks in your handbag for a change, in case they get soiled up or start stinking due to sweat after a day-long outing.

- In your office while doing your work, take out your feet from the shoes as often as possible—this will relax your feet. Also, frequently roll your toes and feet as this will improve blood circulation in them, and you will not feel the sleeping foot condition.

- For infusing *fluidity in your walk* it is imperative that you must take some care of your feet. If you want them to serve you life long, they surely deserve your attention. Do not neglect them or take them for granted, this attitude may misfire some day. Pedicure is essential, your beautician would tell you. File your nails regularly, and clean your feet with pumic stone while taking bath. Also take care of the cellulitis, ingrown toe nails, corns and dead skin. Cleaning between the toe webs is essential to prevent fungus infection. If cracked heels give you trouble, apply special creams (liquid paraffin wax, white petroleum jelly, vaseline, crack cream) after removing the dead skin with scrubber. Massage your feet with oil at least once a week, better if you can do it two or three times. If you can catch hold of your hubby to do it for you, then nothing like it. Otherwise, the next best bet is your maid servant. This will have a soothing effect on your fatigued and aching feet to give you a relaxed feeling. If you get a chance, pamper your feet by taking a bare-foot morning stroll in your garden. The cold wet grass gives a very soothing feeling. After this walk, put on dry socks and canvas shoes, particularly in the winter months. With the enwrapped feet you will feel very much relaxed.

- Elevate your feet whenever it is possible. Put a pillow or cushion under them while sitting on your bed, reading a magazine or watching your favourite channel. Also spare a little while to exercise your feet by rolling them, flexing them towards sole or dorsum. Flex and extend your toes. All this will soothe your tired nerves by improving the circulation. Some of you may observe signs of extra strain on your feet and legs. For example, constant pain which does not subside even after taking off the shoes and sandals, or after usual massage and warm water soaking, or after your usual dose of pain killer. Then, it is time for you to do some thinking about your walking style, daily

routine at home and at work, and also your shoes. Any abnormality in any of these things may leave you with a permanent pain in the feet and calf muscles which is quite rampant in the ladies, specially past thirty years of age.

Many a time some ladies, who wear skirts and frocks, put on as a routine high spike heels and extreme shoe styles to show off their beautiful legs. For, legs are considered, particularly in the Western society, a high point of woman's beauty. Well, the ladies in skirts with high heels may succeed in attracting many appreciating pairs of eyes, but at the same time they invite unwanted strain to their hips, thighs and legs. This, in turn, results in hypertrophy of the affected muscles and also constant pain and fatigue. So, don't ignore these signs if you wear high heels. Consult your family doctor or chiropodist at the earliest.

I see many girls adopting a soldier-like or statue-like postures **while standing** by giving their spines a backward concavity. This exaggerated backward concavity or what we normally call 'lardosis posture' occurs when you put extra strain or tenseness in your lower spines. Some ladies become extra-conscious of their 'question mark'-type posture when told repeatedly to correct it. Consequently, their over-enthusiasm to correct the wrong posture leads them to over-correction. And the 'sway back' is nothing but this over-correction. It takes toll on your femininity and puts you in an awkward position.

Whether you are alone or in a group, or simply posing for the camera, or you are in a fashion show or at any social gathering—make sure that you are standing tall on your feet, confident and upright but completely relaxed. Remember, *relaxed* is the keyword because tensioning of the body musculature will turn its loveliness into ugliness. *To stand upright, lift your head out of your shoulders, your shoulders out of your waist, your waist out of your hips, and stand tall.*

The lower back must be tucked in, all the time. Abdominal muscles should be pulled in, giving you a slimmer look; shoulders must be relaxed, eyes forward and most important, a pleasant smile on your lips.

While entering into a room, a restaurant, an office cabin or the scene of a party, never barge in like a wind or tornado. Instead, make it a point always to stop for a while at the entrance, take a look around, assess the scene, locate your friends and acquaintances, and then step in. Most of the time, the hosts are there at the gate to welcome you. After exchange of pleasantries, introduce yourself to other such guests in whose company you feel that you would be comfortable while enjoying the party. In case, you are going to a party where you are new to the people and the place then take your own time in making yourself acquainted with the surroundings, the atmosphere and the people. Introduce yourself very-very politely to the guests. If you like the ambience and the people, stay there as long as you can to enjoy to the full. Otherwise, bow politely and ask to be excused for leaving early.

In social gatherings or parties, you should stand gracefully with something in your hand, preferably a drink or juice. But, what should be your party pose? Just read on, and you will get the answer. For a correct and relaxed party pose, both your hands should be in front of the lower part of your chest; feet a bit apart—either of them in front and the second one a bit backwards, the gap between them being less than one foot; back knee straight while the front one little flexed, with tilted shoulders.

Having a graceful and commanding stature is what separates the woman who turns the heads from the wall-hangings. At a place where you are being watched, you must stand with authority. Relax yourself with deep breath and keep your body relaxed, while balancing your bodyweight comfortably between both your feet as I have told you earlier.

Raise your chin to create a long, graceful neck. Bring your shoulders back without moving your ribs or back, only adjust the shoulder blades. The shoulder-neck-shoulder line should be straight, not curved inwardly. Press your hips forward by tightening your gluteal muscles. You can release these muscles at intervals. The idea is not letting your back sway sideways.

Few more points for your graceful entry in a party before we talk about lady-like sitting. As you stop at the entrance for a short while to have a sweeping glance at the audience present, lead with your hips not by your head. Don't rush to make your entry. Otherwise, how would the guests notice you? Do not try to become part of the crowd, that is don't push your way through the crowd; instead of fighting your way, always stop to let people move out of your way after having said 'excuse me' in your firm but polite voice. Getting noticed means allowing time for you to be noticed.

Tired of standing and weary of walking? Well, lady it's time to sit down. No, no, do not rush to the chair. Take your first lesson, **how a lady should sit gracefully?** Learning graceful sitting is as important as graceful walking and standing. First, a few words about the physical anatomy of our sitting posture. Our seat bones, also called pelvic bones, are two hip bones along with a sacrum (five sacral vertebrae fused together). They have a rounded tuberocity on each side called ischial tuberocity, which comes in contact with the ground when our body acquires a sitting posture.

Nature has not designed our body to sit at the end of spine or on our thighs as some ladies do. Some ladies, ignorant as they are of a correct sitting posture, just dump their bodies on the sofa or chair as if it is cement bag. Haven't you heard of 'secretarial spread'? Most of office-going women, who spend most of their office time in a tiny chair, suffer from figure problems like bulging of the hips and heavy thighs. Let me tell you that the heavy hips and thighs are due to the defective

sitting position. For example, when the body-weight is allowed to rest on the thighs, naturally they will spread out. Therefore, if you are chair-bound for most of the day then make it sure that you sit on your hip bones with tugged in hips, upper torso erect—ribs cage high, your back being supported properly with an appropriate lumber support, i.e. back rest. This way your body-weight will be distributed evenly through your vertebral column and hip bones (ischial tuberocities) to the chair.

To sit properly in a chair, you are not required to push your spine, the derriere, all the way to the back of chair; instead, leave a small gap of inch or two between your spine and the chair-back, then relax your shoulders. A graceful sitting begins with your choice of the chair. If options are there, then go for a straight back chair of normal height instead of sofa or deep cushioned low-level chairs because neither they are suitable for graceful sitting, nor it is easy to get up from them quickly and gracefully.

If you are short-statured, then avoid sitting on a full height chair. For, it may cause problems as your legs won't reach the ground and you would be sitting on your thighs with your feet hanging in the air. And, it is quite uncomfortable. To avoid such a situation you should opt for a small-size chair in your office, or better if you put a foot-rest under your chair to support your feet; but, in public functions, you should go for a low-lying sofa. So, that were the options for short-statured girls. Now, a piece of advice for tall girls. While sitting on chair, they should always use cushion under their hips so that they do not have to stick out their feet and legs in a haphazard manner. And, there is enough leg space between their seat and floor.

Suppose you are the wife of a top ranking military officer, and you have been invited to a prize distribution ceremony at the command headquarters where function has been

arranged under a beautifully decorated *shamiana*. You are supposed to take your seat in the front row on a sofa which is low-lying and deeply cushioned. There is no dais. When you sit, a small centre table placed in front of you is just not able to hide your legs. Or, imagine an open garden party where you have to take your seat at a deep low-lying sofa. Do I have to tell you how to take your seat gracefully? Or, you know it already? Let's check it out.

Don't be in a hurry to somehow occupy your seat; wait patiently for your turn. First, let the seniors and elders take their seats. And, then you move towards your seat when waved by the hosts/organizers. Now, how to sit? Turn your back towards the sofa and preferably take a corner place on the sofa, not in the middle as this would look indecent. Also while sitting on the corner, you can take advantage of the side handle. Lower yourself slowly to the edge of the seat when the back portion of your legs is also in contact with the seat edge. Do not slide immediately your full bottom on the seat, instead occupy only front half. After a few minutes, place your complete torso on the back rest and feel comfortable. Sit quietly, do not shift and scrumble your position every minute to place yourself more comfortably because this constant shifting shows you in a bad light.

Now, I come to another important aspect of sitting on a sofa. It is—whether to cross legs or not while sitting on a sofa. Usually, it is observed that some ladies sometimes cross their legs so awkwardly that this posture actually destroys their total grace. Here, I suggest that legs may be crossed, if required, at the knee level only. And, if they are crossed at any other point, like thigh or calf level, then the posture may appear odd. For a graceful placement of legs, follow these tips: If you are right-handed, put your thighs together and pointing towards left; shift the right foot to the right with the toe pointing towards the floor; bring the left leg up, cross

above the right knee. The result will be a graceful placement of legs at an angle with the body.

Have you heard of the 'S' curve of the models? No problem, even if your answer is 'no'. I will try to explain it to you. Curves are more graceful than the angles because they look more feminine, more flattering. A fundamental rule for a woman-like sitting is to keep both the knees together. I have observed that older women are the worst offenders of this rule, specially if they are overweight. With growing age, the elderly women tend to become increasingly careless about their gait and postures which ultimately become too faulty.

Now, about the 'S' curve. To sit gracefully you should approach the chair directly only when you are offered by someone (that is, who else but your polite host, or the man in your life pulls it for you). Turn your back towards your right. Tuck in your hips, keep your upper torso (rib cage and shoulders; upper part of the trunk) straight, lower yourself slowly while bending your knees and place yourself gently into the seat. With the thighs reaching diagonally across the seat instead of straight-forward, slide your feet together to the right, bring your left foot around the back of the right foot. And, here you are in the model's sitting posture—the typical 'S' curve.

To get up gracefully, bring your feet parallel to each other from diagonal sitting, lean forward from the hip; if required, take support of the hands to push your body up, otherwise push on your feet, straighten your legs and get up in one swift movement.

Do you know what is **grace in repose?** Well, let's talk about it a little. To my mind, it is probably the most important parameter to judge a well-poised lady—that is, her well cultivated ability to sit quietly without fidgeting and changing postures with every passing minute. Be cautious, that un-

necessary hand movements, gestures and fluttering show you in a very poor light. It simply shows your nervousness, uneasiness, and, above all, complete lack of confidence.

Your ability to remain quiet and at ease with yourself and surroundings shows your real feminine beauty and grace. It adds immensely to your charm. Your hands play an important role in adding to your graceful gestures. Many women fidget because they do not know what to do with their hands. Avoid hand movements while you are sitting. If you are talking to your friends, or even to a larger audience, try not to talk with your hands. Remember, over-gesturing takes away your natural grace. You will know more about hand movements in the following chapter on *Conversation*.

How many times have you slipped from the stairs? Almost every child slips from the stairs, it is a universal experience. Those who do not have this experience in their childhood are either too protected or physically handicapped. *A few tips on how to negotiate the stairs.* While negotiating the stairs you should not look constantly towards the steps; instead, look relaxed, head held high, back straight, rib cage up, knees little flexed. The knees should not be fully extended and locked because that would give your movement a stiffened awkwardness, resulting in a stilted bobbing action.

While you go up, let the thigh pull the legs up and the rib cage pulling the rest of body up; but, do not let your head drop down. Next, when you are coming down from the stairs, take angle instead of putting your foot straight forward across the steps. This would give you a graceful body line and firm footing. Try to evolve a personal graceful style to climb up and descend from the stairs as if you are floating in the air; rhythmic fluid movements, as if the stairs do not exist at all.

Car craze is in the air. Car manufacturers seem to have taken India by storm. Car travel is no more a luxury in the

big cities. But, did you ever think that taking your seat in the car or leaving it demands graceful movements on your part? A tall girl wearing a narrow skirt really finds it troublesome to enter into or get out of the new luxury cars of low height. Have you ever watched such a girl getting in or out of a car? If not yet, then perhaps you may not have an idea that how difficult such a job is. Really, a woman's grace is at stake on such moments. By learning how to get in and get out of the limousines with ease and gracefully, you may add extra charm to your body movements.

If you do not want to become a laughing stock, while taking your seat in a car or leaving it, try to adopt the following method. While getting in, do not put your head forward in the car, instead let your foot nearer the door get inside first. Place that foot firmly on the floor of the car, then slide in your hips and put them on the edge of the seat; thereafter pull the other foot inside and move backwards to place your bottom fully on the seat. While getting out, put your foot (which is nearer the door) out of the car, place it on the ground firmly; with your second foot (still inside the car) push your body weight out till your are able to stand erect. Let this coming out be led by the head.

If you have to pick up something from the floor, or you want to open lower drawers of your office table, do not bend your body like a Giraffe. Instead, lower yourself by bending your knees to do the job, and then get up slowly. This bending of the knees will safeguard your spine against overstraining. And, you will also look graceful.

16

It's Roses all the Way When She Speaks

CONVERSATION is an art. It is a hallmark of feminine grace and sophistication. Conversation is one of the most effective ways of communication. Although several other mediums are also available to exchange views and express feelings, yet spoken language is one of the easiest and readily available means to converse with others. In fact, the words you speak, the way you speak, is a reflection of your personality. When you speak, the accompanying facial expressions and body movements considerably enhance or diminish the effectiveness and charm of your conversation. It is only through conversation that you endear yourself to people around you or compel them to avoid your company.

If you know the art of sophistication in speech, you can win lots of friends and admirers. Then, people would surely feel delighted listening to you. And, strangers also, while overhearing you, may shoot an appreciative glance in your direction. But, is the *sophistication in speech* something rare or heavenly? Or, it is just an imaginary

phrase coined by the poets and litterateurs to exaggerate the qualities of their female characters.

Before talking about *sophistication in speech,* I would like to tell you some basic things about speech. Have you seen a blind person receiving messages, i.e. reading the text through his fingertips which he runs over the words written in Brail script? You might have also seen two deaf and dumb persons communicating with each other. If not, then better if you see the Sunday afternoon special news bulletin for the deaf and dumb on DD1. Then, you would know how the newsreader communicates with viewers without speaking a word through movement of her lips, eyebrows and gestures of her hands.

So, it is really difficult for the visually handicapped or speech and hearing impaired people to express their views and feelings. But the way they communicate among themselves underlines the importance of facial expressions and hand movements in a conversation. In your conversation also, these gestures play an important role. And, when these (facial expressions and hand movements) are used appropriately and gracefully, they add to the effectiveness of your spoken words. **Body Language** is the term commonly used to describe facial expressions and hand gestures. We will discuss body language in detail in the following pages.

Have you ever observed a mother talking to her infant child cuddled up in her lap comfortably? You will see the baby smiling often and moving his/her lips as if trying to speak. The baby seems to look most attentively; but, actually he/she is listening quite attentively. This listening is one of the most essential things to happen to a child before he/she can speak. A child who cannot listen, won't be able to speak. During infancy a child's grasping power is at its peak compared to any other time in his life. That is why in just one year he is able to speak and understand the language. It is the mother who teaches her child the first lesson of language. This language is called mother tongue.

Now, a few words about the speech mechanism of our body. Our speech is controlled by Broca's speech area (area-44) present in the frontal lobe of the cerebral hemisphere. It is present on the left cerebral hemisphere in a right handed person and vice versa.

The speech or voice is produced by the vocal cords, two pearly white strings of fibrous tissue covered by mucous membrane, present in the sound box, i.e. larynx. Actually, speech is the result of vibration of these cords, produced by the passage of the exhaled air of the lungs. Apart from the vibrations of the vocal cords, the phonation (voice production) is also assisted by the movement of tongue, lips, soft palate and nose. The voice has got many components like pitch, tone and other such things.

But then, why am I talking to you about all this? You may not have any interest in this theory of sound production. Please, don't feel bored. My idea is to make you understand the finer points of speech mechanism so that you could use your voice correctly and effectively. Another important aspect you may be unaware of is that speech plays an important role in making your impression. Your speech is a yardstick by which people judge/appraise your personality, your intelligence, your class, your upbringing, your humour. To achieve a charming voice which can make people willing to talk to you or listen to you attentively, you have to learn some basic things early in life.

Here is an example of how a speech bordering on hoarseness has marred an otherwise charming personality. Ms Aneeta Wadhwani, one of our family friends, is the principal of a reputed Gwalior school. She is, indeed, a very smart, charming beautiful lady, with some special qualities like entrepreneurship and untiring zeal to accomplish her goal. However, unfortunately, she does have a drawback, major one at that. Whenever she appears on stage, wielding a

microphone, her image of a charming personality receives a severe blow because her cracking voice betrays—it has all the shades of hoarseness. In just a few moments, all her charm and beauty vanish in the thin air.

Not that Ms Wadhwani is not aware of her personality's major drawback. She knows it pretty well. Once talking to me, she expressed her helplessness, "it has been so since my childhood. Probably, it got aggravated after my joining the teaching profession because I have to call my students in a raised voice." Countering her, I said, "But this all is playing havoc with your lovely personality. You should do something about it." As a solution to her voice problem, I suggested Ms Wadhwani to undergo a special course in speech therapy and special training in voice modulation by a good speech therapist.

My another acquaintance, Ms Madhvee Shah, is also a lady with lot of natural charm and grace. Her husband owns a large jewellery showroom in our town. You will always find her well dressed. She knows her requirements to the last detail. She is quite good in her selection of makeup, hairstyle, jewellery and other accessories. And, you may be surprised to know that looking charming is not the be-all and end-all of Ms Shah's personality. She is equally well read and very articulate in her views. In parties and social gatherings, she seems to be the ultimate in feminine grace and charm. But, like Ms Wadhwani, Ms Shah's voice also betrays her beauty. One can easily listen to her hoarse and high-pitched voice even if she is talking privately to a small group of friends.

Here is yet another example of Ms (Dr) Meena Goyal. She is my colleague. A graceful lady, Ms Goyal is always very polite and gentle. And, she is thorough in the subject she teaches. But when it comes to taking her class, she feels handicapped by her voice. She is hardly audible even to the students sitting in the first row what to talk of those sitting on

the back-benches. Although students and staff members all respect her for her knowledge of the subject, but then what to do when one is not able to hear what she is speaking?

These are just a few examples. I have come across lot of such women. When these women speak in hoarse, high-pitched voices, they just do contrary to what Shakespeare expected of a woman. His words are echoing in my ears: "Her voice was ever soft, gentle and low; something very rare but excellent in a woman."

I believe that most of the women, howsoever well educated, well dressed and good looking, are totally unaware of the flaws in their voice. Therefore, they don't care about faults in their speech and distracting elements in their spoken language. Maybe, you also belong to this category. One thing you must keep in mind is that it is very unlikely that anyone is going to tell you about your faulty speech. For those who are not close to you, for example your colleagues, visitors, acquaintances will seldom take this trouble, fearing your displeasure and annoyance. And, those who are close to you are so accustomed to your style of speaking that they hardly notice it. Even if they notice it and tell it to you, you may not feel quite bothered to give any heed to their advice."Oh, it is OK. How is it going to matter anyway?" That may be your casual reply, reflecting your carelessness about your faulty speech.

Have you ever noticed that your sentences often end up trailing in a mumble; your 'ings' often fall in pit; you often use some offending words and phrases which are not abusive in the literary sense, but then they are not civilised either. Is this your problem? Well you may say, "No, not at all, who says?" Even if you have replied my question with an emphatic "No," I advise you to do two things. One, try to give a concerned ear to whatever you speak. In other words, listen attentively next time to your own voice. Well, if you cannot

do that, the next best thing is to record your conversation as often as possible, or read out loudly from a newspaper for ten-twenty minutes and record it, then play it and analyse your voice and speech delivery. Second option is to take a close colleague or friend of yours into confidence and ask him/her to analyse your voice-speech. This will certainly help you to overcome your speech flaws provided your friend is sincere in his advice.

Notwithstanding all the hi-tech methods of communication available in this modern age, speech still remains one of the most potent means to exchange views. Innumerable times in a day you approach the people around you through your voice. For strangers, your voice is your first introduction. It creates a picture about you. The keyword is *your speech tells your background, your intelligence.*

Imagine yourself as a lady who has all the education, training, skills and charm. She enters into the interviewer's chamber for the job of a secretary. And, the moment she is asked a question, her hoarse voice betrays all the charm, so beautifully cultivated. The aura of feminine beauty represented by her gets spoiled in no time by her faulty pronunciation and poor diction.

Or, consider yourself as a dazzling beauty sitting pretty in a party. As soon as a smart handsome man approaches her for personal interaction, her voice plays havoc because of faulty grammar and unpleasant style.

Here, I also wish to recall an incident when I accompanied my younger brother Sharad to meet a girl of a reputed family for the purpose of marriage alliance for him. She was very pretty, a graduate and well versed in all the household jobs expected from a young girl. After serving tea, she sat with us alone for a few minutes. We tried to talk to her. To our utter dismay, she was hardly able to speak a single sentence in Hindi without the heavy rural accent prevalent in the

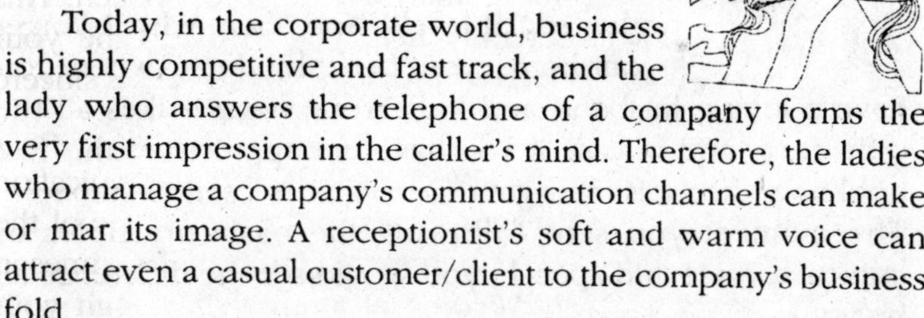

countryside of central India. Then it was just out of question to expect her speak anything in English, which is today a necessity for the metropolitan lifestyle. We were so disillusioned by the whole afair that we could not stay there for a single minute more, what to talk of accepting the marriage proposal.

Today, in the corporate world, business is highly competitive and fast track, and the lady who answers the telephone of a company forms the very first impression in the caller's mind. Therefore, the ladies who manage a company's communication channels can make or mar its image. A receptionist's soft and warm voice can attract even a casual customer/client to the company's business fold.

A receptionist's job just doesn't end after telling a caller about the character and style of functioning of an organization. By her soft and warm tone, a polite frontline lady officer can take steam out of a fuming caller who has a lot to complain to the company. Her concerned voice would go a long way in cooling the frayed tempers of a dissatisfied customer.

How to tackle a caller's phone if you are working as a frontline officer in a star hotel or in any other service oriented organization? As I have said earlier, the role of the people manning a company's communication channels is not limited to just passing on the information asked for. They, in fact, are the first introduction of the company to a stranger. How best they discharge their responsibility would be reflected in the caller showing further interest in the company's affairs.

The image conscious business houses and public relations organisations are very discerning in selecting their frontline staff. In no uncertain terms, they make the job aspirants aware of their challenging and sensitive responsibilities. And, this is all but natural as it matters a lot in this competitive world to have a polite, enthusiastic and helpful public relations staff. A cold, indifferent voice would definitely put off any willing customer to take his business to some other organisation where he is welcomed by a charming voice, which is oozing with warmth and enthusiasm.

But how to make your voice pleasant, warm and full of enthusiasm which can enhance your charm tremendously, giving a boost to your image among your office colleagues, or in your business circles and other social levels. And, then, why to forget your home, your beautiful home, where you have a loving husband and kids. Your voice makes all the difference, and in case if you have not appreciated this fact uptil now then it is the right time to give it a serious thought. The moment you start following the basic principles of attractive voice and speech, you would see the difference all by yourself.

Before giving you lessons in voice improvement, I once again repeat the speech mechanism of your body. The phonation (voice production) is done by the exhaled lung air as it passes through the larynx, your voice box, where vocal cords are situated. The cord's vibrations are modified with the help of lips, tongue, nose and soft palate. Your total mouth cavity along with its walls (cheeks) plays a very important role in determining the quality of your voice.

To improve your voice the first lesson is to develop the correct breathing habits. It is often observed that poor breathing habits coupled with imperfect postures lead to the production of a faulty voice. Do you know why the singers sing in a standing position? Or, why does a person addressing people from a podium stand up while delivering his speech? The main reason is the lungs expand and retract more efficiently in the erect posture, thus enhancing the quality of voice. But, mind you, here I am not suggesting you to get up from sofa while talking to your acquaintances at a party.

You might have also noticed that when you are tense or nervous, your breathing becomes shallow which leads to production of poor quality, low-toned voice. Correct breathing means natural deep breating, as we have during sound sleep.

So, if you have a problem with your breathing, make it a habit to do morning yogasanas, specifically *Pranayam*. This is a special breathing exercise which will definitely improve your breathing. After a month's practice of doing *Pranayam* regularly, you will notice the changes in your voice. Besides yogasanas, swimming and running also help in improving your breathing and consequently your voice.

You may feel that practising deep breathing is very easy. Yes, easy it is. But, be cautious not to make a sound when you take deep breaths, or stop for taking breath. Otherwise, it would show up in your voice, and quality of your voice instead of improving would further deteriorate. Here, take the example of a singer. Surely, you won't like him to take a deep breath in the middle of the song. So, always try to maintain a firm **tone** of your voice sans any huffing and puffing. Here I am not able to resist myself from mentioning the living legend Lata Mangeshkar, whose velvet voice has charmed people not only across the length and breadth of the Indian subcontinent, but also audiences across continents. Truly, she is the nightingale of India of whom every Indian is so proud.

Do you think Lata Mangeshkar's voice and singing abilities are totally God-gifted? No, the magic of her singing does not lie only in the God-gifted voice. The training and perseverance to use it in various modulated forms as per requirement have played a great role in transforming Lata into the Melody Queen. She has said umpteen times in her interviews that it is *Sadhna* (the perseverance) and *riyaaz* (the training) which have taken her to the pinnacle of achievement.

The **mellowness** (melodious attribute) is another important component of the tone. The pleasant **resonance** of a silky voice like that of Asha Bhonsle haunts every one irrespective of his status, rich or poor, illiterate or highly educated. You can improve the mellowness and resonance

of your voice by training your vocal cords in a particular way. For that, first listen to the nodes of 'Harmonium,' the basic musical instrument of Indian origin which is similar to piano-accordion. Practise holding on words like *moon, noon, ring* and the like. Then try holding on vowels *a, e, i, o, u* which then should be coupled with *m* and *n* sounds. For example, *H-ah, nay, ni, no, noo, M-ah, M-ay, M-ee, M-ii, M-oo.* How do you find this exercise? Does it seem a bit difficult to you? Don't worry. Just approach any teacher of light classical Indian vocal music who can very well teach you the voice modulation.

I would like to caution you not to carry the wrong message by my mention of our two legendary female singers. I have no desire to say that you should always try to speak as if you are singing, because if you try to do so, it would look third grade. The key word here is *voice modulation* which you can learn very well by watching or listening to commentators, announcers and news readers on radio and television. Some of them are really marvellous. To name a few, Mr Devkinandan Pandey, Mr Jasdev Singh, Vinod Kashyap on radio. And, among those appearing on the national network of Doordarshan, Ms Nithi Ravindran, Ms Meenu, Ms Sheela Chaman and Mr JV Raman are ideal for voice training.

Remember, no matter how good are you in grammar, or how vast is your vocabulary, what counts most is correct pronunciation. And, to learn that, dictionary is just not sufficient. The best practical way is to watch television regularly and observe minutely good news readers and those conducting debates or giving commentaries.

The shrillness of voice or for that matter its harshness depends a lot on the **pitch.** It is seen that mostly when women keep the pitch lower in their routine talking, their voice quality improves considerably. Your low-pitched voice is, generally, of good quality when you are talking to a smaller group of people, or when you are talking in low tones. But, the moment you get agitated or when you are required to address a large audience, chances are that your voice would crack. So, one should be careful on such occasions. Remember, when you speak slowly your pitch is at a low level, and the moment pace of your voice increases, the pitch is raised to a higher level, automatically.

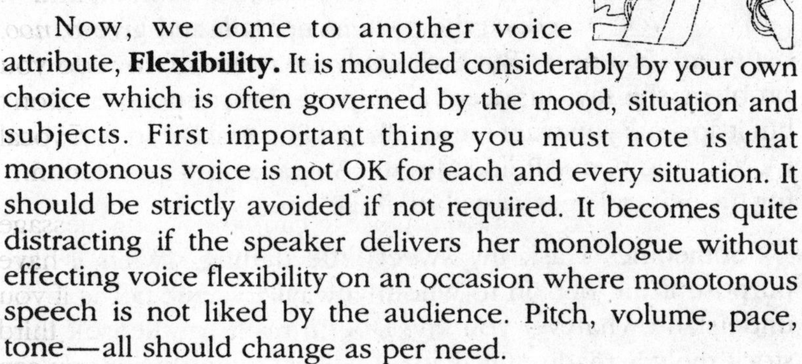

Now, we come to another voice attribute, **Flexibility.** It is moulded considerably by your own choice which is often governed by the mood, situation and subjects. First important thing you must note is that monotonous voice is not OK for each and every situation. It should be strictly avoided if not required. It becomes quite distracting if the speaker delivers her monologue without effecting voice flexibility on an occasion where monotonous speech is not liked by the audience. Pitch, volume, pace, tone—all should change as per need.

You can dramatise your voice by giving pauses at right places. Expressions like "What are you saying?" and exclamatory words such as 'Oh,' 'Ah,' 'Yes,' 'No,' 'What,' etc. also make your talk lively. All this helps in projecting an appropriate image of yours. Who can forget the dramatic dialogue delivery of legendary actors like Raj Kumar, Dilip Kumar and Amitabh Bachchan. But how did they succeed in imbuing their voices with a sort of magnetism which attracted millions of their fans? Of course, by imaginative and innovative ideas. But in our day-to-day practical life 'drama' effect is not required all the time except for some special occasions which demand such effect. Most of the time what you need is a plain and simple approach—how to put your voice to effective use in a most attractive way. Remember, the projection of your voice should not look artificial, but natural and charming.

My daughter, Shubhangini, a sixteen-year-old lovely girl, has a habit of rushing her thoughts through her mouth, just like her frequent rushing from one room to another in our home. She is always in such a tearing hurry that often it

becomes difficult for us to understand what does she want to say. Shubhangini reels off the words and sentences so jumbled-up that they lose their clarity. So much so that one has to strain one's ears to grasp the gist of her narration. Maybe, it's all due to overenthusiasm of her young age.

I have often advised Shubhangini to reduce the pace of her talk and give pause between sentences. But seemingly unaware of her speech problem, she says innocently, "Papa, I always speak so slow, but it appears you want me to talk like Shri Atal Bihari Vajpayee ji". You know, our Prime Minister Vajpayee ji who is famous for his oratory, speaks with definite pauses.

Sometimes I ask my sweet little darling, "What is the purpose if the person to whom you talk is just not able to understand whatever you say? Does it make any sense?" Her stock reply is ready, "OK Papa, I will try honestly henceforth to speak slowly, don't worry". But let me tell you she is yet to try honestly.

Changing our speech habits is indeed a very difficult task because we do not hear ourselves often. Therefore, most of the time we are not aware of our shortcomings. First pre-requisite for bringing a positive change in your speech is the awareness of shortcomings in your day-to-day speaking. Then, you must have some role models among the people around you or TV personalities who really speak well. Thereafter, impelled by an unflinching desire to improve your speech, you can clinch the goal.

Already, I have talked about three speech training techniques. One, reading the newspaper aloud for fifteen-twenty minutes daily, and concentrating on the style, pace, tone of your voice instead of the text meaning. Second, listening to accomplished news readers on radio and television and following correct pronunciations and speech mannerisms. Third, and the most important, record your voice (conversation) and analyse it as you replay it.

You can take inspiration from persons who have succeeded in attracting millions through the magic of their modulated voice. One such example is of the great voice-charmer, Mr Ameen Sayani. He was not born with a golden voice. Instead, he developed a sort of magnetic effect in his voice which ultimately charmed millions across the globe in seventies through his famous radio programme Binaca Geet Mala. **Well, how to put that charm in your voice?** Here are some guidelines which would surely help you if you try sincerely.

1. Have **kind words** on your lips for every occasion in your daily life. Like, if some stranger opens the car door for you, say a brief 'hello' and 'thank you.' Do not forget to praise a child's painting when the proud parents show it to you. Don't forget to say thanks when you are invited to a party even if you do not want to attend. **Be enthusiastic** in your voice tone and appearance while bidding farewell to guests at the end of the party you have hosted, even if you are feeling very much tired. And, when you leave a party, say enthusiastically to the hostess how much have you enjoyed the party. Do not be miser when you speak these words. Do not feel shy, say them 'loud and clear' as the listener feels very much pleased, listening to these words. Believe me.

2. Is the joke over? Should we start laughing now? I often face these questions from my friends whenever I try to cut a joke with them. Cutting a joke or telling a story is an art which very few people know. An able story-teller builds up slowly, slowly the interest of the listeners and tries to sustain it till the end. He does not go into the finer details, instead keeps himself on the main track. The constant charming tone and making voice felxible and dramatic as per the narration requirement enables him to sustain the listener's interest. Remember, monotony has no place in story-telling and joke narration.

3. Have you ever tried speaking standing in front of your dressing table mirror in your bedroom? Well, if not, then try it and analyse your lip movements, eye movement, movement of the jaws and various facial expressions. Try to speak in different moods and feelings, like sorrow, happiness, astonishment, surprise, remorse, and then watch your facial expressions. You will learn about many new things. All your 'facial expressions' are the handiwork of your facial muscles. They play a very important role in making your speech lively and meaningful.

Dead pan face is the expression often used by theatre directors to rebuke their artists who fail to animate the facial expression appropriate to the delivery of a particular dialogue. Suppose the heroine has to respond in affirmative to the hero's love proposal. If her affirmative response is not accompanied with the sparkle in her eyes, or sans the desired coyness, or without the matching enthusiasm on her face, then naturally she fails to live up to the expectations of her director.

Muffling of the words is a major fault of speech delivery. It may be due to stiff upper lip, or stiff jaw line, or inflexibility of the tongue and its incorrect placement in mouth. The movements of tongue and lips during the speech process are referred to as *articulation*. If these movements are faulty, the whole words and sentences may disappear or become meaningless, or they may carry an entirely different meaning. Many a time congenital problems like tongue-tie, cleft lip, cleft palate or other defects of maxillo-facial region may be responsible for it. Sometimes, painful jaw or gum or tooth may also affect the speech temporarily. Apart from the organic causes, the faulty habits of young age, if not pointed out and corrected timely, may lead to permanent defect in speech delivery system. And, curing such defects poses quite a challenge to the speech therapist.

4. Have you seen someone with cleft lip or cleft palate? How does he speak? The voice of such a person has got a nasal twang for every word. Have you ever noticed your own voice when you suffer from a stuffy nose? How much it changes? You know, N, M, Na are the nasal sounds; they have to vibrate through nasal passage to have a pleasant note. Whenever they are not routed through nose, and, instead, take a mouth route, they are accompanied by an unpleasant twang. While these (N, M, Na) require a nasal vibration for a pleasant note, other vowels or consonants if routed through nose produce a very unpleasant sound. This nasal twang can be corrected by proper speech therapy, provided there is no major tissue or bony defect.

   As female voice is naturally high-pitched than the male voice, it gets out of control much more easily, sounding cracked and shrilled which obviously indicates that the person is under strain and is nervous. So, avoid sounding nervous; keep your chin up, keep cool even in adverse circumstances.

   To have a melodious resonance in your voice, it is essential that you speak with relaxed jaw and lips; otherwise, your voice will sound stifled or suffocated.

5. Even if you are putting your views in a board-meeting discussing some crucial policy matter on which depends future of your company, try to express your ideas in a soft and subtle manner. An aggressive, harsh or loud voice is not feminine. It always distracts your listeners. Consequently, they are reluctant to show interest in whatever you are saying. It is simply foolish to think that if one has to stress upon a point, or if one has to win an argument, then one has to speak at the top of one's voice so as to compel the listener to pay due attention. Generally, it has been observed that cool persons are better equipped

to handle the arguments with ease as compared to agitated and tense ones. So, make it a thumb rule to never raise your voice whatever may be the situation or provocation; it will safeguard your voice against many ill-effects (shrilling, hoarseness, cracked voice) and distraction of the listener.

6. You can make new friends, develop new relationships and strengthen your old friendship, solicit cooperation from strangers, win new acquaintances, and gain in knowledge provided you know how to charm people with your conversation style. For inculcating a pleasing and meaningful conversation style, you have to put your views across your listeners in an unobtrusive manner. And, be cautious not to make your voice harsh and loud. Once you succeed in developing this style, you would be surprised to see how people start responding to you in an entirely different way—they would feel happy in your company and would lend on eager ear to your talk. All this would give you immense pleasure and would go a long way in making your life meaningful.

Powers of an able and charming conversationist are boundless as she can have her way as per her desire. Developed conversation skills can take you places. Be it social, political or professional front—you can be winner all the way, provided you have skills to convince the others. What is the job of a sales representative, after all? Her ability to convince the prospective buyers about the utility and value of the product she is selling.

But mind you, there is no room for superfluous ideas and artificial things in your conversation style. Its basis cannot be false or bogus. It all has to come from your heart, in a natural, genuine way.

Often, shy people who are otherwise very warm and friendly are just not able to convey their feelings to the person across the table. And, this goes against them—

they are sometimes construed as high-headed, individualistic persons. You should not fall prey to such wrong notions. When you are introduced to somebody in a party or at a meeting, repeat his name with a longer tone instead of a quick slurr. Say, "how do you do Ms Ranjana Mehta! It is a pleasure meeting you". Make it a point to **keep your tone friendly to appear friendly.**

Smile is the jewel of your face. To be a good conversationist, **smile as often as possible**—whether you say something, or you ask for some favour, or when you do some favour, or when you are introduced to somebody. Haven't you heard the phrase "pass on your sweet smile through the receiver of your phone". Yes it is true. Keep a small mirror in front of you whenever you receive a call from or make a call to your friend. Watch your face—whether you are smiling or not? The moment you see smile playing on your face in the mirror, the person at the other end can also hear your smile. Smile, of course, is produced by the lips but your eyes can also reflect smile, and in the same way your voice can give an impression of smile.

With a genuine smile on your face and in your voice, you instantly put the other person at ease. He feels easy, comfortable in your company. And, believe me, in this world, full of anxieties, worries and tensions, a genuine friendly smile makes a lot of difference.

Giggling and laughing is not required in the normal course of conversation. Reserve it for special occasions, like when you have to charm your man, or when you are at a party with your close friends, or on a picnic with your near and dear ones. Otherwise, it can send a wrong signal.

While showing interest in the person in front of you, be sincere in the real sense. It won't work if you try to appear

sincere for the sake of sincerity. Because, anybody who is a bit intelligent can immediately differentiate between a fake and genuine sincerity. Concentration is essential when you are in the midst of conversation with somebody. Do not allow your thoughts to wander with your telephone or electricity bills. Don't carry your depressions, frustrations with you as this may mar the pleasure of your conversation. Your conversation partner may not be interested in sympathising with your sorrows or listening to your complaints. Maybe, his or her idea is to just spend a few happy moments with you in a light conversation. Do not fool yourself thinking that people are interested in your problems and frustrations until and unless they are your very-very close friends. And, you also know very well, the friends who are genuinely interested in sharing your depressions, are really very few in a person's life. Maybe one or two, to whom you can open your heart. Otherwise, people will immediately brand you as a big bore and will laugh away all your sorrows and frustrations at your back.

7. Today, a working lady is required to deal with all sorts of people. Some of them are decent and well behaved while others are arrogant and rude who just don't know how to deal with women. For them, politeness is a far cry. And, the question of lending a helping hand to a woman just doesn't arise. Well, when you encounter such rude, ill-mannered and hostile creatures, how would you tackle them? You have few options. One, say "Excuse me," and get away from the scene as fast as possible. That is easy and sure way to avoid them.

   Second, confront them with equal amount of rudeness and arrogance, and chances are that visualising a potent opponent in you, they would make a hasty retreat. Third, and the last, way is to maintain your composure and coolness; whatever the provocation, do not lose that. Ignore the slur and return it with a compliment; reciprocate

their rudeness with perfect courtesy. Return the hostility with the most friendly smile you could muster. Take the criticism in your stride and say sincere thanks for the interest she/he has taken for your improvement. Return their bitterness with all the sweetness at your command.

Have you heard the phrase "the lady with golden smile and with honey coated tongue." Well, you may not have heard it. But, here what I want to emphasise is that having a golden smile and a honey-coated tongue is probably one of the most difficult things to do in this world. Not a single person living in this world can claim that she/he has never been affected by the criticism or rudeness, or never felt provoked to take immediate revenge from the person speaking ill. Even Lord Krishna and Lord Rama have lost their tempers in extreme circumstances. A person not giving in to the provocation and keeping his cool even in adverse circumstances is just like Buddha. Well, I am not asking you to become Buddha or Gandhi. But, you can at least sincerely try to acquire this noble quality of not getting provoked.

By simply pretending that an awkward situation or a tense moment does not exist, you can succeed in changing the adverse circumstances to your advantage. By your deep-seated friendliness and decent, composed behaviour even the most difficult of the persons will ultimately bow down to you. Actually, it is a game of nerves, the person having stronger nerves will get the upper hand and ultimately succeed. If by chance you happen to meet a hard nut who defies this golden universal rule then remember that incident or situation for record sake, but in no case react in the rough and rude manner of that adamant person. Here, you should be doubly cautious because most of us tend to be provoked easily by adverse remarks.

8. In the beginning of this chapter, I was talking about the **sophistication in speech.** What is this sophistication? It has been derived from word *sophia* meaning wisdom, divine wisdom. In the literary sense 'being sophisticated' means 'to give a fashionable air to the worldly wisdom'. Some people have a wrong notion about "being sophisticated". They consider it as something delicate, tender, fragile in the context of the fair sex. But, actually it means how well informed you are about different subjects. A skilled conversationist is quite at ease while changing from one subject to another during her talk, giving correct information on varied subjects. And, her skill lies in focusing on the subjects which interest everybody present in the group. For becoming such an accomplished speaker, you are not required to be a college professor. Instead, such an ability is present in almost everybody. You can make this ability to work wonders for you only if you are curious to listen, read and note down the new facts and information as and when they come before you.

As I have emphasised earlier, how do you speak is as important as what you speak. Sophistication is not a quality restricted to the elite of the society or people having bagful of money; neither it is something artificial nor an affected style. Instead, it is all real and natural. A woman endowed with this skill is always at ease in any situation, whether she is in the company of a senior government officer or a celebrity, or has been invited to a neighbour's pool-side dinner party.

To be conversant in various topics of national and international importance, it is essential that you subscribe to one or two good national dailies, like *Hindustan Times* or *Times of India* or their Hindi versions. With regular newspaper reading you will be able to keep yourself abreast with the latest happenings in the arena of sports, politics, social events. The Saturday and Sunday megazine

sections of popular dailies give you a wide variety of topics to read. If fashion and latest trends in dresses interest you then you can choose from magazines like *Femina, Gladreg, Elle.* In Hindi also, you have a wide array of women-specific magazines to choose from, like *Griha Shobha, Manorama, Meri Saheli.* Notwithstanding the saying, "now the politics has become the game of scoundrels," it is advisable to keep yourself well informed about the national and international political scenarios. And, to make your task easy on this front, two quality magazines are quite handy—*India Today* and *Outlook.*

It is a common observation in any given social circle that ladies most of the time are busy discussing about sarees, jewellery or other accessories; or they discuss their families, husbands and children. These are among the most common topics on which talks of Indian ladies centre, irrespective of their education, social background and working or non-working status. Seldom one comes across a lady who can confidently talk on business, market, finance, global trends, corporate world, government policies, or debates in the Parliament.

Reading through my preceding remarks you may think that I am critical of the Indian woman because she lacks in business and other related spheres. Well, I have no intention of belittling the Indian lady by such an observation. But, here is your chance, if you can fill this gap in your knowledge. For, the woman who reads the business pages would find herself singled out in the men's world and would command extra respect in her circle.

"I cannot become an 'encyclopaedia,' and why should I become? I don't understand. There are so many more interesting things in the world to do, like shopping; going on the hill stations; or visiting the Bahamas or Florida or Suncity, and why not Rome"—this text within quotes,

many among you might feel, is just the right reaction on my advice of making yourself knowledgeable. In response, I would say go to any place you like, because visiting new places always gives you new thoughts and topics of discussion with your friends. But keep your camera and pocket-diary always handy to record your moments of happiness. In fact, mind is a bottomless pit where you can store as much information as you desire, and chances are it will never complain. It is probably the only computer available in the market which has got limitless capacity to store the information and knowledge.

Here, I would like to caution you not to allow the feeling of becoming knowledgeable enter into your head. Never allow the arrogancy to overwhelm your serene sweet-self because then all this information and knowledge is of no use. It is highly deplorable on your part to use this sophistication as an instrument to belittle others. The key word here is politeness, gentleness. These qualities would place you on the high pedestal of sophistication as you acquire more knowledge and information. It is Mother Nature's rule that as the mango tree becomes laden with the ripe fruits, its branches bow down towards the earth. In simple words, as you ascend on the path of more knowledge, try to become as humble as possible, as polite as possible. Never try to show off your knowledge in front of others as this will belittle you, instead of them.

17

Your Home: Your Signature

YOUR home, sweet home—a place where you unwind yourself after a hectic day, a place which provides you much needed solace and peace of mind in this turbulent world, a place which you love so dearly. The home of which you are so possessive is the place which you share with your near and dear ones. You identify your total being with it. And, you will not like to trade it for anything in the world. Whatever it may be.

It is not just the four walls, a floor and a roof which make a home the place of your dreams. Rather, it is a place which invariably tells your taste, your lifestyle, your class. ...hort, it reflects your total outlook towards life. Your total personality is reflected in the way you keep your home, not only the values and ideas you believe in. Taking shelter in your bed at night and leaving it in hurry the next morning is not the only purpose your home serves. But, it has got a much larger meaning, the meaning of being an abode, a nest, a place of your own

creation where you have a deciding role, the role of a homemaker.

"A home away from your home"—scream the advertising campaigns of even the most luxurious hotels of the world. Have you ever analysed why do they do so even when they know very well that the hotel rooms are, by any standard, far more beautifully decorated, furnished and well equipped than most of the homes from which their clients come. This is probably to drive in the plain fact that there is no place in the world which can match the comforts of your home.

Sometimes you go out of your town or country to attend a business conference for a few days. In an alien land, even after receiving best of the hospitality, you start feeling "home sick". Or, when you go out with your husband and children for a week-long vacation, travelling in the best available mode of transport, staying in the best of the hotels, enjoying the sight-seeing and breath-taking locales. In the mid-way of your vacation, suddenly one night you start feeling home-sick, or your children may ask at the breakfast, *'Mama, Ghar kab chalenge'?* (Mother, when would we go home?). This home feeling is present in everybody, irrespective of status, money and position. Have you ever heard of any man, howsoever busy and big businessman he may be, howsoever busy itinerary he may be pursuing, living all his life in a hotel? No, no one loves to live in the guest house or hotels for all his/her life.

The first thing everybody does, after acquiring a bit of money, is to have a place of his own. This is a universal rule. And, those who are not able to do that, those who are living in working women hostels or as paying guests suffer from a complex of being 'homeless'. This feeling of homelessness is as harmful for one's mental well-being as the feeling of being rootless. And, it invariably gives rise to the feeling of insecurity, which sometimes becomes so powerful as to drive oneself almost crazy, if not mad.

Need for home might have its roots in the stone age when the caveman living in the forest felt the necessity of having a shelter. A place where he can relax, sleep, feel at ease; where he can keep his belongings, live with his woman, make love to her, and raise a family. Maybe, after having enough of his wandering lifestyle, the caveman wanted to give stability to his life by building a home which would have given him a feeling of something (home) he owns and someone (his woman) is waiting for him there. A feeling of possessiveness, a feeling of belonging creeps in even with a mere thought of home.

Have you seen someone living without a home of his/her own? Well, I have seen many. What a pitiable life they lead, just absent-mindedly wandering from this place to that place, living somewhat American pattern of life. They are just rootless with little attachment and concern for the place and people around them. You just can't imagine how empty they feel within—a state of vacuum. With whom to confide their inner-most feelings, joys and sorrows? Nobody is there. Their lonely existence reminds me of a song of famous Indian singer K.L. Sehgal—*Ek bangla baney nyara, Sonney ka bangla, pyara sa bangla* (oh, get me a home, a lovely home made of gold, my sweet home).

Home remains a home, whether you are single or married, living in a joint family or in an ultra-modern nuclear family—of course, with some differences in various set-ups. You should be at ease with your surroundings by making your home a comfortable place to be in. That sounds like a common sense. Yet, how many times you have felt uneasy or not playing a perfect hostess unlike Mrs. Khosla, your neighbour. Sometimes the reason for this social paranoia is awkwardness born out of discomfort. For example, you just bought a brand new sofa-set with light pink velvet upholstry. It is so pretty, so

good, that you yourself become nervous while sitting on it. Now here is a news for you—your husband's sister is coming for a fortnight to spend her summer vacations with you, along with her three naughty tiny-tots. You place an urgent order with your tailor to stitch double layered full sofa covers by tomorrow evening, the train time of your dear sister-in-law *(nanadji)*.

Some ladies are comfortable with bone china cutlery, some are with silver and crystal, while others feel just nervous while handling them. Well, if you don't feel comfortable with expensive cutlery fearing its breakage, or spoiling them then best is to forget them altogether. Instead, go for modern stainless steel or good variety plastic wares. These days they are available in a variety of colours, designs, shades—ranging from bright to soft. Things which suit your taste, fit well within your budget are the best things. Now, if you are wondering what your dinner table cutlery has to do with your style sense then the simple answer is, everything.

You don't require a budget of ten lakh rupees to decorate your living room unless you have got plenty of money (surprisingly, these days many people have bagfuls of money). And many a time, even with lots of money gone into decorating your house the result won't be pleasing to the eyes if you do not have real taste and 'eye' to do your house. Though interior decorators can always advise you about decoration and furnishing of your house against heavy fees, even then you require your own imaginative ideas and sense of beauty—how actually you want your dream house to look like. Here, I would again remind you that a house is a mirror image of the lady who owns it. It reflects her attitude, her intelligence and her creativity.

My Gwalior is a very beautiful city, easy going, no hurry. Everybody watches what you are doing. Every winter, we have a month-long Annual Trade Fair. You can buy anything from a rope to the latest car from more than two thousand

make-shift shops doing business at the fair. Since last two-three years, the Mela Commitee (Annual Trade Fair Authority) has started inviting handicraft artisans from all over the country. About two thousand of them come every year to exhibit and sell their products at very cheap prices. 'Cheap' I am saying because if you purchase the same thing from an upmarket show-room or departmental store in any large city then the cost may be three-four times. I myself could not resist the temptation of buying many such ethnic items for my home. They are quite unusual type of decoration pieces.

Similar experience I again had when I visited a small art gallery-cum-sales outlet run by an enthusiastic and enterprising young man, Vijay Chawla, in my town. It was really a feast to the eyes to roam in all the rooms of that 'Select Gallery'. It was full of very lovely pieces of art, all hand-made, like big earthen flower vases, unusually large-sized earthen pots. Madhubani paintings, Terracotta Shilp and all that. There, I even saw high class ladies indulged in a shopping spree. They just seemed to be carried away by the ethnic craze. Watching all this was so heart warming because ultimately we Indians are coming back to our roots, i.e. to our cultural heritage, at least for decorating our home interiors.

To tastefully decorate and furnish your home, it's better to work in stages, in instalments. Basically, it's a question of resources at your command. If you can afford it then furnish your home in one go. But, my advice is you should wait for good items till you can really afford them. You know we cannot change our sofa or carpet every year (although some people do that also). Chart out a tentative schedule for acquiring bigger items like dining table, dining set, carpets, etc. one by one. Just as with imaginative use of accessories, you can even diversify your limited wardrobe, similarly with a little imagination you can convert your balcony or lounge into a beautiful cosy coffee place where your husband can

enjoy few moments of happiness in your warm company, with roses of your small garden providing a beautiful natural setting. A cane furniture with heavy cotton cushions or improvised ethnic wooden furniture just polished by polyurethane would combine well with some natural indoor plants.

I have seen many ladies often becoming tense the moment they know that they have to host a dinner party even for members of their very own social group. Reason: They think that for every party they host, their house decor should look different from the previous one. Well, if you have surplus money then frequent changes in house decor is no problem. But, in case you have no money to flaunt through your new house decor, don't feel frustrated. Sit calmly with pen and paper, and note down the proposed decor changes. With your own imagination you can provide so many changes in your interiors which won't cost you even a penny. By changing the cushion covers, calendars, window drapes, and few wall hangings and show-pieces you can give a different, new look to your place which would surprise your guests. The keyword here is not panic reaction, but instead an imaginative planning which will solve your problem of old home decor.

Today, hundreds of books and magazines specialising in home decor and style are available in the market. These can set your imagination on fire. But, here, be cautious. Don't just give in to every other suggestion or model of home decor highlighted by these publications. Remember, once you opt for a change, it requires money and meticulous planning. Also, you must have a fair idea of the end-result. Because, it may happen that you may not like the new decor once it is in place. One thing more. Never feel envious of those celebrity houses as they have acquired that picture postcard look after a thorough planning. And, lot of money has gone into making that planning a reality. But certainly, with little creativity at your command and your sense of self-image, you can make a home of your choice.

For families living in one-bedroom apartments in Mumbai and other metros, paucity of space is a major problem. Peculiar situations many a time throw a real challenge to the homemake who sometimes has to entertain one or two families for dinner. There is no separate dining area in the house; only a make-shift arrangement substitutes a dining room. Well, do not mind. Whatever the situation, you can come out with flying colours, thanks to your creative imagination. Think a little bit and let your centre table be converted into a dining table. With small mats, trays and small-size dinner plates you can very conveniently entertain your guests. Do not forget to add your personal touch by placing few fresh flowers in a small glass vase at the centre of the table. A little thought about the soft music and pleasing soft light will help you in creating a relaxed and pleasant ambience.

Do you think linen napkins would go well with the straw-mats? Must you have separate glasses for water, soft drinks and wine, or you should go for all-purpose wide-based crystal glasses? Whatever your choice, you must be aware that serving pieces and tableware would be a reflection of your style. A savvy hostess knows very well that little touches are very important. Like, a clean towel at wash basin along with guest-size medallion scented soap in the bath; a well made bed for coats and shawls if you do not have enough hanger space in your ante-room.

And then, the last but not the least, before every party keep yourself ready with a master shopping list of the grocery items and other things to avoid the last-minute dash to the market. Make the schedule a day before the party in consultation with your husband, provided he is ready to lend you an eager ear. On the party day, prepare your vegetable dishes, sweet dishes, salads, soups, two or three hours in advance. And, don't forget to go for a bubble bath an hour before the party to keep yourself calm and confident. And, surely, you will stand out as a perfect wife, a perfect hostess.

18

How to Win Hands Down

THE way you relate with people, the way you project yourself to the society, matters a lot. Because, it is among the most important factors which ultimately decide whether you will be a winner or a loser in this highly competitive world.

The "Techniques of masterly human behaviour" (MHB) are of immense help for achieving all-round success, commanding respect and love of people around you, and creating a positive long-lasting impression even on strangers. These techniques are very simple and down to earth. Their successful application requires a little imagination but lot of patience. So, to succeed in your chosen field learn them fast if you have not already done so. Maybe, you have an idea about them, but you may not have given a serious thought to master them. Never mind, it is never too late to learn something which can equip you with a very effective tool to project yourself impressively.

There is an old saying "The way a woman behaves usually reflects the way she feels at heart", and there cannot be any doubt in this regard. These words aptly highlight the characteristic feature of a woman, apart from echoing another popular phrase "the way a woman looks usually reflects the way she feels." So, how to make yourself a woman liked by most, if not by all. Let's dwell somewhat deeper.

Well, it is a difficult task I must say at the beginning itself. More so, if you are a carefree, fun-loving type of creature. Because, then you must be in the habit of taking things casually and very lightly. Also, for a care-free person, bothering about the norms of behaviour of civilized society can't be a priority. 'I don't care'—this one-liner most often used by the fun-loving creatures is an indication of their self-centred lifestyle. Mostly, the users of this one-liner are college-going young girls of rich or super rich parents, living in metropolis or megapolis.

A person, not the least concerned about norms of civilized behaviour, may say: "Why this discussion of masterly human behaviour (MHB)? Does it highlight something new? Who does not know how to behave? Does anybody learn walking or speaking? One does all these things as naturally as taking breath. Every woman behaves as she deems fit at a particular time or situation. Then, why should she bother for something which she already knows? So, what is the point of discussing all this."

I am afraid that some of you may also support the above viewpoints. My answer to all these arguments is: The MHB is an art in which nobody is perfect, howsoever intelligent, well educated, well placed (socially or financially) she/he may be, because it is an art which one has to master. To make the MHB concept more clear let me fall back on the meaning of it as contained in the dictionary: "a skilful presentation, pleasing to the senses, learnt through sustained perseverance".

So this MHB is also to be learnt through a burning desire to improve upon those aspects of your personality which have a bearing on your social and professional interaction. Initially, you may feel a compulsion in following the MHB. But in due course of time it becomes a habit, a habit liked by all, envied by some.

I feel very happy when I see young energetic girls in their late teens, highly ambitious and pursuing their goals of higher education through stiff competition. To watch their progress in the toughest branches of medicine, electronics and business management is indeed a source of immense pleasure for me.

After getting placement in the business field or in a job they are certainly entitled to feel contented and a bit proud of themselves. And, I consider it quite justified. Why not? Didn't they toil day and night to attain the position where they are today? As the years pass by, they are also rewarded for their professional excellence. And, they further ascend the ladder of promotions and accomplishments.

But, **the success has its own problems.** Most serious is when it goes into the head. The success has different side-effects on different women. It makes intelligent ladies more mellow, polite and sober. But, not so intelligent ladies start wearing success on their collar and try to flaunt it whenever and wherever they find the opportunity. Even their parents, friends and peers become victims of their heady success. The statement which such women want to make is that they have arrived, i.e. they have become successful; gone are the days of their struggle when dressed poorly, they used to travel in government's public transport; now look at the expensive jeans and shirts, the boots, the diamond necklace and rest of paraphernalia which this newly found success has given them.

This high-headedness becomes the very first thing which is being noticed by others in your personality. Your every

plus point, charm, beauty are shadowed by this shortcoming. Nobody is able to notice them. But, everyone is quick to observe your proudy, high-headed behaviour which is highly distracting. Remember, all your achievements when acknowledged and clapped by others become jewels in your crown of glory. But, if they are being drummed up by yourself then others are least interested in appreciating your so-called scroll of honour. And, sooner you would find yourself left alone to listen to the harsh noise coming out from your drums

So, avoid to become the captain of the one-man self-promotion brigade. But, then, why people at all indulge in self-praise? Don't they know it's not liked by anybody. Actually, people who clamour for overnight fame consider self-praise the easiest way to achieve their goal. They are impatient people, they just don't want to wait for people to recognise their achievements in due course of time. They themselves want to announce to the whole world their so-called accomplishments. Earlier the better. And, their impatience plays the spoilsport, making everything look discoloured and stinking.

So, the first and the foremost lesson of masterly human behaviour is: "Avoid self-praise, screw your head tightly on your shoulders as you ascend the success ladder, and remain polite and soft as far as possible".

Some people, blinded by self-esteem, do not consider others' accomplishments worth praise. Instead of complimenting somebody's hard work and sincerity, they seek pleasure in belittling his/her achievement because it satisfies their ego. Considering themselves extraordinarily talented, they just don't want to recognise virtues in others and dismiss them as non-achievers. Thinking that God has gifted a rare, intelligent brain to them only, they see others just as ordinary people not capable of doing great things in life. Among women, such egoistic type mostly belong to the nouve rich

class representing the yuppy-puppy culture. Obsessed with their 'I don't care' attitude, they are completely engrossed in their petty, self-centred acts. They have a myopic vision of the happenings around them.

The yuppy-puppy culture women are always busy in flaunting their wealth, high family status and high contacts. They will not let go any occasion to show off their costly dresses and jewellery. These birds of the so-called high society are also expert in cooking up stories. For example: "Oh, last year when my husband went to deliver his speech at the Davos World Economic Summit along with the Prime Minister, I thought of accompanying him for some shopping at Rome and Paris. But, at the last minute I dropped the idea. You know I cannot tolerate these politicians and serious-looking type of individuals as I am a fun-loving person. Moreover, I do not like Davos, a dull city."

Here's another bird chirping in another scenario. She is the so-called social worker belonging to high society and the wife of a big industrialist. How vast and multi-dimensional is the canvas of her social work is clear from her telephonic talk with another lady: "I do not know what to do, with so many engagements at hand? Only yesterday, the Joint Secretary in the Ministry of Women and Child Welfare, Mr Khanna, who is very close to us, was asking me, 'Bhabhi ji, why don't you accept our offer of heading the delegation which we are sending to China for the world conference on women welfare?' And, you know it is his third telephone. I am in a fix. You know, how busy I am these days. There are meetings of the Slum Welfare Committee. Then, there is that Adult Literacy Project which I have started in a JJ colony in trans-Yamuna area. But Mr Khanna is insisting so much, I don't know what to do".

The lady on the other end of the phone had become quite fed up with this monologue of self-proclaimed greatness. Unable to bear this anymore, she quickly conceded, "Yes,

Bhabhi ji I know that you are too busy to entertain such petty proposals, but to whom the ministry people can look forward to head the delegation?"

But, you know, the real behind-the-scene story was just opposite. Actually, the industrialist's wife was trying her level best to pressurise the ministry people to include her name in that delegation at any cost. Yes, she is ready to pay any amount. But, to create an air of self-importance she is floating all sorts of stories.

These high society birds have one more shortcoming, that is, when a fellow lady compliments them for their gorgeous looking Banarasi saree then instead of accepting it gracefully with slight nod of head and thank you, they start boasting about their *Khandaani* (family) tradition. They would make you believe that most of their sarees are crafted by traditional weavers on their family looms. And, it has been their family tradition for the last two hundred or so years to only wear these exclusive sarees woven by their family *Khandaani* mastercraftsmen in Orissa. But everybody present in the party knows very well that Mrs Dhamija's family has earned their fortune only recently in the garment export business. And, not long ago all the Dhamija brothers were dependent on a small cloth shop in an obscure town in Haryana for earning their livelihood.

So, I hope that now you know **how damaging is this blowing off the self glory trumpet for your social prestige. You must resist it at any cost.**

Here, I would like to give you the examples of three Bollywood heroines who, though devoid of stunning looks, made a mark in the industry. They are Jaya Bachchan, Shabana Azmi and late Smita Patil. By any parameter, they could not be labelled as glamorous and oozing with sex, the two foremost qualities demanded of any silver-screen actress. Yet, they became successful and found places in cine-goers hearts.

They received accolades despite tough competition. And, they didn't fall prey to the obscene body show which is considered an easy way of recognition for new heroines. Then, how could they succeed? Any idea? The secret of their success, you know, is that they put their most subtle charm of beauty to its best creative application. It was their ability to express the most genuine emotions on their faces. With this, they succeeded in building a rapport with their viewers. Theirs was the most natural and effortless display of emotions of the character they were playing. Here, I also recall another accomplished actress, Madhubala. Who can forget the serene and soothing effects of her hypnotising eyes? The child-like innocence of Madhubala's face would remain etched in her fan's mind till eternity.

Now, we come to another important aspect of feminine behaviour. I strongly believe that the **most important point in the feminine behaviour is genuineness (honesty) and childlike innocence.** The person standing in front of you should feel the warmth of your honest behaviour. He/she should be able to appreciate that you are sincerely interested to relate with him/her at an equal level without any airs.

How actually you conduct yourself in a conversation would tell a lot about your personality to other conversationists. Here are some tips on how to participate in a talk. While meeting someone for the first time at a gathering or party, **try to become a 'good listener'.** Knowing how to listen is as vital for an ideal conversation as knowing what to say next. Often, I have observed that chatter box type of ladies have a very good presence of mind. But, when it comes to what to say and what not to say they seem to be totally blank. They also seem to be in a tearing hurry to tell everything about them to the person they are meeting for the first time. It places them in such a bad light that the meeting which might have laid the foundation of a long lasting association

ends in a disaster. This generally happens with those ladies who, though otherwise behave decently, do not have the patience of listening to other persons' views.

Be brief. This is my advice to those of you who have a tendency to dominate a talk. No talk can please if it turns into a long monologue. Get to your point as quickly as possible, and know when to stop. Haven't you heard the saying "speech is silver but silence is golden." Just keeping your mouth shut when other person is talking would convey to him your genuine interest in his talk.

Remember, interest is always mutual—a sort of give and take. It is absolutely unfair on your part to start conversation with "how are you?", "how are your kids?" And, before that poor lady could answer, your eyes shift from her face and you start looking for some other known face in the crowd. This is highly irritating. It is a sort of insult to that lady. You can only understand it if you yourself pass through the same experience. No doubt, we are all hard pressed for time, and we want to utilize this opportunity (party) to meet as many acquaintances and friends as possible. But, one should not behave like this. Believe me, this is the surest way of losing a friend.

But how to listen? Seek first to understand, then be understood. Develop a natural enthusiasm that gets you to asking the questions as your questions give others the opportunity to express themselves which they like very much. Offer your full concentration, whether talking on phone or talking to someone while sitting in your living room. Don't allow TV or other such things to divert your attention, it looks irritating to the other person.

All our actions take their hue from the colour of our heart whereas landscapes do their variety from the light. That's why attention and consideration given even to an ordinary

acquaintance is a reflection on the qualities of your heart. It gives you an image of 'lady with heart, that too golden heart'.

When in conversation, try to maintain a constant eye-contact with the person instead of looking to the wall hangings in the room. To clarify what do I mean by 'attention' and 'consideration' I give you an example. Suppose, a friend is telling you about her domestic or office problems. But, instead of sympathising with her or suggesting a solution, you switch the conversation towards your own difficulties. This is the most objectionable response. Though offering advice in such a situation is an interested response, I would suggest you not to give advice unless you are requested to, as most people simply want confirmation of their ideas, not advice.

It is very difficult to offer a correct advice unless one has taken right lessons from the struggles in his life. Moreover you can simply give advice, not impart the wisdom how to benefit from it. You must remember that **unsolicited advices are often thrown into dustbin because the supply of advice always exceeds its demand.**

Unfortunately, people generally have quite a false impression about becoming advisers. They think that the surest way of showing your concern and sympathy for a person's problems is to offer advice. And, by acting advisers, they can also show their intelligence. Actually, as I have said earlier, the person who has confided his problems and worries in you, just wants confirmation of his ideas and actions, not advices. For such a person even a simple sentence like 'Yes I understand your problem' spoken by you is more than sufficient to show your concern for him.

God has simply made the basic infrastructure while creating you. Now, it is up to you, what you make out of it. It is simply a matter of training yourself how to relate with the people in a socially acceptable way. A lady is supposed

to be more mature, intelligent, and considerate in her behaviour than a man. However, much depends upon the type of job, profession, to whom you are interacting with, and your specific requirements.

But, undoubtedly, the fundamental quality of a lovable personality is to give due respect, love and care to the persons who come in your contact, irrespective of their status and your liking. Only then you can expect anything in return. And, better if you don't expect anything in return, not even recognition or appreciation of the fact that you have done anything for them, then what to expect the return of love and concern from them.

Remember, if you oblige someone and through your behaviour compel him to take note of it, then don't be foolish to expect that you would be seen in good light. Instead, there is a strong possibility that you would be branded as a desperate publicity seeker notwithstanding your goodwill gesture. Best thing is, forget the matter altogether. Just no expectation of return of love and concern. This "no expectation" mental frame will be very much helpful in keeping your mind cool and composed.

The fact is, you may not be knowing your shortcomings at all which are robbing your personality all the time, because nobody shall be pointing them to you and why should they? As they know very well that you will not take kindly to the fact because you don't like that anybody should point out your mistakes. But mind you, some of your shortcomings can be so distracting that they completely mar your personality, you may lose your man, your job, or you may be superseded in the promotion ladder because you do not know how to relate with the people.

To respond warmly and decently does not require doing great things or spending lavishly. Small things matter a lot when we talk of decent behaviour. It just demands your

attentiveness and proper application of your intelligence. With these two weapons in your armoury you can surely succeed in transforming yourself as the 'most sought-after woman' (MSW). So, how to go about achieving your goal? First thing, try not to react even if feeling quite slighted. Suppose, someone very close to your heart does not keep a promise (like taking you out for dinner or to the movie or getting you a new dress). Though you may be feeling like becoming a non-entity due to his ignorance, do not try to humiliate him. Perhaps, he could not keep his word due to his own pressing problems. In such a situation, your angry reaction would show you as a selfish woman quite unconcerned about her life partner's problems. It may, in fact, scar you relations with him permanently because nobody likes criticism. Moreover, if it is done without going into reality.

Criticism, you know, is a common human reaction which even fools are able to do. But, large-heartedness and forgiveness stand out as distinct qualities of those who are really decent and kind. And, you know very well that everybody likes second type of people. Therefore, you would be highly respected and immensely loved by your man if you simply ignore his fault. He would really appreciate your large-heartedness. And, next time he would certainly keep his word.

"Her presence lightens up the place. She is like a cool refreshing breeze coming out directly from the seashore or the valley of flowers."

Have you ever heard these words in your praise? No? Do you want someone to shower such praise on you? If your answer is 'Yes,' then read on.

During my MBBS days, I used to visit quite often the house of my classmate Jyoti Mehta. Our houses were on the same street. Her mother was principal of a reputed post-graduate Girls College—the Home Science College of our

district, Jabalpur. Sometimes on Sundays, Jyoti's mother, finding some spare time, also joined our chit-chat. On one such afternoon, out of curiosity, I asked her, "But, Auntie, how do you manage your big college so efficiently? Don't the students create problems for you? How do you get the cooperation of your staff; don't they sometimes pose difficulties for you?"

Jyoti's mother was sipping tea. In response to my enquiry, she smiled. Conceding that she faced lot of problems in the beginning, she said, "Earlier, I used to shout at my staff too much. Students were also the target of my constant scolding. Although apparently they never reacted to my angry outbursts, it was clear to me that I was not liked by my staff and students alike. They used to share their resentment in my absence. It continued for few years."

Pausing for a moment, she said, "But one day I realised that if my teachers and other colleagues do not work with enthusiasm and interest desired of them, maybe it's due to my own fault. Perhaps, it points to the failure of my interpersonal skills. Thereafter, I tried to change my attitude towards my staff. Instead of blatantly criticizing them, I made it a point to first highlight their good qualities and then I used to humbly suggest the change or improvement I desired in their work culture. To my utter surprise, this small change in my approach resulted in completely transforming the working atmosphere of my institution. Things improved dramatically. Teachers became quite sincere in taking their classes regularly. They even started discussing their personal problems with me. Because, the previously blocked communication channel between me and my staff gave way to free exchange of ideas and views. All this brought many positive changes. And, the one which I was very happy to notice was the remarkable improvement in the teaching standard. I felt proud when students' parents used to tell me that they are satisfied with their daughters' studies. It also gave them a sense of pride

that their daughters are studying in a prestigious institution, like ours. Believe me son, I never felt so satisfied in my life as I felt during those days".

No doubt, Jyoti's mother was really feeling proud and satisfied while telling her experience. It was clear from her glowing face. This was an incident of late sixties. But, believe me, things have not changed since then. With decent behaviour and a proper understanding of others' qualities and weaknesses, you can make things work for the welfare of all. No matter whatever you are—student, job aspirant, professional, executive or businessman.

How often do you watch your husband doing shave while getting ready for his office in the morning? You may say, "Umpteen times, what is new about it?" Well, have you ever seen him shaving without putting the lather on his face? Well, no. Because, using of razor becomes much easier after the softening of beard and it shaves perfectly.

And, you know, criticism is like cutting (as the razor cuts the hair), which is resorted to, to correct something/someone. But, the problem is nobody likes the cutting (criticism) because it hurts, and it hurts immensely. Sometimes it inflicts an incalculable damage to your relationships, to the spirit of cooperation and camaraderie. So much so that it kills all the enthusiasm of working together.

Here, I would like to give you an example. On a hot June afternoon, things were moving normally on the shop floor of a large tyre manufacturing unit near Delhi. Floor Engineer Sukomal Pandya was supervising the carbon mixing with white rubber. Suddenly, two workers fainted and fell down, maybe due to heat exhaustion. Obviously, the work came to a grinding halt. The two boys were removed to an open space and given first aid to bring them back to their senses. After half an hour, work was again in full swing at the shop floor. No problem. But the same afternoon in another part of the

unit, two boys again fainted. They also could not bear the excessive heat of the place where moulding of raw tyres was being done on huge machines. Work was again stopped for a short while, and it took one hour to repair the damage to the material and machines. Before the end of the shift at 4 pm, the chief engineer came along with the company's vice-president for their usual round. Both of them expressed their anguish at the two accidents. But, the vice-president, exceeding limits of decency, rebuked Sukomal in front of all the workers.

Sukomal, a qualified engineer and tyre technologist, was feeling demoralised and depressed as he was being unduly blamed for the accidents. In fact, it was not due to any lapse on his part that these accidents had occurred. But being too junior to air his resentment, he continued to suffer silently. No more, he was his earlier enthusiastic self. He was just not interested in continuing his job. And, within a month's time, he left the company to join their rivals.

Now, what do you think? Was it OK for the vice-president to behave in such an abnormal way? You know, minor accidents are a routine in a tyre unit. And, for them to criticise Sukomal and that too in front of his juniors showed the vice-president in a poor light. It did not improve the things at all. Probably, a little tactful handling on the part of vice-president could have saved the company losing a talented technical hand.

But things were not so bad at the Andhra Bank, Gwalior branch where I do often go for my banking needs. Its young Branch Manager S.K. Goyal is a very nice person. One day, it was a pleasant experience for me to see a young pretty lady managing the bank's cash counter quite efficiently. She, Nirmal Mittal, was very quick in her job, and not for a moment the pleasing smile left her face. Nirmal was a new trainee at the bank.

After collecting my cash from the counter I went to meet Mr Goyal. He was courteous as usual. I told him about my appreciation of Nirmal's pleasing manners and efficient working. He laughed and said, "Yes, she is very polite and decent with the customers and also quick in her job. But, perhaps you don't know the other side of her story".

I became curious to know more about Nirmal's personality. "Tell me. Is it something different?" I asked Mr Goyal. He replied, "In a way, it is. Not long ago at the end of day, she often used to keep us all hanging in the office till late evening because she could not do the balancing job. And, my chief-accountant even went to the extent of suggesting me to fire her. He complained to me that she did not know the basics, and how long others would keep on helping her with the balancing job".

The phone interrupted Mr Goyal to stop talking. After answering the phone call, he continued, "One day after the end of public dealing, I called Nirmal to my cabin and told her, 'Nirmal, our customers are very pleased with your services. I also appreciate your sincerity and efficiency, how quickly you dispose of your work. I would like to see you progress fast. But, I have heard that you have some problems with your balancing job. Maybe, I may offer you some help in this regard'. She was quite willing to accept my help. Then I tried to explain the whole process to her in the easiest possible way. And, you won't believe Dr Agarwal, in a week's time our chief-accountant came to me saying, 'Sir, I do not know what has happened to Nirmal, she has improved tremendously'. I just smiled because I knew what has worked."

It is very easy to find faults and criticise someone but it seldom helps in improving things. Remember, criticism can bring about a desired change or improvement only when it is used with the appreciation of the qualities of the concerned person. Constructive criticism supported by honest pats at the back can do wonders. In other words, this cutting

(criticising and fault finding) becomes much less painful if you inject xylocain (local anaesthetic drug used for minor incisions). That is, genuine appreciation and unadulterated praise are as effective in making criticism bearable as xylocain in making incisions tolerable.

Therefore, always keep in mind that calling attention to one's faults in a subtle manner works wonders, not telling him how incompetent he is.

Last year, my daughter Shubhangini was entrusted by her principal to give a speech on 'Importance of Personal Hygiene' in front the school assembly during morning prayer. She had two days at hand to prepare her five-minute speech. While drafting her speech, Shubhangini wrote and re-wrote it several times. Ultimately, she showed to me the final draft.

After going through her proposed speech draft, my reaction, in fact, was quite critical. I wanted to tell her the reality, "Shubangini you have miserably failed in preparing a good speech. Your piece shows as if you do not know the ABC of personal hygiene. It would put you in a very bad light in front of your entire school".

But, not willing to demoralise Shubangini, I somehow concealed my true reaction on her piece. For, I knew that this would shatter her confidence completely. And, even if I helped her with a good written speech after criticising her, she would remain shaky. This would have marred not only her first-ever speech performance but would also have dampened her spirits to undertake any such activity in future. Therefore, I tried to encourage her, "Well, you have written a very good informative piece. But this is more of an article which would go well with your school magazine. It just doesn't give the impression of a speech. For that a different style is needed". This way without denting her self-esteem and hurting her confidence, I tactfully managed to enable my daughter to give a commendable speech.

To find positive points of your interest in someone's personality which you can appreciate and praise is pretty difficult. It is difficult because our mind has not been trained to do that. Instead, what we generally find is the unusual eagerness among us all to pinpoint mistakes, shortcomings and faults in others. Every Tom, Dick or Harry can do this because it is most easy thing to do. It comes naturally to human beings.

If you have to develop yourself into a person with a warm heart and an understanding mind then you must depart from this common fault-finding behavioural trait. Yes, I agree, it's not easy. For this you have to specifically train your mind. Forget targetting a person for his shortcomings. Instead, appreciate him whole-heartedly for his qualities. Though a bit difficult to inculcate, this quality of being able to appreciate others is a beautiful human characteristic.

Mr Satish Ajmera, a successful businessman, runs several prestigious textile showrooms in my town and other cities. He has more than two hundred employees working under him. Mr Ajmera is today a changed person. Rather, I would say he has undergone tremendous transformation in his behaviour with his subordinates.

In Mr Ajmera's own words, "I used to get terribly upset with my employees even on a slight provocation. And, I won't stop short of giving them a complete dressing down. There was simply no question of a second thought if I had already decided to come down heavily on an employee. But, one day it occurred to me: Was it proper to behave in such a rude manner? Thereafter, I resolved to change my behaviour. Now, you won't believe that I toss a coin to decide what should be my reaction to various mistakes committed by my employees in their functioning. If it's head I try to calm down and tell in a polite manner the erring employees to mend their ways. And, the coin showing tail means, I must scold the employee for his fault. But, I always end up adopting the first course

because the coin which I toss has head on both its sides".

So, Mr Ajmera knows that his coin has got no tail. And, he has intentionally allotted the hard option of scolding employees to the tail side. This shows that Mr Ajmera wanted to get rid of his rude behaviour at any cost. We can all follow his example to turn decent in our behaviour even with those people whose acts we don't like.

My friend Alok Mehta is a very interesting person and truly a gentleman. He is executive editor of *Dainik Hindustan,* a national Hindi daily. Always very enthusiastic in whatever he does, Alok is an old hand in Hindi journalism. Once he told me about his experiences of dealing with raw hands among journalists whose follies sometimes used to make Alok quite critical of their budding talent.

It is quite common for any leading newspaper to go for new talent so that novel ideas and current trends could be given an expression through their writings. Sometimes, many experienced people also leave the paper, so to fill up their vacancies, new staff is recruited. According to Alok, "The trainee journalists and sub-editors do require some time to adapt to their working conditions and fulfil job requirements. You know, working in a newspaper is quite demanding on one's private life. Generally, there is no regular fixed working schedule for journalists. Most of them have to meet deadlines, no matter if it calls for working well past midnight. Therefore, we do give due time to trainee journalists for adjustment, but at the same time they have to be corrected whenever they commit mistakes".

Alok continued, "While dealing with trainee journalists over the years, I have evolved a completely new strategy to handle them. Earlier, I used to pin-point their faults in no uncertain terms. And, sometimes I was quite rough in my behaviour with them. Then, one day I realised that things

were not taking shape as per my expectations. Though the performance of new recruits improved, but they hesitated to talk to me and often expressed their subtle resentment to my ways. I decided to change myself. First of all, I decided to put myself in their place. Then, after analysing the matter impartially and honestly some questions propped up in my mind. Like, 'Alok what were you when you joined the paper as a raw hand?' 'Were you much better than them, didn't you commit mistakes'?"

Now whenever I pin-point my new subordinates their mistakes I begin as "Well, you have done this wrong, no doubt about it; but you have not done so bad as I used to do in my days as a beginner. It is true that nobody is born with power of judgement and aptitude for correct decision, it comes with experience. And, I am pretty sure that you will know things better in days to come. I am always with you and I do not find it necessary to criticise you because I am not equipped with that kind of wisdom. However, don't you think that it would have been better if you had done it this way?"

Expressing satisfaction with the way things worked out after his adopting the new approach, Alok said, "Avinash, you may not believe, but my new strategy clicked very well. And, now I find it pleasure to work with the trainees instead of getting upset over their shortcomings as I was prone to, earlier. I consider it a better proposition to put myself in their place before putting them in the dock".

It is true that it makes even the quinine tablet palatable (have you ever touched it on your tongue, it is so bitter), if it is taken with honey. Same goes with the **criticism also, one does not mind it if you put it in a unconventional way, a sweetened way. After all, you want that person to improve and that too without its usual side-effect, i.e. resentment.**

Many a time, in our hurry to criticise our subordinates we forget that to err is human, that we are all prone to becoming targets of criticism. By our repeated over-critical reactions we, in fact, end up making the concerned person non-receptive to new ideas. This results in the blocked mental faculties. Ultimately a situation comes when he is unable to comprehend what we want to communicate to him. Then, the very purpose of criticism, i.e. improving his personality, or his well-being, is lost because he develops a feeling of resentment towards us. And, the whole exercise turns into an ugly display of temper and misbehaviour. Things are spoiled not just during moments of critical arguments but for whole life as the concerned person will never be able to feel normal in front of you.

Have you read the great Indian epic **Mahabharata?** Do you recollect why this bitter battle was fought which claimed millions of lives? Why Duryodhana, eldest of Kaurav princes, harboured so much hatred for Draupadi, the queen of Pandavas?

At the root of Duryodhana's hatred for Draupadi, there was an incident when Duryodhana felt very much insulted at the hands of Draupadi. The incident goes like this. Once Duryodhana along with his younger brothers visited his cousin Yudhishter's kingdom, Indraprastha, in their hey days. In one of the palace rooms there was a small quadrangular pool of water. Actually, the pool was not visible. Instead, the artisans skilfully made the pool to look like a carpet.

When Duryodhana entered that room, he mistook that pool as carpet and stepped over it and fell into it. Draupadi who was standing there in the balcony saw Duryodhana falling and laughed loudly, saying, "The son is also blind as his father" (King Dhratrashtra, Duryodhana's father, was blind). The laugh and saying of such nasty words from his cousin's wife had infuriated Duryodhana no end. He was burning

with rage. And, he took the oath that one day he would make the arrogant Draupadi bite dust. As we all know the slighted Duryodhana ultimately took vengeance by asking his brother Dushasana to disrobe Draupadi in the court of Dhratrashtra. And to top it all, they had won Draupadi in gamble from Yudhishter.

This ability to laugh at others everybody has got. We all indulge into it but seldom we realise that how much easily we make our enemies, those who will surely never miss a chance if they get the opportunity to get at your neck. They may not get it for many years to come but whenever they get it, they will use it. Even if they don't get it, then also the grudge will always be there.

Here, the lesson is, develop the ability to laugh at your expense, at yourself, on your own mistakes and shortcomings, instead of laughing at others. This ability will place you in good light.

We all commit mistakes, sometimes by ignoring the rules of law, at others forgetting some important engagements. Many a time we even forget to honour a promise to someone very special to us, maybe our child or the beloved. Though we commit mistakes quite frequently, more often than not we do not have the courage to admit them openly. Openly, I mean with open heart. Most of us lack the quality of accepting our mistakes gracefully.

If you turn up late for an appointment, it's natural for the other person to feel upset. But, you should not give him an opportunity to complain. Like "Madam you are late. I have been waiting for you for more than half an hour." You should be quick to tender your apology, "I am extremely sorry that I kept you waiting. I am so sorry for that, I have wasted your valuable time. Kindly excuse me."

And, to your utter surprise you would find that person's anger and resentment vanishing into thin air. Overwhelmed

by your apology, he would repeatedly say, "No madam, no, please do not worry for my time. It is a great pleasure to meet you. No, do not feel sorry because I understand that you are too busy." Actually, your self condemnation has made him mellowed. You had already accepted that your late arrival had caused him trouble. Then, what has been left for him to complain about?

So, decide yourself which is better—self-condemnation, or your condemnation by someone else. Self-criticism is far better than being condemned by anybody else.

Often my wife due to her domestic preoccupations is unable to reach her clinic on schedule. But, without giving her patients any chance to say anything, she begs her oft-repeated pardon, "Oh, I am sorry that I am late. But I did not intend to be late, as I knew that you must be waiting for me. I am so sorry, please excuse me." Although she has to say these words quite often—at least twice a week, still these words have almost a magic effect on her patients. They start assuring her, "No madam, no. Please be comfortable. No problem, it is alright".

I often enjoy this unique way of exchanging pleasantries between my wife and her patients. But at the same time, I also appreciate her modesty that she is so courteous with her clients.

Now, I give you example of another lady. Ms Sangeeta Shukla is a lady with difference because she is never to be found without a lovely smile adorning her beautiful face. She is Assistant Professor in the Department of Zoology, Jiwaji University, Gwalior. Like my wife, Sangeeta also has problem in reaching on time for her job. Her house is seven-eight kilometres away from the university. She says, "Although I try my utmost to reach university on time, my son often keeps me engaged, or sometimes, there are some visitors to entertain, so I get delayed. And to add to my problems, I have a strict

boss who is very particular that all the staff members should reach in time what may come. He is pretty rough when it comes to giving a dressing down. Whenever I get delayed, I enter meekly in his chamber, and before he is able to raise his head I start begging his pardon, 'I am so sorry that today I am again late, I always try my level best to be punctual. But somehow I failed to keep it up today'."

Telling about her boss's reaction to her apology, Sangeeta says, "Looking on my apologetic visage and finding me on the verge of crying, he says, 'No, no, don't worry. But be careful next time.' Of course, this scene is not a daily occurrence. Otherwise, how could I convince him about my sincerity. Even then once or twice in a month I have to face this awkward situation."

So, learn from the examples of these ladies. **If you are wrong, admit it gracefully.** Because, it will increase your prestige, make you modest. It will always put you in good light. On the other hand, if even after committing a mistake you continue to behave arrogantly then be sure that soon you would be having a long list of bitter enemies. Never try to defend your wrong doing with silly excuses because anybody can see through your silly defences. No one would believe them. So, it's better to brace yourself with a genuine apology and say it loud and clear.

That is what Dr B.R. Shrivastava, MS, MCH does. A very busy surgeon indeed, he has to look after his patients at J.A. Group of Hospitals where he is posted as surgical consultant. Also forming part of his hectic daily schedule is the cancer hospital where he is one of the trustees. Then, his other commitments are at other private hospitals where he is called for consultations and surgeries.

Whenever my wife calls Dr Shrivastava at her nursing home for some surgery, he is never able to make it on time.

But before the anaesthetist or fellow doctors are able to say anything he starts apologising very profusely. And, looking to those self-condemnations one has no other choice except to protest "No, no sir, don't worry for the delay. You are well in time. Don't feel sorry. It is more than enough that at least you are able to come. Please get on to your job, don't worry sir". And then he flashes a bewitching smile in your direction which is very infectious. This unique quality of Dr Shrivastava has won him many hearts.

In this chapter, the things that I am advising you to adopt in your behaviour are not theoretical, neither they are superfluous narration of bookish-classical set of principles. Instead, most of them I have learnt at a great cost, the cost of being at the receiving end, of becoming the target of admonition for not being intelligent enough to imbibe them in my behaviour at the right time.

No doubt, one can improve oneself through one's daily experiences provided one is ready to listen to one's own heart. Remember, **life matures only those who are ready to change the bad habits of their behaviour without any** *ifs* **and** *buts*. In every intelligent and considerate mind, there is a feeling of remorse after every episode of misbehaviour, a feeling of self-admonishment. This feeling or remorse provides you a golden opportunity to resolve firmly to never repeat that misbehaviour. This self resolve is very essential. This is the key for self improvement. And, unless this feeling becomes quite intense in your heart, nothing is going to change, nothing is going to improve—you will remain as ill-mannered as before.

No amount of advice or condemnation by others can do any good to your bad behaviour unless you firmly resolve in your mind that "enough is enough. Now is the time that I should change myself." This is the resolve which you must make as often as required. Promise yourself that you will not

hurt anybody by your words and by your behaviour. Whatever may be the situation, howsoever adverse the circumstances, you will not lose cool of your mind. And, once you succeed in following this resolve in letter and spirit, you will see that the desired change has started taking place.

I often go with my friends to the temples and other places of worship. At these holy places, my friends pray to the God to give them money, property, happiness and all the comforts in life. And, what is wrong with that. Does not each of us desire same things in our life? Do not we all wish God to shower his choicest pleasures in the form of assets and comforts on us? So, what is wrong if my friends also desire them. But my point is, in addition to pleading to the God for fulfilling our desires, we should also pray to Him every morning to give us the ability to be considerate and helpful to any needy person who comes in our contact. Pray the God to be kind enough to make you understand others' point of view also, to equip you with a caring heart and considerate mind so that you become a lovable person, held in high esteem by people around you.

My mother used to say that children should be made to grasp the values and family traditions in their tender age. For example, when a stranger or someone needy comes to your door, offer him a glass of water, and if you can afford provide him some rest at your outpost. If some known person even of lower status comes just casually to deliver a message or some items, offer him a seat, a glass of water, and if possible some sweets and fruits.

My grandma at Meerut used to teach us that offering hospitality to visitors is our tradition; it is the sign of generosity and prosperity of reputed families. The ladies of such families (usually addressed as Bahuji, or Bibiji) were usually highly respected by the visitors to their house. And, the women over many generations had been feeling honoured by the respect and regard symbolised by such etiquette. But, alas,

the old traditions are no more to be seen in our families, howsoever rich and well-to-do they may be.

Here, I would also like to draw your attention to another positive aspect of hospitality. But, first, a poser for you. Tell me, howsoever rich and reputed you may be, but how does it matter to someone? After all you have not gifted him anything from your riches. Except flaunting your wealth, or feeling a cut above others, thanks to your big bank balance or pile of currency notes in your chest, what have you done? Then how does it matter to anybody that you are playing in riches. The thing what really matters to anybody is how do you treat him—with respect or high-headed behaviour. Offerings like water, tea, sweets are just a way of expressing your respect towards your acquaintances. Such a gesture definitely shows you in good light. Postman, telephone lineman, electricity lineman, drivers, messengers, peons, staff from your husband's office—they all deserve a better deal from you whenever they visit your home. A single cup of tea would make them feel respected or cared by you. And, they would remain loyal to you for years to come.

Hundreds and hundreds of visitors daily throng the residence of Shrimant Madhav Rao Scindia's Delhi home at 27, Safdarjung Road, who represents my Gwalior parliamentary constituency. Most of the visitors come from far-flung areas of his vast constituency. The volume of visitors swells up during election time. But always, without fail, they are welcomed by a glass of water, some tea and sometimes eatables too, depending on the weather. This is a routine practice at his place, and, of course, it costs money and calls for efficient management. But, all this is going on routinely and smoothly for the last so many years.

For showing etiquette towards common man, I give due credit not to Shrimant Scindia but to the houselady, Mrs Madhvi Raje Scindia, the real strength behind the success of Mr Scindia.

This simple gesture shows how much caring and concerned is the houselady about the ordinary people of her husband's parliamentary constituency.

If you are a well-known person, hundreds of invitation cards, greeting cards and letters you may be receiving each year. It is at all not possible to go to every function where you are invited, but it is definitely possible to send a loving note along with some flowers to the person who has sent you the invitation. My learned friend, Dr Veerendra Gangwal, a reputed industrialist and president of the M.P. Chamber of Commerce is very particular about responding to invitations.

In Dr Gangwal's words, "I always make it a point not to forget to send a prompt reply to any invitation or communication addressed to me personally, because I know this is the only way to show that how much I feel for that person. If you fail to respond to these routine communications, your popularity and social image would certainly take a nosedive. Same goes with the telephone calls also. If I am not available in my office then my assistants make it a point to remind me about all the phone calls received in my absence. It may appear a very small thing but I have learnt it very early in life to respond to all the people who in a way honour me by their invitations. Surely, it has paid me rich dividends".

Courtesy does not cost you a fortune, never more than a few minutes and a small amount of money. But, believe me, it enhances your stature, contributes immensely towards your image building exercise. A concerned note to an ailing friend or colleague, wishing "Get well soon. We need you very much," if sent with a bunch of flowers will surely strengthen your bonds of friendship with that person. If you find that your friend or colleague does really need a helping hand then do not hesitate to extend it. A genuine, sincere help would definitely put you a class apart from the modern-day hippocrats. And, it's also an insurance for your future. For chances are that you would always find that person by your side at the time of crisis, without your asking.

I have always believed that a lady born in a rich family and then married in a wealthy family is an "unfortunate person" to begin with, because the God has deprived her from the hardships, painful emotions, and the troubles of lesser beings, which form the essential components of basic learning of the Masterly Human Behaviour (MHB). Very few ladies born rich are able to visualise the problems of underprivileged people who are lowly paid and toil to make both ends meet. Sometimes, they even can't manage the two square meals for their families. Normally, these underprivileged people are considered as unfortunate. But I would term the rich and wealthy persons as unfortunate because they have been spared the daily grind of life.

You can find hordes of ladies belonging to neo-rich families posing as social workers and the so-called social reformers out to 'reform' the society. Ironically, the realities of big bad world are far removed from the airconditioned ambience of their bedrooms and living rooms. If you are well placed in the business circle or your husband is a player in the corridors of power then you may be rubbing shoulders with such nouveau rich social reformers. They would do anything for being seen at right places, such as residences of foreign ambassadors specially western, or at seminars and meetings held routinely in all the big cities, specially Delhi. They never hesitate to 'buy' the chief guestship or special guestship of any bogus social service organisation which can sing praises eulogising their so-called kind and caring personality. Today, this mockery of social service has been indulged in unabashedly by the publicity seekers in our cities.

My simple request to you is, if you belong to a rich and reputed family then try to dissociate yourself from such blatant display of newly found status and wealth. If you really want

to do something, if you really want to relate yourself with underprivileged, in a honest manner then do not play with their emotions. Because, everybody is now able to differentiate between publicity-mongers and genuine caring heart. Do not fool yourself that your lie will not be caught, people may not say on your face, but definitely at your back they will say, "Here comes another farce who is ready to shed tonnes of crocodile tears at the drop of a hat".

So, my contention is, try to become a genuine person, honest person with caring heart, otherwise for how long you can carry this drama of mockery. It will be a great strain on your nerves. Believe me, it shall be of no use, it will not give you any pleasure or satisfaction of doing anything genuine for anybody. And, at last when you are at the fag-end of your life, this mockery becomes a very costly affair, because, the burden of your whole life drama (a farce and total lie) becomes too much to bear.

Elegance

Generally, people use the word *elegance* to describe something which is decent, graceful and serene. More so, when this word is used in the context of a lady to describe her dress, her visual appearance and other parts of her attire. But I think, more than dress and visual appearance, this word describes your behaviour.

The very first criterion for *elegant behaviour* is to keep your mind cool and composed while dealing with people. Generally, routine human interaction on day-to-day basis does not require much skill and intelligence. But, whenever you are facing an adverse situation or dealing with the agitated people, there is every possibility of bitter arguments and heated exchanges flying in the air. Heated arguments, frayed tempers, high-pitched voice are part and parcel of any confrontation,

whether at your home, or office, or at any other place while shopping or travelling.

Here, I would like to remind you of an old saying that intelligent people never buy a confrontation in the first place; and even if by chance they are forced in such a situation, they try their best to avoid it or bypass it. By avoiding I mean they try to keep quiet and do not retaliate, i.e. they do not give the other person a chance to misbehave with them, whatever may be the provocation.

To this many of you might say that certainly these type of people should be called as cowards and spineless creatures who are not able to save their prestige and honour. This is a very very normal reaction because none of us would like to be at the receiving end in a confrontation. Everybody would resort to tit for tat; or slap for slap, bullet for bullet.

But, to my mind there can be some other, better way of dealing with an adverse situation, apart from the usual aggressive reaction. The other way can be called as soft approach or an approach with reasons.

While handling a confrontation in an aggressive way, i.e. using harsh arguments, insulting and taunting language, abusive and high-pitched voice, you may win on some occasions. But, remember, not all the time. With your occasional success in a confrontationist bout, you may feel elevated, boosting your ego and self-prestige out of proportion. And, then there is every possibility that in future you would try to be one up on your opponent in any confrontation with your aggressive approach.

Here start your problems because there is always a possibility that sometimes your opponent may be more at ease with abusive language than yourself. He/she may score over you in the game of shouting and high-pitched arguments; he may be more adept at hurling abuses and derogatory remarks than you. Then what would you do? Start weeping,

or beat a hasty retreat? Whatever you may do, but one thing is certain that you would do it with a disgraced face and deeply wounded prestige.

But, then, you may ask what one should do in the face of utter humiliation and insult? Should one allow without even a murmur any Tom, Dick or Harry to send one's prestige and self-respect for a toss? Doesn't that uncultured fellow require to be taught a lesson of the lifetime?

But, here again I would emphasise that it is always in your own interest not to react angrily or violently in an adverse situation. You must go for a soft approach or an approach based on reason.

First of all, you should understand that there is no dearth of uncivilised people, shrewd, calculative, mean type of people ready to take advantage of your decency and simplicity. They have just no compunction in exploiting you for your soft and mild behaviour. But despite all the treachery and meanness polluting our environs, I would still advise you to never try to be one up on the uncivilised creatures. For, you cannot compete with them in the field of indecent behaviour, like shouting and heated arguments, because it is their exclusive domain. You stand no chance.

Secondly, by lowering yourself to their level you would expose yourself to a much more vulnerable situation. Because, nobody would utter a single word against those who are notorious for their indecent behaviour. But would you, a qualified, soft-spoken, graceful lady, like to be branded as a cheap, third-grade woman who does not hesitate to use abusive and indecent language? So, whatever may be the compulsion, be strong in your determination that you would never stoop to the level of your opponents if they resort to uncivilised behaviour and rude language.

Thirdly, always remember to put your viewpoint or argument or criticism in a gentle and mild tone. Never think of raising your voice or showing your resentment in the shape of anger or insulting comments. Don't forget that your opponent, whether a family member or your office colleague or anybody else, after all is a human being. So, always try to put your point with a soft voice sans any false ego or inflated prestige.

Your behaviour should not reflect any desire or attempt to humiliate or insult somebody. Your approach should always be just and reasonable. There is every possibility that the person, sitting in front of you, may be very agitated and excited about something or may have very strong views on a particular issue. In such a case best course before you is to try to convince him with solid reasons and valid arguments. But, you must do all this in a sugar-coated tone as that will surely have a soothing effect on his frayed tempers.

To put your intelligence to best use while dealing with angry, agitated persons, a pre-requisite is that you must not allow yourself to be carried away by the highly charged atmosphere. Remember, your intelligence works at its peak when you remain calm and composed, as cool as ice. No instigation or provocation, howsoever insulting it may be, should be able to stoke the flame of anger in your mind. Most important thing is that you should know how to control your anger and hatred. If you succeed in controlling these negative emotions, you can surely come out with flying colours of any adverse situation or overwhelm a difficult colleague or an adamant opponent.

19

How Do You Relate with Your Man? (What Does a Man Desire in a Woman?)

LAST May, I went to Bilaspur, a small town at the south-east end of my state, to attend the marriage of my niece. Very close to Bilaspur is Amarkantak, a hill-station-cum-pilgrimage centre. At Amarkantak, my school-time classmate Ms Aruna (name changed), 46, is vice-principal at a Navodaya School. Once in Bilaspur, I could not resist the temptation of visiting the serene and beautiful Amarkantak which is the birthplace (source) of holy river Narmada. I was also quite excited at the prospect of meeting my childhood friend and classmate Aruna.

When I along with some of my relatives reached the sprawling complex of Navodaya School, children were nowhere to be seen since it was summer vacation. Aruna came out of her small bungalow to welcome us. She appeared quite contented and happy while talking to us. Later on, after lunch, on the pretext of making a round of the school complex we (me and Aruna) moved away from other guests. We talked enthusiastically about our childhood memories and the time we together spent in the primary school. Suddenly, I asked Aruna, "But why did not you marry uptil now? Don't you feel alone here? Haven't you ever felt the necessity of a life-partner?"

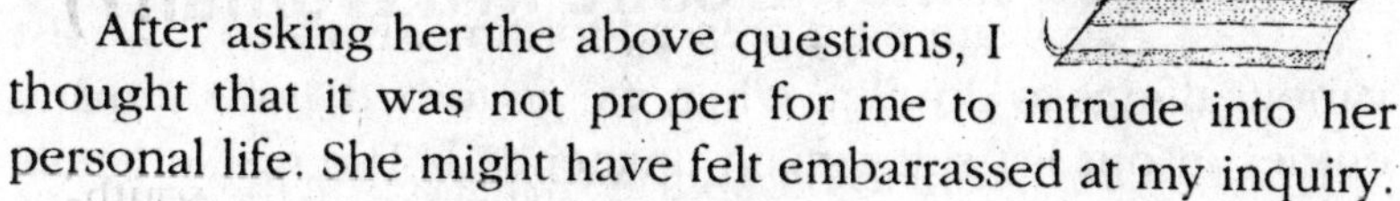

After asking her the above questions, I thought that it was not proper for me to intrude into her personal life. She might have felt embarrassed at my inquiry.

But, belying my fears, Aruna remained unperturbed at my queries. Showing no signs of embarrassment she admitted frankly, "If I say that I never felt the pinch of the absence of a man in my life then probably I would be fooling myself. But somehow life passed by very quickly. And, when I felt I was comfortably settled in life, it was too late for any matrimonial alliance. You know, our society is a typical lot of mixed values. They see an unmarried woman beyond twenty as an abnormal creature, as if due to some grave shortcoming she could not marry at the right time. This attitude further discouraged me for going into any sort of relationship with anybody.

Now, here I am a lady past middle age who has failed to relate to a man altogether. Although I am happy and satisfied that I am drawing a handsome salary, I am independent, sometimes I feel the pinch for a companion. But I don't allow that to trouble me for long as I have engrossed myself completely in my profession. I have identified myself totally with my students. No remorse feeling at all. After all, I chose it myself. Nobody has thrusted the unmarried status on me, so why to feel sorry at this stage."

The number of unmarried ladies in our society has not risen suddenly in the recent past. Actually, it has been a phenomenon since ages. Some women willingly choose to remain unmarried as they opt for celebacy, sadhveehood or

become nuns. Others fail to get suitable life partners due to poverty or their unattractive visual appearance. And, yet some others in single-minded pursuit of their careers and professional excellence just don't give much importance to matrimony.

Let us first take the women of last category. In today's world, no doubt we all are hard pressed for time. Each day, we list various things to do. But, when we go to bed at night many entries in our list still remain unattended. The result: letters needing replies keep pouring in, stacks of files keep piling up in your office, and calls to be returned wait endlessly. No different is the lifestyle of today's woman in big cities. Living a fast-paced life like her male counterparts, she does not have the time to stop, assess, relax and to listen.

Too many friendships are carried via the five-minute phone calls if not by the internet or E-mail. Love relationships, if not of serious type, fall by wayside, or, if the chemistry clicks between the two then it must bloom overnight as the young lady does not have the time to wait till the next Valentine's day to have long courtships. And the result—you never get past the superficial level because you never had the time to listen and respond to your own heart, then what to talk of responding to other's heart. So, this is the life, the true life of a busy lady, today's woman, who is independent and career oriented.

Shefali Kapadia (name changed), 27, is a business promotion executive with a reputed cellular phone company of Mumbai. After her BE in telecommunications, Shefali did her MBA from a prestigious management school of Ahmedabad. And, she joined this company, her first job, very recently, about a year ago. Since beginning she had this burning desire in her to become independent and stand on her own feet. So, here she is, drawing twenty-five thousand plus perks every month. She feels quite contented.

Nowadays, Shefali's parents, living in a small town of Gujarat, are searching a match for her. She is also willing to settle down in matrimony as she feels this is the right time. She has got many male friends. Many of them are her old classmates while some are colleagues and business acquaintances. But they are all just friends. Among them, she could find none whom she could rely upon or whom she could call her real boyfriend. So, they are all just friends. Moreover, she is in no hurry to somehow get her match fixed. She wants to take her time to find a suitable man. After all, it is the matter of whole life.

Once, Shefali also thought of a "live-in" arrangement with her close friend Suhas who was her classmate. When Suhas came to Mumbai on his first transfer in a textile company, he had no place to live. But, the live-in idea could not fancy Shefali for long as it appeared too outrageous to her. However, she is enjoying her new-found independence and financial abundance. So, not very keen on the marriage right now, Shefali wants to let the things shape on their own.

Supriya Chaudhary, 30, after doing her CA, works for a multinational company as the financial adviser at their Lucknow office. She knew Pushpa Raj, 34, since her college days when they were together in college. He was senior to her by three years. Later on, he joined a business group at Madras. Though both were deeply in love, they were struggling to establish their careers. Moreover, their family circumstances were not conducive for them to get married at that time. Therefore, marriage was not a priority for them. Consequently, Raj left for his posting in Madras, and Supriya joined a multinational company at Lucknow and continued to live with her parents.

In Madras, Pushpa Raj came in contact with a girl, Malini, the only child of a millionaire. Malini lived in a beautiful mansion having sprawling lawns and a swimming pool and equipped with all the luxuries. Pushpa Raj had never seen

such a luxurious lifestyle, what to talk of enjoying it. It was a heavenly feeling for him. He easily fell for Malini's luxuries, ultimately ended in marrying her, completely unmindful of the fact that Supriya is waiting for him at Lucknow. When Supriya came to know about Raj's marriage, she was a broken lady.

Another man, Suyash, came into Supriya's life six years after Raj parted company with her. Last year she met Suyash, a young industrialist from Delhi when her company sent her to Goa for a financial management seminar. Suyash was a faculty member at that seminar. The frequent interaction between Supriya and Suyash over the five days at the seminar brought them close. On the last day, they parted company to soon meet as the new business associates. Their acquaintance was hardly six months old when Suyash proposed to Supriya. He even came down to Lucknow to meet her parents.

Supriya, though happy at the strange turn of events, was in a fix whether to trust Suyash or not. Won't he turn out to be another Pushpa Raj? At this juncture, brother and *bhabhi* (sister-in-law, brother's wife) helped her to arrive at a decision. And, Supriya became Mrs Suyash the very next week. Her honeymoon in Europe was one of the most cherished times in her life. But even during those memorable days, she sometimes thought about the failure of her first love affair. How she failed to handle her man the first time? Was it all due to her fault? And then why she succeeded this time even when she did not try at all? Was it not Suyash who was bestowed on her by the God? These questions kept crossing her mind. But she had no answer. Do you have any?

In the case of Shefali, don't you think that she is the exact prototype of modern woman who at any cost wants to preserve her privacy and independence. But before you decide to follow Shefali as a role model, here is a piece of advice: Your career, your independence, your freedom, your

professional excellence, all this is welcome. There is nothing wrong in striving hard to achieve them. But, remember they are not welcome at the cost of your femininity, your womanhood. You are a woman first then a career person. Keep your femininity intact, because that is your identity.

Man always relates with the woman in you not with a career person. If the 'woman' becomes absent then how would the chemistry of man-woman relationship would work. If you want that the man should relate with you then do not lose your femininity howsoever well educated, high positioned you become. You should maintain your charm, allure and career simultaneously.

Here's another woman, Romilla, whose case is entirely different from the two I have just talked about. Many friends who once used to visit her to seek solace now feel pity for her. Being single at 26 is fine, but think of being alone at 36. Most of the men assume her single status as an accident, a destiny rather than a compulsion because she still has got her sensuality intact.

That day Romilla was thinking aloud as she was sipping her beer, lying in the lounge chair in her balcony facing the garden. She is not afraid of her singlehood at this age also. Acually, she had rarely been alone. She had relationships all along, right from her high school days. In fact, she has lost the count now of men who had come in her life. Romilla held the view, why to bother for something which has passed; why not to look for the future which is lying ahead. She always had been very positive in her approach, but this time around things were a bit different. Although she was not sure why? Maybe, this time she felt that it was her last swing and most likely she and Nalin would settle down.

In Romilla's words, "Nalin wasn't the first man I'd slept with, but certainly I thought that he was going to be the last. We rushed our relationship too quickly. But, then suddenly

one day he said that he wanted to call it off." Romilla continued: "I begged and begged like a pauper to Nalin to take me back. Then every week, once or twice, he would come, sleep with me then go. This made me more depressed as I felt being used and cheated. But, gradually, it seemed to me as if our relationship had got a new lease of life. And, I was happy that after all it was me whom Nalin wanted."

Then after six months, Nalin told me that he had someone else in his life who was his colleague, and he had ultimately decided to part company with me. I was in for the greatest shock of my life. I never felt so cheated. Although I had undergone some sour relationships in the past, none of them gave me so much heartache as the one with Nalin. Because, in his case I was trying my best to make our relationship endure. I did not know what to do, so I gulped few sleeping pills with some milk. By the morning I was in a pretty serious condition, but I was saved by the timely medical aid made available to me by my neighbours, a doctor couple. Stomach lavage and those glucose drips for days together. Nalin shrugged this off as a bad joke. 'Nothing serious,' he said, 'Why did you do it, why don't you become practical'?"

After this incident, Romilla tried her best to persuade Nalin not to break their relationship. In her words, "I started making him late night calls and not putting the receiver back at my end. I wrote him long letters, but to no avail. Then one night he told me what he really thought about me, 'a whore'. This rudeness and arrogance has knocked me hard and brought me back to my senses. Now, I am starting life afresh, with no hangovers. No more Nalins for me, I am getting him out from my system, completely. Oh, no doubt, this was an experience of life time. An obsession, perhaps."

About relationships, another girl, Kalpana (name changed), says, "I have become matured over the years. I think the reality is that relationships don't last for ever. Now I believe

in myself. Even six months after my boyfriend had dumped me unceremoniously, I was pretty miserable. I was suffering from great inferiority complex. Then, one day I saw that a new couple had just shifted to the flat opposite to mine. Akash, a handsome tall guy with broad shoulders and thick moustaches, had come to live with his girlfriend Rashmi in that flat. They seemed quite in love, but soon I found out that Akash was more outwardly type. He used to watch me whenever I was out of my house. He was extremely sexy looking, a debonair man to whom any girl would fall for. So what if I was also hooked by his masculine looks. So, when he made a pass at me I responded happily. It was a simple kiss and a bit of caressing, but I never felt so turned on."

Continuing about her encounter with Akash, Kalpana said, "It seemed to me that he never felt happy with Rashmi who was working in a foreign bank whereas he was the unemployed son of a rich businessman. During our brief encounter which never crossed the kissing and caressing limits, he often told me that he had become quite fed up with Rashmi. After that first kiss, he was always on my mind, every minute of the day. The fact that he was living with someone else did not bother me at all. It was none of my concern.

"I often used to go to Akash's flat whenever his live-in partner, Rashmi, had gone to attend her job. Actually, I had an obsessive urge to know what was he doing, what was he eating, whether sleeping or taking bath. I would stand for hours in my kitchen, gazing at his window. When he got a temporary job, I would get up at six in morning to watch him leave the house. At night I would often see him in his bedroom or living room. Whenever I felt the urge to hear his voice, I would phone him but won't utter a single word. I loved his talking and shouting when he wanted to know who the hell I was, not responding to his 'Hello'. Although we never slept together, both of us liked to kiss and cuddle whenever we

could. Then gradually, he started cooling off. I felt very much hit around, dejected, yet continued pestering him. I would send him cards, poems, long love letters but to no avail. He started giving silly excuses like 'Rashmi may be back any moment', or, he has to go out to keep an important appointment. Few months later, they moved to another house, far away from mine."

This was the story of Kalpana's crush at a young age. Now, at a mature age of 45 and mother of three grown-up children, Kalpana says, "Frankly speaking it took me months to forget Akash. My already buised self-esteem due to ditching by my boyfriend plummeted even further. Now, I often feel that love in young age sees no rules. Truly, it is said that it is all fair in love and war. But how stupid I was. Isn't?"

Few more real life incidences of obsession in love I can quote here but before that I would like to talk about **obsession** itself. As I understand, it means a siege, a state of mind which is impregnated by a fixed idea from within or outside towards an object or a person. The people with obsessive tendency are so much occupied with the thought of a person about whom they are obsessed that all the time they are thinking about that person during their waking hours.

Women in our conservative Indian society are not too free to express their feelings towards someone, particularly men. Even if they are obsessed in love, they try their utmost to hide their true feelings due to the fear of society. "What the people would say?" This is the million dollar question before them. Although they feel as strongly as their male counterparts about love, they are somehow able to exert control over their feelings and expressions.

On the other hand, men are more articulate and extrovert while expressing their feelings towards their lady love. They have less inhibitions. And, as a universal rule, it is always the man who first proposes and expresses his love towards the

lady, not the lady in question. But, as I said earlier, it does not mean that the lady in love does not feel as strongly as the man, but she desists from frankly expressing her love or attraction.

My learned friend Dr Purshottam Dutta, MS, and famous ophthalmic surgeon, says that obsession in love is something akin to 'childish behaviour'. A woman or man, overwhelmed by obsession, see no reason but fall headlong for whomsoever they fancy in their minds. On the part of a woman, it is absolutely childish or rather foolish to behave in such a manner. It definitely lowers her prestige and also exposes her to the possibility of rejection. Because, her over-indulgence or constant pestering may or may not be liked by her man. Or, he may like this childish possessiveness in the beginning. But, soon finding it quite distracting, he may chide the lady, "Come on baby, have some reasoning. How I could do that." Or, he may turn off the woman, saying, "I have other things to take care, please call me day after tomorrow."

Remember, almost always invariably, it is not possible to find someone as obsessed as you are with him. He may not respond to your love feeling with the same intensity as you expect him to. Then, what would you do? Feel dejected, cheated, insulted or rejected? Yes all this is quite possible, and, mostly, it happens with those who are in hurry to express their love to their men. It is better that while expressing your love to your man, keep something for a later date. Keep some of your mystery intact. Keep your ways subtle and low profiled. That would help you and keep you in command of the situation.

"But is it really possible, when you are immersed headlong in love with your dream man?" asked Sangeeta Mitra, 29 (name changed). Sangeeta, copy editor with a glossy woman magazine of Mumbai, tells about her first crush, "I started modelling when I was still in college completing my graduation in journalism. Once I met Mukesh who was ace tennis player

in the city and was also ranked in the national circuit. He was in my college doing his B. Com. I would sit for hours together to watch him play in our gymkhana club. I joined the health club in that suburb five-star hotel which he used to frequent. I made sure that I look my best every day in case I bump into him, which I did often. He was warm and friendly as usual whereas I flirted like a mad. Whenever he used to wave a goodbye towards me, I used to be on cloud nine. So much was my obsession with him."

Sangeeta continued, "One day he came to the college in the new red coloured sports car presented by his father on his twenty first birthday. Oh, I was unable to speak for a few seconds when he came out of it and waved in my direction. I had even forgotten to respond to his waving. I don't know what happened to me that I could gather the courage to ask him to bunk the class and take me for a ride. Somewhat hesitatingly, he agreed and we came out in his new trendy car. On our highway drive, he kissed me first time and cuddled my organs. Few weeks later, I saw him in the manhunt of a fashion magazine. Soon he was advertizing for some reputed brands. He was a perfect man for me. Other girls were also mad after him. But, I always thought of myself a class apart from the routine girly stuff as I was modelling and was quite good looking too."

Love affairs never have a smooth sailing, especially the one-sided ones. Sangeeta was also in for a great shock when one of Mukesh's friends told her one day that Mukesh was going to be engaged very soon to a girl from a rich business family of Delhi. In Sangeeta's words, "I was horrified. I found myself in such a state that I was violently sick all the night. But, the news did not put an end to my obsession, rather it made it worse. I found out where he lived and also got hold of the address of his fiancee. I started sending love letters, flowers, gifts to him and anonymous letters to his fiancee in

Delhi telling her that Mukesh was seeing other girls at college. And, he accompanies them to late night parties, discotheques and hotels. He changes his girls like his shirts.

Sangeeta continued, "Now, I had started showing my undying love for Mukesh in my letters. He also knew that I was madly in love with him and would do anything to get him. Few more months passed like this. Then, for one of my assignments I went to Delhi to shoot for a TV commercial. There, I made it a point to call on Mukesh's fiancee, Kavita, who was a real sweet girl with a very-very innocent smile, matched by an equally mild behaviour. She was like a tender untouched rose bud covered with morning dew drops. When Kavita came to know that I was a classmate and friend of her fiance, she almost bent with all the politeness and modesty. Her humble manners were very heart warming and sincere. For the very first time in my life, while sitting in Kavita's large mansion, I felt belittled and ashamed of my dirty deeds targeted against this little sweet girl. I felt like weeping and confessing that those all anonymous letters were my handiwork, and I should be punished for that, and that I was her culprit. But I did not have those guts. However, I resolved that enough was enough; from now onwards, I would not hurt Kavita anymore. I would be like her elder sister and would safeguard her interest all my life. Mukesh and Kavita now are a happily married couple. In fact, they live very close to my building. They are my very good friends. I often visit them. They have always maintained highest standards of grace and decency in their behaviour towards me. Not even for once, they ever made it known to me that they knew who was writing those nasty anonymous letters."

Here, I would also like to quote my long time friend Manorama (Sihare) Singh's views. Says she, "It is not possible, most of the time, to hold back your feelings for someone if you feel strongly about him. Whatever you may name it, obsession or infatuation, it does not matter. Love is blind."

Narrating her own experience Manorama says, "I know it from my own experience. Me and Dr DK Singh waited for full five years before we could marry. But we always felt very strongly about each other. Sometimes we could not meet for weeks together as he was working at Jabalpur and I was doing my MD at Indore. After doing MD, I went to Delhi to join as Senior Resident in a large hospital, and he remained at Jabalpur. But throughout our pre-marriage relationship, we felt very strongly about each other. That bond of commitment made our lives pleasant and worth living. No thought of any other person ever crossed my mind during those five years, although there were enough opportunities and temptations. I always felt myself duty-bound towards Dr Singh. Now both of us are touching fifties and our commitment to each other is as strong as it was in our young age. Touchwood." Manorama is now working as Professor and head at one of the most reputed medical colleges of our country.

A woman always loves to be loved and taken care of. She always feels happy when she is admired for her beauty and her looks. She likes to be told constantly that 'You are beautiful and charming'. A woman feels flattered when told by her man that she is sensuous and alluring. She feels pampered when her man takes extra care to make her feel comfortable and happy. When treated like a princess, a woman starts behaving like a little girl in front of her man, despite her age, high education and high professional status. In fact, her behaviour is just like that of a little school girl. She giggles, pretends as if she is annoyed. When alone with her man, dream man, she feels as if she still is in her teens. She likes to be helped in getting in and out of the car, or while stepping down from a high step or platform. And, all this she wants throughout her life from her man with whom she shares her happiness and sorrows.

But what about the man? What does he want from his better half? How does he like his woman to behave and relate?

Of course, the likings and fancies differ from man to man. Some men like their women to be highly glamorous and sexy looking while others want their women to give the impression of soft-subtle beauty without any hint of being made-up. Some like the raw freshness and rustic beauty as found in our countryside while others would like to give their hearts to the urbane, sophisticated, high society movers.

So, how to generalise the opinions, male preferences and choices for the fair sex? Is it possible to generalise? Well, the answer is fifty-fifty. Yes and no, both.

First, we talk about 'No'. How is it possible to say anything in a general way for something so special. Special in the sense that the lady is special and the man is special. They have their own thinking, own likings and dislikings, desires and fancies depending upon the social, familial and cultural background, their job, profession, etc. There is an old saying, "A man may love or flirt with highly glamorous and sexy looking lady, but for a wife he wants someone similar to his mother".

Well, here some of you may question, if mother may be an uneducated family woman living in a remote village, while her son is living in a metropolis with an MNC job, then would he still like his spouse to be like his mother. My answer is yes. The son wants his wife to have the *motherly qualities* similar to his own mother. Because his first exposure to the womanhood was through his mother. And, secondly, glamour doll type of wife may make a man feel on cloud nine, but glamour is not the only quality which can sustain a marriage. It is just not sufficient.

I must admit here that today "glamour" is a very-very misunderstood and misused word, even by the woman herself.

Most women feel that glamour is something which they can wear, and make them pose in such a manner as if they are out of this world creatures. Generally, a woman takes glamour as a tool to ascend the ladder of success and project her in the most desirable fashion. Literary meaning of the word glamour is: The supposed influence of a charm on the eyes, making them see things as fairer than they are; studded charm, a groomed beauty.

No doubt, today's young and educated man does want his mate to be beautiful, charming and glamorous too, but in a natural way. Not made-up or artificial type. She should be glamorous but in a subtle way, which is not shocking or astonishing to the eyes of the onlooker. Rather, her appearance should give the feeling of a soothing freshness of the morning sea breeze.

Today's Indian male is still conservative in many ways like his traditional counterpart. He loves glamour, but on the silver screen and in glossy film magazines only. In his personal life, he wants someone whom he can take home and tell his mother, "Look here, Mom, she is your daughter-in-law." Let's now talk about some real-life experiences of men about the fair sex.

Anil Sharma (name changed), 29, young IPS, says, "I met her when we were at JNU. She was doing her language course in Russian and I was doing my MA in history. What I liked most about her was her enthusiasm and zest for life. Beautiful of course she was, but always naturally beautiful as if she had just washed her face with soap and water. Notwithstanding the fact that she belonged to a modern, typical neo-rich metropolis family, she always chose her outfits with great care which never included minis or low cleavage blouses. Mostly, she wore shirt and trousers, and sometimes skirt and blouse too. But all her clothes were well styled and matched. Her subtle way of beauty attracted me towards her. She was

a lovely companion for dates, and now she is a lovely mother of my two kids. I love her very much because she is never eager to hog the limelight. Even then, she is often under the limelight without any efforts, as she is **charming and alluring naturally."**

Dr Suresh Sharma, 42, is my colleague at the medical college. According to him, for a man to get attracted towards a woman, she should be endowed with some special qualities and characteristics. The foremost among them is, her attractive visual appearance. In fact, the building of any future relationship very much depends on this crucial parameter of visual appeal. If a woman is not beautiful and charming then chances are that men won't look in her direction. Dr Sharma strongly believes that sayings like "Beauty is always skin deep" are sheer nonsense, nothing but nonsense. No one likes to be seen with ordinary looking or below average looking women.

After all, why a man wants to meet a woman, in the first place? What is the attraction? What is the need? Why at all he needs a woman? (Here, instead of pondering over my questions you might say, "You don't know sir? Very sad. And, still you are doing this portrait?)"

Before explaining, let me put you some more questions. Why do you want a friend? Why do you want a sister or brother or father or mother. Have you ever felt the pain and sufferings of those who are orphan or single in their family? A man needs a companion because he always wants to relate. First, he relates to his family members—relatives. And, when he grows and reaches in his late teens, he starts feeling the desire for the opposite sex. Yes, it is the *sex* which drives a man towards a woman. *Sex* is one of the most basic instincts, like hunger and anger, which the man has acquired in the most raw and naked form from the animals, as it exists in them.

The very first impression which a man carries about a woman is always based on her looks. It is the looks which decide

the future course of events. Whether he would take a second look, or gaze intently. Or, he would give no look at all as if he has not seen anything.

Here, I would also like to give the views of Dr Rajoo Vaish, MS, MCH, consultant orthopaedic surgeon of Indraprastha Apollo Hospital. Dr Vaish believes that generally there is no such thing like the "Love at first sight". This sort of thing is possible only with those who are either very shallow type or move with their heart on their palms. For such people anybody would do.

Elaborating further, Dr Vaish says, "You may appreciate the looks, the features, the dress sense or the total visual appearance but nothing beyond that happens. The maximum which is possible in the first meeting is the first impression, but not love. Those who say that they were hooked on to their lady love at first sight are in fact trying to say that they were attracted towards her."

For love to blossom there are some pre-requisites to be fulfilled. In medical terminology, for love equation to click, some essential chemical reactions must have to take place. After the looking (first visual impression) is over, the lady charms her way to the man's heart by different ways. Let's see how did some women find the way to their man's heart.

Somaya moved into Robin's heart almost unknowingly because of her sheer intelligence and graceful behaviour. Robin, 23, doing his B.Tech from IIT, Kanpur, concedes, "Of course, it were her looks which first caught my attention in the college corridors but later on her analytic wisdom impressed me most. She is real genius. She does give an impression of a next-door girl, but her indepth knowledge of physics, in which she is doing her M.Sc., impresses me most. I have decided to propose her because she has got everything a man can desire for in a life partner, a beautiful face, charming personality and to top that her intelligent looks."

Most of the time, the choice of a girl for a young upright, upwardly mobile man is governed, apart from her "looks," by her style of gestures, body movements, i.e. body language, her conversational style and behaviour pattern. No need for me here to emphasise the education, her professional qualification, her career prospects, and so on.

Pradeep Khanwalkar, 41, says "I was not lucky to fall in love with someone." General Manager of a recently launched car company, Pradeep continues, "Although many attractive young girls came in my contact during my college days and afterwards, nothing came through out of those friendships in my early years. So, I decided to go for an arranged marriage. Through newspaper advertisements and relatives, my parents collected a large number of photographs of the eligible girl candidates. During my bride-search spree, I met about thirty girls. I went to far-off areas to meet those girls and their families, sometimes all alone and sometimes accompanied by my elder brother. In the whole process, I was very much confused, not able to decide whom I should accept as my life partner. Ultimately, my choice narrowed down to three girls. It took me one more round of meeting with them, all three, before I could decide for Sunayana, the young lady from Calcutta. Now you might be interested to know how I could decide for her. Of course, her looks played a major role in my selection, which were classical Indian type. But, then, her attitude towards life and self confidence played no less role. In our second two-hour meeting I could make up my mind that she was for me and would prove to be a good life partner. And, now after twelve years of marriage behind us, I don't regret my decision."

20

Final Touches on the Portrait
• Philosophy of Life
• Management of Life
• Glance through Different Seasons of Woman's Life

AT the outset I must clarify that I have no intention to give you teachings or sermons because neither I am a Father of a church, nor a Shankaracharya of any *mathapeeth*. Also, I have no desire to talk about the 'wisdom of life'. because this also requires that the man should be extraordinarily intelligent and genius, which I am not. Instead, I am a simple man who sincerely and humbly desires to share some of his thoughts with you.

So, I would be talking to you about very-very routine things, trivial matters which are often forgotten and misunderstood but they carry immense importance if remembered and properly executed.

For example, your **thinking power,** or better

called, **thought process.** This is something which goes on in our mind round the clock during our waking hours. Even during sleep this goes on and manifests itself in the form of dreams. Do we give any importance to our thought process? No, we don't. Most of us are not even aware of its existence. But the fact is: 'It forms the very basic framework of our personality'.

What you speak is what you think. Isn't it? Can you speak without first thinking or without framing in your mind what do you want to speak? Well, some people take their own time to form their appropriate replies while others don't seem to require such time as they can reply instantaneously. And, there are also some people who can speak on any topic for hours together even if they do not know the ABCD of the subject. Here, don't forget some chatter-box type of ladies who can talk for any length of time on their favourite topics like their neighbour's daughter's latest love affair, or about the sarees and jewellery, and what not under the sun.

It always makes a good sense to think properly before you speak anything. Think twice before you utter any word from your mouth. More you speak unnecessarily more you are bound to commit mistakes. Whether you agree with me or not, the fact is those who speak bare minimum are given respect in the society. And whenever they speak, their opinion is given due weightage. Secondly, speaking requires a great deal of your psychic power—energy which if you do not speak unnecessarily can be conserved and utilized in more productive and fruitful activities, like reading books for upgrading your knowledge.

Many a time silence is the best policy because by remaining silent you don't have to regret later on that you have spoken wrong words. By keeping yourself mum and quiet, you could at least be sure of one thing that you won't be caught speaking something inappropriate.

Thinking (Hindi equivalents: Vichaar, Sochana, Dhyana) is of numerous types. It can be directionless, purposeless, negative, destructive, damaging; full of depressive or violent ideas; full of hatred, jealousy towards others. In its positive form, thinking can be full of optimistic, happy, enthusiastic, creative and constructive ideas. Such ideas are like flowers in a garden spreading their fragrance all around, attracting everybody with their heartwarming colours. Beautiful ideas are like small children loved by everyone because they are innocent and always give disarming smiles.

Since ages, it has been recognised that *wisdom* resides with those whose minds are free from the thoughts of first category mentioned above, i.e. thoughts of harming someone, destroying something or damaging some structure. Wisdom is accompanied by the peace of mind and happiness. In fact, all three—wisdom, peace of mind and happiness are real sisters who cannot live separately from each other, as they are very fond of each other's company.

So, the first step towards "betterment of your life" is to resolve firmly to throw unhealthy ideas and thoughts out of your psyche. This self-resolution would pave the way for reaching the new frontiers of happy state of mind leading to high levels of creative energy.

I am of the firm belief that you cannot teach a person anything; you can only help him to find it within himself. And, that is what I am doing. I am simply trying to make you aware of the hidden treasure within your innerself. I am attempting to point out your true potentials and strengths.

Making Oneself Happy

Happiness is quite a deceptive word. Simply, because it means different things to different people. And, then, why 'happiness' is so elusive? Why can't we attain it despite our trying hard to become happy. Is it not true that we all like to feel happy? And, for achieving happiness we try our level best. Like, we go to parties, movies, clubs, picnics or undertake sight-seeing trips and so on. But, maybe, the activities you undertake for feeling happy may not be leading you towards your goal. It is possible that the way of your happiness may not be in those activities I have just mentioned.

But, here I would like to tell you that no single activity can be categorically said to be pleasurable for all the persons at a particular point of time. For, different persons derive pleasure from different activities, at different times. Like, some people derive pleasure in meeting old friends and relatives, while others feel happy by calling on someone they love. Mothers feel happy when they cuddle their tiny tots in their arms. So the activities which give the people pleasure are as varied as the persons themselves. Here, the most important thing which you must remember is that people are about as happy as they decide to be.

In fact, happiness, enjoyment and pleasure are the subjective feelings present in our mind at any given point of time due to one or many reasons. And then, it will not be wrong if I say that, "Happiness is an inside job; it does not depend on any external factor as we generally believe, but much of it is governed by our mental attitude". In support of my belief, I would quote the gem of words uttered by one of the greatest Presidents of the United States of America, Abraham Lincoln who said, "Most people are about as happy as they make up their mind to be".

Happiness, like love, cannot be borrowed from somebody, neither it can be purchased from the marketplace like sugar or butter. It is a habit, it is a feeling, it is state of mind, it is something which many wise people are endowed with, or they acquire it simply by their 'easy going mental attitude'. Here is another famous old saying, "The foolish man seeks happiness in the 'distance' (distance of time) while the wise man grows

it under his feet". In fact, it also does not depend on the actual number of 'blessings' (comforts-luxuries) we manage to scratch from the life, but only on our attitude towards them.

Some people think that 'youth' is the happiest period of one's life while I strongly believe that a person who is able to think most interesting, useful thoughts at any given age is the happiest person. Happiest are the people who give most happiness to others because it is a contagious phenomenon. A happy person can change the whole dullness of a meeting or gathering. Always remember that people love to see happy faces because they themselves want to be happy.

My friend Shiv Barua, 42, is a noted scholar and writer. He often emphasises in his lectures that *"there are two things one should aim in one's life; first to get what you want (i.e. to become successful), and after achieving that enjoy it too. Most of the people get the first thing in their life but only the wisest of mankind (selected few) achieve the second."*

My another friend, Dr G C Baijal, supports the views of Shiv Barua. Dr Baijal, Professor and Head, Department of Ophthalmology, J.A. Group of Hospitals and G.R. Medical College, Gwalior, adds another dimension to our debate on happiness. His argument is: even after acquiring palatial bungalows, farm-houses, cottages at Nainital and houses in metros and having big bank balance why should someone not feel happy all the time and enjoy himself? Why should the thought of insecurity, unhappiness, uneasiness, feeling of discomfort, cross his mind, at all? Why doesn't he enjoy his hard earned success? Why this preoccupation with the feeling of insecurity and the fear of unknown?

Do you have any answer to these posers? Let's try and find out.

Creating Happiness

"You don't find happiness, you create it. It comes by enjoying small little daily routine happenings (things) in our life," says another close friend, Dr Harish Chandra Setiya, a reputed eye surgeon of my town.

What Dr Setiya says is quite meaningful. Read again what he says. Read it three-four times, and then think. Is he not giving us the clue to our complex question—why do we not become happy even after acquiring so much wealth and prosperity? What prevents us from becoming really happy? The answer is: we ourselves prevent our own feeling (happiness) to enter our system. We constantly try to attach some tag to it, that is, we make it conditional. Like, "I would be very happy when I am able to buy the Cielo car," or "I would be very happy when I could furnish my house as per my liking and choice," or "I would be very happy when my husband becomes the vice-president of his company."

We wait for that particular day, for that particular thing to happen. Only then we would permit ourselves to feel happy. So, you make your poor heart slave of your unending desires. For example, it would be allowed to feel happy after you succeed in purchasing that dream house at Maharani Bagh.

"Happiness is like honey—you cannot spread it without getting some on yourself," opines G L Bhojwani, industrialist and gentleman par excellance who has built up his own empire of factories, real estate projects and trading setups. Explaining further, he says, *"Success is getting what you want; happiness is the feeling you get. Well, you may or may not get happiness. All this depends, not on luck, but on the way you feel about it."*

Some people feel that they would be really happy when all their problems are solved. In a way, they are absolutely correct in their expectations because problems keep them nagging all the time, like a pin stuck in your seat. But would

they really feel happy when their current problems get solved. No, it just doesn't happen that way. End of one set of problems is no guarantee that another crop of problems won't come up. And then, who does not have problems on this planet? Does Bill Clinton not have them? Or, Bill Gates, the computer wizard (supposed to be the richest man of the world) does not have them. If Clinton has his budgetary deficits to be explained to the Senate and Ms Paula Jones and other women at his neck, Mr Gates' problem is how to beat his competitors, and expand his software empire to the virgin markets of the world. So, happiness is not the absence of problems but the ability to deal with them effectively.

"How to remain easy-going, jovial and happy all the time despite the stresses and pressures of life?" People often put this poser to my friend, Mr Paras Kumar Gangwal, 50, a successful businessman. A thorough gentleman, he looks after his large business set-up spread over many states. In reply to the above question, Paras tells people what his father had taught him, *"Make business a pleasure and pleasure your business, and don't hesitate to share your joy and fortune with others, this way it doubles up immediately." He further says, "Life is for living, not for thinking of problems, or sleeping with them. To live freely, one must liberate oneself from the negative thoughts and fears."*

Overpowering the Fears

What are these negative thoughts and fears? How they take root in our mind, and what factors aid in their growth and sustenance? What can we do to get rid of them?

Numerous are the fears. Anytime, you can think of any number of fears. Some are momentary while others have an overpowering grip over your mind. Basically, all the fears grow from a feeling of insecurity, and the dread of unknown. Like, what would happen to me or my business if this deal does not click? Or, what would happen if the aeroplane in which I am travelling crashes? Or, I am afraid that I would miss the Calcutta-bound Rajdhani Express as this is hell of a traffic jam at Connaught Place. Or, if I suffer a heart attack tomorrow, what would happen to my wife and little children?

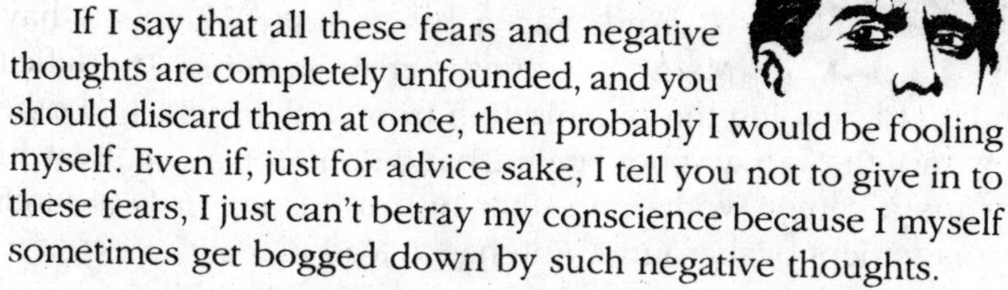

If I say that all these fears and negative thoughts are completely unfounded, and you should discard them at once, then probably I would be fooling myself. Even if, just for advice sake, I tell you not to give in to these fears, I just can't betray my conscience because I myself sometimes get bogged down by such negative thoughts.

Who to blame for this? The blame cannot be passed on to any individual. Because, our lives have become so much complex and tense that day by day it is becoming increasingly difficult for a person to remain calm and at ease. Every morning, the newspapers portray before us the real, ugly side of our existence— burglary, theft, dacoity, killings, kidnapping, rape and what not. Think of any negative aspect, and it's there in the newspaper. All this compels one to think, is this world really a place safe to live in?

No more only disease and war are the primary causes of death. Even a fun-drive in one's new car may lead to death due to road accidents. We have road accidents too many. Seventy thousand people die in India every year from road accidents and more than ten times of that suffer serious injuries. Are our roads safe enough to drive—you have genuine fear here. Regarding untimely accidental deaths, who can forget the 'Uphar Cinema' fire tragedy where sixty people lost their lives, in June 1997 at Delhi. Did these unfortunate people, enjoying the 'Border' movie in best of their moods, know that they would be dead in next few minutes?

All these shocking incidents shake our confidence in the justice of nature. But we forget that it's only when normal and natural course of events gets disrupted somewhere in

the way, all hell breaks loose. Then it makes little difference whether it's the overcrowded school bus which rolled down Wazirabad bridge in Yamuna, killing several innocent children. Or, the Dabwali inferno at a school function in Haryana at whose altar again several little ones were sacrificed.

And, what would you say when you see Ms Anu Aga, now chairperson of Thermax India Ltd, leading the organisation from a chair which just a few months ago was her late husband Rohinton's seat. By no means a career woman and having no finance or business management background, Anu has to lead in reality a Rs. 600 crore organisation in this highly competitive world.

People may have all the kind words for such a lady. But, when it comes to actual business they shy away because sympathies and emotions have no place in a good business sense. But, it seems, even destiny has no mercy for Anu. Barely had she steered Thermax through the crisis of her husband's death, fate dealt her another cruel blow. Her 25-year-old son Kurush, just back from England with a degree in Engineering, died in a head-on car collision. But, see Anu's courage. Despite her enormous personal grief, she made it a point to visit and comfort the family of the staffer who also died in the accident.

Then, after a few weeks, Anu was there to address a press conference about the joint venture her company had entered into with Culligan for water purifying technology and products. One marvels at the strength and courage of Anu. How could she handle simultaneously her shattered life and company?

What is Anu's outlook of life? What has made her so strong to withstand even the worst upheavals in her life? Her simple reply is: "I very strongly believe in this prayer— *'God, give me serenity to accept the things I cannot change, the courage to change the things I can, and the wisdom to know the difference'.*

I learnt not to get upset over the things I can't control".

But is all this so easy to do as said and read? No, it is not. It requires a great deal of maturity to handle seemingly larger than life problems. But, how to acquire this maturity? "Through faith in the Almighty God and faith in oneself." This was the reply which my question elicited from my friend Ramesh Saboo, a top industrialist and former national president of Indian Junior Chamber. Saboo said, "From my experience I have always found faith in the God and in my abilities quite helpful to steer out of adverse situations".

It's our habit that we feel insecure for something which has not yet happened or may not happen at all. It is not good for your mental peace that you unnecessarily keep worrying about something untoward happening to you. If you ask someone why he or she earns the money, the usual reply may be "To buy comforts and amenities for the self and family." And if you again ask the same person that why after acquiring reasonably good money and assets he wants to add to it, then he may reply, "I have to stock for the bad days, who knows what may happen tomorrow?"

This reply can also explain why a person goes, all the way, sometimes even out of the way, to become wealthier and wealthier day by day, probably because he fears the bad days, the bad business or ill health or some bad luck. No doubt, if you have saved some money or have some assets then at the time of crisis you don't have to look at others with a begging bowl in your hands. But, here is another more important question: Can the money always bail you out from crisis? The answer is, sometimes it can, but not always. Then, what is the sure-shot remedy for crisis situations? It is one and the only "faith" which could give you strength to tide over the adverse circumstances. Remember, it is the single most factor which helps you realise your true potential so

that you could handle any unforeseen crisis efficiently and intelligently.

At the time of a major crisis, a common phenomenon is that we become absent-minded or deeply stressed. During crisis, our mind loses its capacity to take proper decisions. Our thinking is overwhelmed by fear of failure, rather disaster. This fear goes very deeply in our heart. This can happen to me, to you and in fact to anybody because this is one of the most natural human reactions in the face of a crisis. No body is exception.

I can vividly recall the days when my father was on his deathbed. It was in January 1995 when he suffered from the cerebral haemorrhage and was lying unconscious in our home. All my brothers, sisters, their children had come from distant places to be by his bedside. Although my house was crowded with friends and relatives, yet I felt very-very lonely, and often at nights I used to weep holding hands of my father who was unconscious. For days together before his death I could not sleep or eat, and had stopped attending to the patients as I was not in position to behave normally.

Frankly speaking, I was deeply disturbed, although being in medical-profession, I was mature enough to understand that his end was very near and whatever I might do, I won't be able to save him. His end came at the crack of dawn when I was busy in arranging the suction of his throat. Even many days after his death, I could not become normal and felt so blank emotionally that I was just unable to attend even to my routine professional work, what to talk of writing. It took me more than three months to gather myself, streamline my thoughts, and come back to my writing desk.

So, like every human being, I have also passed through hard days. The days, when life seemed without meaning, not worth living. This book, in fact, is a collection of all my sweet-sour experiences. **The philosophy of life** or the **wisdom of**

life concept has not occurred to me on one fine morning. Instead, it has developed over the years through pleasant and unpleasant happenings, and varied experiences. But the dynamic rules which I had followed all these years, even in the worst of times, have helped me tide over many a crisis. And, then, why can't these rules be helpful to you as well. Here, I am grateful to the God who has given me the privilege to share some of my beliefs with you.

But, still I feel that this kind of work—encouraging you to do confidently whatever you want to do, suggesting ways to feel happy, to be at peace with yourself, to get the best out of what the world has to offer, to accomplish your goals and feel contented—is a task which requires more ability than I possess. That is why when I sat down at my desk to start writing this book, I prayed the God to sit by my side and give me the wisdom and intelligence to write something which can be of real help to the women of my country. Something which can take them to the path of happiness, success, self-esteem and self confidence.

I do not know, while I am writing this last chapter, how much successful I have been in my endeavour. But, my faith in His kindness, His friendship has increased manifold. He has been constantly at my side, guiding me at many places to come out with the best of advices. He is my partner, He is my friend, no doubt. But beyond that, God for me is the real driving force. I thank Him for all the beautiful thoughts He has given me while writing this book.

Faith in God

Mr Justice Shrawan Shankar Jha, 50, of Madhya Pradesh High Court, belongs to a family of scholars and educationists of Jabalpur. He was my senior at the university. We have many common friends. So, when he was transferred to the Gwalior bench, we again rebrushed our old memories. Now

our common interest is tennis which allows us to spend some time together daily.

One day, Justice Jha referred to those people who do not get proper night sleep. In the name of sleep, some of them waste many hours in the bed by just counting the stars in the sky. Worries, tensions, anxieties keep them awake till the wee hours of next day.

Such people often seek advice from him regarding their sleeplessness. Justice Jha tells the people to follow a method which he himself has been following for many years and enjoying a sound sleep.

Talking about the magic formula, Justice Jha says, "My grandfather Pandit Lajja Shankar Jha used to call all the children to his room before the bed time every night. Then, he would sing prayers, bhajans, devotional songs in praise of God. We all children in our effort to match his pace and voice used to sing in competition. A convention, adhered by all in our large joint family, was that nobody would eat anything in morning without taking bath and offering morning prayers. Similarly, in the evening also, without doing 'Sandhya' (special evening prayers) nobody would have dinner."

Justice Jha explains further, "Even at this age and with so many things to tackle and give attention to, coupled with the job pressure and other problems, my childhood formula still works. Before sleeping, I sit up in my bed and recite all those prayers in my mind. And, while doing so, I hear clearly the loud voice of my grandfather, as I used to hear him forty years ago. This simple method makes my mind so light and tranquil that I have never found any problem in getting my sleep."

Well, the faith in God provides you the much needed confidence to overcome your doubts and the feeling of insecurity. It also enables you to shed your inferiority complex. Lack of self-confidence is one of the major drawbacks in the

personalities of our women, specially the young ones. This I could tell from my experience. Apart from routine interaction with the women, I also got the opportunity of teaching more than three thousand lady doctors during last twenty-four years.

An important characteristic feature which I have observed in most of the women, is lack of confidence. Large-scale prevalence of this shortcoming among the members of the fair sex has a lot to do with the trends prevalent in our society. Still a boy is given preference over the girl child even in highly educated, upwardly mobile families. Then, what to talk of the low strata of our society. A girl is constantly made aware of the fact that she is a second grade citizen.

In a society, where girls are teased and taunted at public places; where incidences of bride burning and torturing the innocent daughter-in-law are order of the day, it is not surprising if the young girls and ladies are shaky or lack in confidence. And, for them, most vital decisions affecting their life are taken by their male relatives.

If you want to succeed in getting recognition as a "woman of substance" or want to fight to set right the age-old wrong precedents of our society, then keep the God in your heart, and your path would become less troublesome. With single-minded faith in God, you can get anywhere. You must learn to pray Him that He should provide you the strength to conquer your weaknesses and ill-founded self doubts. Nothing is impossible in this world. Remember, the degree of your success depends on the intensity of your devotion to God. Indirectly, your single-minded devotion towards God also propels you to strive for your goal more sincerely. In other words, you feel confident enough to go that 'extra mile' to succeed. And, sooner you hear the knock of success at your door.

Do you know the secret method of eliminating your inferiority complex or your self-limiting deep sense of self

doubts? This method is not a long list of do's and don'ts. You simply fill up your mind with the nector of faith. Let your mind overflow with thoughts of positive ideas about you. Yes, about you. Because hitherto you have portrayed yourself in negative colours. So, it's time for you to change your tracks. Think that come what may I will reach the victory post, or whatever may be the obstacles I will overcome them all, in my tryst with destiny.

It was only due to tremendous faith and confidence in their capabilities that the Indian Army could force ninety thousands Pakistani officers and soldiers to surrender unconditionally in the 1971 Indo-Pak War.

Bachendry Pal and Santosh Yadav could scale the highest peak in the world, the Mount Everest, thanks to their unfalling faith in God and themselves. So, there is no substitute for the faith and confidence. These are the first two essential components of a winner's profile. If you want to be called a lady with guts, or want to command respect only due to your individual achievements and accomplishments, and not because of being the daughter-in-law of some big businessman or any other similar tag, then start filling your mind with firm and clear positive thoughts about your potentials and abilities.

It is a common observation that without being egoistic and dangerously over-confident, a normal lady with normal and reasonable thinking, can take on the challenges of life and achieve success. Of course, lot many other factors, like education, vocational training, formal upbringing, family background, etc. also play their role. But, even if all these parameters are in place, chances of success of a young educated woman in her chosen field would depend a great deal on her self-confidence and faith in her own capabilities.

Recognise Your Strenths

But the question is where to 'shop' for self-confidence and faith? From which departmental store or duty-free shop could these commodities be purchased? Sadly enough, no, these exclusively human qualities cannot be purchased from any shop. Sorry, these are not on sale. Yet, surprisingly, without paying even a penny, you can have these qualities in abundance provided you resolve once for all to refurbish your personality with them. These are available to every woman, whether an ordinary one or a professional, or a socialite. Only requirement is, all of them must at once shake off their complexes and negative thoughts.

There is no end to what we can achieve provided we are able to recognise our strengths and put them to good use. You only need three things to get to the top—talent, ambition and the initiative. As the saying goes, "**Always aim for the moon, and if by chance you don't get there, don't worry, you will fall among the stars.**" The message implicit in this saying is, you have to take the initiative irrespective of the result which may not be as per your expectation. But at least it would give you satisfaction that you have tried your best. Maybe, next time the result would be to your liking.

Surely, you don't want to be like those who never dare to take a plunge in the deep waters and pass their whole life sitting at the river bank. Remember one important thing, nobody would help you, nobody would ever look into your direction until and unless you yourself make the first move towards your goal. And why should anybody bother for cowards who just don't try to achieve their goal.

If you have done your planning, your home-work and are confident of your judgement, plus-minus twenty per cent (that's for normal state of indecision) then do not hesitate to make your move. And, if the issue is very important for you,

stand on your ground firmly. Sooner, to your surprise you would see that you have moved closer to your goal. Another important aspect is, a confident person evokes in others an assurance for himself. If you have confidence in yourself, you will see that other people (your colleagues, friends, relatives) too have confidence in you. In fact, they want to be assured that you can do the job. Only then they won't hesitate to associate with you, to help you in your efforts. But, always, you will have to make the first move.

Regarding your habit of sharing your fears every now and then with others, my advice is that it's better if you avoid this. Unless it is utmost required to do so, shun this tendency with iron-will, because people in reality do not want to sympathise with you even if you take them into confidence. They give you a negative marking unless they are your true well wishers. And, you very well know how difficult it is to find true friends in this world of rapidly changing values.

I have seen many ladies who open up their heart to everyone they come in contact with, in the hope that people would understand their problems. But no, it doesn't happen the way they think. Most often than not, they are called fools. So, try your best to keep your fears close to your heart, do not share them. Instead, share your enthusiasm, hope, joy with the people because they like the things that way. Actually, they have their own cups full of problems, negative thoughts, fears, etc. Then, obviously, they do not have the time to ponder on your fears. The only people who enjoy hearing about your troubles are lawyers and doctors, and they are paid for it.

Let me now tell you about a simple exercise on how to build up the much needed self-confidence and faith in yourself. This three-step exercise is described below:

***First step:* Honest self analysis** gives you the idea about what is actually holding you back. It concerns with knowing afresh about your insecurities, inferiority complexes and self doubts.

***Second step:* Believe in yourself** to constantly feed your brain with positive ideas about your strengths and potentials.

***Third step:* Have courage to surge forward** to experiment with the new ideas, explore new avenues, possibilities and opportunities.

Before discussing these three steps in detail, I would like you to feel absolutely convinced that this simple exercise is capable of transforming you from a lamb to tigress. It is a sureshot method. Thousands have benefited from it. Then why not you?

What was that thing about which our late Prime Minister Shri Lal Bahadur Shastri talked at Ramleela Maidan, New Delhi, during the 1965 Indo-Pak War, or George Bush had in his mind while ordering American fighter planes to bomb Iraq in 1991, or Alexander the Great had in his mind when he spoke about his destiny—the desire to conquer the world?

Yes, you guessed it right—it was the confidence, the common quality of these three great men who played decisive role in the world history.

Courage, in fact, is your resistance to fear, a mastery on fear but not the absence of fear. Don't be afraid of taking the big steps forward as your bold initiative would finally decide whether you would be taken seriously by the people or they would just ignore you. As I have stated earlier, confidence which we have in ourselves gives birth to the confidence which others have in us.

Remember, success in any project undertaken by you does not solely depend on your earnest affirmation of self-confidence but also upon the confidence which others repose

in you. What people think of us, is largely a reflection of our own faith in ourselves; our own attitude of mind will therefore induce the confidence of others in ourselves.

How to Acquire A Winner's Profile

If you are a corporate woman or a business woman or self-employed professional then obviously you know very well the need of surging confidence and faith. The two very important prerequisites of any team leader. Whether you are leading a small team of hardcore professionals or a pack of your employees, you have to ensure that you firmly believe in what you say. Well, arrogance and high-headedness are just not required. They won't allow you to stand out as a leader. Only a strong belief or faith in your own capabilities would give you the confidence to interact at equal ease with your boss and subordinates.

Unlike her male counterparts, a woman executive has to face a peculiar problem of proving her eligibility for the job she is doing or intends to undertake. Her male colleagues generally are of the view that the best place for a woman is her home. Her fiefdom should be the kitchen instead of the board room of a company. And, this is despite your good education, training and fulfilling other criteria of the job you are in. Also, the sad fact is that you are assessed more critically than your male counterparts. Their mistakes, shortcomings can be overlooked for any number of times but not yours. Simply, because some of your male co-workers may derive heavenly pleasure in belittling you. Naturally, all this takes a great toll on your self-confidence.

So, it is doubly important for you, a woman, to prove your mettle and potential. To do so effectively, the first and foremost requirement is that you shed off your fears and self doubts. They are of no use except that they take unnecessary toll on your ability to work normally (that is, better) and, secondly, they drastically reduce your faith in yourself. And,

see the irony inherent in this situation—all this is there despite the fact that you have all the knowledge, intelligence and ability to perform well.

So, when you have all the qualities expected of a successful woman then what actually blocks your way to success is the lack of encouraging and supportive atmosphere at your workplace. I shall rate you highly lucky if you have got that kind of working environment at your office. But, if you are not that lucky then also you should not bother.

"Best policy is— learn to ignore them, develop your own happy and enthusiastic mental make-up (that is, a positive thought process) in which all unwanted jealousy-filled criticisms are taken care of automatically. Sooner you develop that thinking (mental attitude) the better. Otherwise, you won't be able to preserve your power of creativity and zeal for achievement. And, in no time you would find yourself consigned to the junkyard of had-beens."

In today's fast changing global scenario, finding women executives in the corporate world is no surprise. In fact, they are occupying key positions in business organisations. The business community is slowly becoming aware of the women's ability of analysing problems in an entirely different perspective. Women can be dependable if they are given the chance to prove themselves. Gone are the days when we considered them eligible only for the jobs of personal secretary, typist or telephone operator in any setup. Now, they are occupying the cabins exclusively meant for higher managerial positions.

But, no matter how fairly people are treated at their workplace, no matter how pleasant their working conditions are, they just cannot really give their best until they have the freedom to show their true acumen, their real potential. This is more relevant in case of women than men. A lady has to

be given chance to prove herself in this era of team-work.

By and large, a woman is considered to be highly emotional and sensitive in comparison to her male counterparts. But, emotionally mature women, who don't carry their domestic emotional turmoil to their office, are proving successful in top jobs. Well, if a woman wants to succeed then she has to exert greater restrain on her emotional feelings. Be careful, people are waiting eagerly for any opportunity, to take advantage of your sensitivity and easy emotional vulnerability.

No matter how shaky you feel inside, never allow your face to reflect you inner turmoil. You exterior should always portray you as a picture of strength and confidence. And, you will see that your personal crisis is blown over; no one is able to catch you, and you are a winner, ultimately.

For acquiring a **winner's profile** you require certain more things, apart form genuine self-confidence and faith. And, one among them is **creativity.** What is this creativity? How would you define it? Besides its dictionary meaning another description which appears close to the perfect definition of 'creativity' is—something to think in an imaginative fashion, to bring out something new from nothing, or to design, produce, make or propound a new idea, more useful and attractive than the existing forms and shapes.

Some say 'creativity' is a hereditary trait, only the family background decides it. Others believe that creativity is the exclusive fiefdom of men because most of all-time great writers, poets, musicians, painters, film directors, novelists were men. For example, Leo Nardo da Vinci, the great Italian genius who painted the 'Monalisa'; Shakespeare, George Bernard Shaw, Leo Tolstoy, T.S. Eliot, Beethoven, Yehudi Menuhin, Alfred Hitchcock, to name a few from the foreign soil. And, on the Indian scene leading the pack of creative

men are — Rabindra Nath Tagore, Sharat Chandra, Bankim Chandra, Munshi Prem Chand, and many more.

It is true, to a large extent, that men have always outnumbered women in the field of creativity. But for this sorry state woman is not entirely responsible, soley because she was always supposed to look after the family front which in itself was a more than a job. Even today, situation is still same for majority of Indian women.

The Greatest Creator

If I say that the woman is the greatest creator in the world then I will not be wrong because she produces the human race. Every human being comes into existence in the womb of woman, and remains there for nine months before actually coming into this world. So, I firmly believe that after Mother Nature, woman is the greatest sculpturess. She moulds a child's personality as she teaches him/her the basics of human behaviour. Whatever a child becomes on growing up, he/she carries in his/her life the indelible impression of his/her mother's teachings. Woman is also akin to a musician who gives a rhythm of life for child and for the whole family. So, in my opinion woman is the greatest "Srajak" (creator) in this world.

I am sorry that I have drifted a bit from our topic—a *winner's profile.* To me creativity is similar to imagination. But, we combine both of them as in **'creative imagination'** (CI). It is never inherited from birth. Instead, it is something which you have to develop on your own, in your thinking. CI has its roots in your ability or courage of becoming different from others. If you don't want to become part of the crowd, you have to develop it.

Battles of life are not always won by the stronger and smarter persons. Remember, one quality which always stands out in a winner is his ability to think differently. No matter,

then whether he is smart and strong as per the norms set by the society.

Knowledge is power if applied creatively. Otherwise, thousands of Medical graduates (roughly 15,000 to 16,000) pass out every year in our country, but only handful of them excel in the field of specialisation and get accolades. In fact, education is not like filling of empty bucket (your mind) with water, but it is like lighting a fire to think creatively. The world is a big classroom where the class-teacher is life, you and me all of us are sitting on the benches as students. Successful among us would be those who are prepared to learn throughout their lives.

According to great American industrialist, Mr Jone Rockefeller of Rockefeller Foundation, if you want to succeed, you have to forge new paths and avoid following the treaded ones. Mere experience without imagination to use it in a constructive way or vice-versa, i.e. creativity without business ability, is likely to be more harmful than of any advantage to you. The calculated freedom to commit mistake with caution encourages creativity in workplace. That is why many business houses emphasise for building a creative and healthy environment to achieve long-term goals. They want to ensure better performance and productivity not just for today but tomorrow also.

The creative mind is always inclined to see the familiar things as old fashioned. That is why younger lot of people in any set-up behave and think in a new way. But, they are often cooled down by their seniors as inexperienced and novice. Well, a balance has to exist between creative enthusiasm and the risk factor of a blunder. So, being creative does not just mean the courage of doing something different from normal routine. Essentially, it means responsibility of thinking in the right direction. A person bubbling with enthusiasm can surely succeed at most of the things he attempts, provided his energy is channelised imaginatively.

Experience — Your "Account of Mistakes"

Let me tell you a story to further explain this. A young smart boy was being interviewed for the post of sales executive in an MNC, by the Vice-President (VP), marketing. He asked the young aspirant "What experience have you gained in this line after completing your MBA?" The boy replied "Oh, you mean my account of mistakes?" The boy was selected immediately because he knew that mistakes in life are termed as experiences. And, it is true to a great extent. So never be afraid of failures and mistakes, surge forward always with courage.

What is the recipe of success? *Maybe, you don't know. Then note down— 'just courage' with 'just amount of wisdom' along with ample confidence, makes the dish of ultimate taste, and that is success. Who, in this world, does not want to be successful? Stock reply to this question is, "every one," because success is the ultimate aim of human excellence. We all want that success should come to us and we should be able to taste it, at least once. Let me talk it first in your perspective. What does the word 'success' mean to common Indian woman?*

Surely, you want to be called a successful mother because you always loved your mother, and, secondly, you very much love your tiny tots. But, then, you are a wife also, a devoted wife who along with the husband wants to be labelled as a "made for each other" couple. In your ad company also, everybody says that you are a wonderful copy editor. And, you are now in a senior position. So what, if you are simultaneously a mother, wife of a demanding husband and a wonderful copy editor.

Not only that. Your mother-in-law also likes you very much. Says she, "Before anything else, you are a devoted daughter-in-law to whom I love like my own daughter." And,

here you are, a woman who is trying to justify her each and every role.

Roles are aplenty. The husband wants you to play the role of a seductress like Rati, Abhisarika, Menaka or Urvashi (the most glamorous beauties of Lord Indra's court, the King of Heaven) in the bedroom. He does not want you to say that you are tired or sleepy. He wants you to behave in the most sexy way. Your children want you to cook them tasty dishes. They also want you to spare some time for them—help them to get dressed for the school, help them in their homework, serve them food when they want it and where they want it, in the bedroom or at the dining table. If they fall ill, they want you to sit by their bedside all the time.

Then your mother-in-law is calling at the top of her voice "Bahu, meri chai kahan hai?" You are running from this room to that room of your home, trying to satisfy everyone. Then you are supposed to get ready for your office where you would be required to deal with your difficult boss and not-so-helpful colleagues.

But who cares for you and for your problems? Everyone of them—your family members—have become habitual of you doing things for them. They won't hesitate to say, "If you won't do it, who would do it?" Your friends and colleagues think that you are the creator of your own problems. Why can't you ask your husband and other members of your large family den to share some of your responsibilities? Why should everybody expect something or the other from you? Why can't you expect anything in return?

Whatever they may or may not think about you, the fact is that you are trying your level best to become all things for all people around you, whether at home or office—a sort of *super woman*. All roles rolled into one—the mother, wife, daughter-in-law, sister-in-law *(Bhabhi)*, aunty, and a career woman.

The success at family front is completely different from the one you achieve in your profession/career. Two are entirely different things. Success of the first kind requires masterly human behaviour coupled with a considerate heart filled with passion, love and care whereas the second type is based on totally different criteria which we will discuss shortly.

Poor Lady or "Super Woman"

Super woman status is often a self imposed position which many women try to acquire for them. They try their best to adjust everybody whosoever comes in their contact. They want to play the role model to the hilt of perfection. But mind you, they are not of selfish type. There is nothing wrong in becoming or trying to become a super woman. But, remember, in the process of acquiring this status one loses many things and the foremost among them is your personal comfort.

Sometimes the ritual becomes so tiring that it wrecks you both physically and emotionally. You may at last succeed in acquiring that status, but at what cost? Cost is really heavy—you have stopped caring for your clothes, make-up, body shape and other fine details of your personality about which you were so particular before marriage. Now you have fused completely your identity with your family. Nothing matters now, it is you, your kids, and your hubby. Super wife, super mother, super host and super daughter-in-law.

Here, let me tell you one important thing. Though I cannot tell you a sureshot formula for success but, I can give a sureshot formula for failure. And, that is, trying to please everybody, which is just impossible because expectations of people will grow in proportion to the level of efforts you put in to please them.

An important factor contributing to your success at the home front is the size of your family—whether small or nuclear

family or joint family consisting of brothers and sister-in-laws, mother and father-in-law and other relatives. Other factors having a bearing on your success are: the education level of your family members; the type of city you live in whether big city like Delhi or Mumbai or small city like Allahabad or Agra; vocation of your husband, whether he is in business, or service or pursuing some profession. Apart from these factors, your own personality which includes your education level, your tastes, attitudes, ambitions, dreams too play a role in your success at the family front. And here, don't forget your ability to deal/interact with each and every member of your family including your kids and hubby.

If you have opted for one and the only role of simple home-maker (housewife) then chances are that you can do justice to your family to the desired level of satisfaction. But, in case, you have decided to play a double role, i.e. working in two shifts, one as housewife and other as career woman, then I can only say, "Oh God, please help this poor lady."

Don't get astonished with the use of expression 'poor lady'. Because this expression aptly describes the prevailing circumstances of the society in which you, a career woman, lives. No doubt, our conservative Indian society has opened up considerably in the last two decades. And, consequently, the Indian woman has emerged out of a sheltered existence. No more, she has to live under the shadows of her family, her husband and in-laws. But, still there are hiccups and pitfalls. Still she has to get recognition as a bread earner, or as a true professional. Her ability to strike a balance between the home and office fronts is still at a test stage. It is like a tight-rope walking.

Despite best of her efforts, the career woman sometimes shows strains of overstretching. If she gives a bit more attention to her job, her children and husband immediately start complaining. And, the moment she tilts the balance a bit

towards her home, her profession suffers, where she is the loser in the face of tough competition. That is why it is commonly observed that many able administrators, professionals and real geniuses belonging to the fair sex, opt for long voluntary vacations at the time of their childbirth and other such events.

By and large, it is a fact that in spite of remarkable progress and upliftment of women in our country, and despite their elevation to the highest posts in the administrative hierarchy or professional careers, women are still unable to project themselves as true professionals or career women. Perhaps, it is because even after becoming economically independent, imbibing ultra-modern outlook and values in their lives, they are still very much Indian at heart. A heart who cares for traditional Indian values, family ties and emotional bondage with the family. This attitude of hers has kept the values and age-old traditions of the Indian society alive and intact. Despite mastering best of professional skills, and grabbing career opportunities, she still wants to be recognised first as a loving wife and caring mother. It is because she firmly believes that she would be able to attain fulfilment and completeness of womanhood only after becoming a perfect wife and mother.

It is this thinking of the Indian woman (some term it as her weakness) which has landed her in a cesspool of conflicting ideologies. And, pressed between two fronts— the home and the office, she is compelled to perform even beyond her capacity to fulfil the expectations desired of her by the people. But, lately, a consolation for her is that her husband is becoming more and more adjusting, if not sympathetic towards her.

So, in the light of all these circumstances, let's talk about the success in your profession which is totally different from the one at the home front, in terms of perception and factors involved. Though, it's another matter that much of the former

(success at the professional front) depends upon the latter (home front).

Success Stuff

Now, let's try answering some questions, like what is success; how a woman can get it; and then what factors infuence it, and why? Though there is scope for me to write here a voluminous **success digest,** I promise to discuss here only the salient features of this digest. I will explain the words which have a direct bearing on our success story. So, let us begin our "success journey."

Dreams, the sweet dreams. Everybody loves dreams, the dreams of becoming rich and famous. Some people dream during night while others have them during day time also. Whether dreams occur to you in the day or at night, you always like them as dreaming does not cost you anything; on the contrary, dreams give you pleasure. A wise man once said, "What the life is without an impossible dream to cherish. Don't let weeds grow around your dreams".

We all know that all great men were dreamers. Every great idea has its generation through a dream. If you can dream of success, you can get it also. Some see things in the soft haze of a spring day while others see it in the flame of fireplace of their living room during cold winter nights.

Here, another quote I would like to tell you is, "Keep a pen and notebook at the side table of your bed along with a battery torch, as many a time great ideas strike at 3 a.m. in the morning". I follow this rule religiously. I even keep a small dictaphone to record ideas and thoughts about my ongoing writing topic. I often come across many ideas before I actually fall asleep or during the sleep. My experience is that whenever I have relied on my memory to recall in the morning the ideas which occurred to me in my bed during night, I have found my mind totally blank. Nothing could I recall.

Dreams are a must, but not the building-castles-in-the-air type. So, you must have the wisdom of discarding useless and unrealistic dreams as they would lead you only to a fool's paradise. Anybody can wish for riches, and most people do, but only a few know the definite way to become rich. A definite plan coupled with a burning desire to become rich would lead you to the path of glory and success provided you play your cards tactfully.

Using the terminology of chemistry, I would say that success is the ultimate result of a chemical reaction taking place between many chemicals (factors, prerequisites, ideal situation). Out of these chemicals, we have identified till now just one, and that is dreams. Remember, a person with big dreams is more powerful than the one with mere the facts.

Dreams lead to **ideas.** They are at the root of all big fortunes. A small idea which may appear simply useless to begin with, can ultimately turn out to be a goldmine if properly explored. How could Jamshed Ji Tata in 1886 have planned a steel plant based on the iron ore mines of barren lands of Orissa, if it was not due to his dream. And, in case of Dhirubhai Ambani also, it was just an idea which took him from a remote town of Gujarat to the business capital of India, Mumbai, and has made him a proud owner of one of the biggest corporate houses of our country.

Ideas are product of imagination, wild imagination. They rule the world. But, the beautiful ideas are virtue of a beautiful mind. The word 'beautiful' used here is in the context of a happy mind, open mind which has got the ability to think creatively. You should never underestimate the capacity of your mind. It has got unlimited power of creativity which gets exposed under conducive circumstances.

If you visualise a successful venture, then plan it tentatively, weighing its pros and cons. By all means, you should give a

fair trial to this idea in your actual thought process, exploring all the possibilities. No matter, even if you give it up later on. At least, you have tried to embark on something new, something constructive.

Success or failure in any given business depends more on the mental attitude than mental capacity. If you want to become a billionaire, develop the mental attitude of a billionaire. The mental framework of a successful person is imbued with the capacity to look quite far into the future. It is possible that when he would have been planning to capitalise on an idea, others may not have even an inkling of such an idea. Therefore, always try to stay ahead of competition. Those who start early are bound to reach the final mark earlier than late starters.

In the race course, for any given race, few horses run. And, mostly, in a race lasting fifteen to twenty minutes, the difference between the ultimate winner and the runner-up is hardly a second or two. One can say what is the value of one second in 1200 seconds (the actual duration of a race, i.e. 20 minutes). But no, this minutest of difference means a lot, as one is called a winner while the other a loser.

So is the situation in the real life. The difference between a successful person and a mediocre is only a **little bit of extra effort**. This little bit counts a lot. But, most of the people feel shy of trying this extra bit, or sometimes they actually do not know what this extra bit is. Some of you may draw the conclusion that 'extra bit' means more hard work. No, by extra bit I don't mean hard work only but working sharply also.

Have you heard that story of wood cutter? A man with very good physique was given a job in a firewood cutting company. On the first day of his job, he cut a large log into small pieces. But the same man on the last working day of his first week (at the job) was able to cut just one-fourth of his first day's output. The supervisor asked him why he was unable to match his first day's performance. The wood cutter replied, "I have put the same amount of labour and the same amount of interest, still my output remained lower. Why, I don't know?" The supervisor, an experienced man, disclosing the reason, said, "Because you forgot to sharpen your axe."

Another step up the ladder of success is ***"Organise yourself"*** *before you move forward. What does this mean, organise yourself? You might have this question in your mind. To find an answer, just read on. Your day-to-day activities, which may although appear quite insignificant, speak a lot about you. Success is yours when you learn how to do all things well—simple as well as difficult things, because a genius is genius in every field, not only in the field of his/her specialisation.*

In fact, success is not a one-time phenomenon it is a ongoing process. One cannot say suddenly one fine morning, "OK, now I have become successful so I quit today."

The way you utilize your extra time, the time you get after discharging your professional and career responsibilities, often decides the way the society would interpret you. If you indulge in backbiting, talking all nonsense about your colleagues and neighbours, go for useless shopping or partying then be sure that you would be considered just another ordinary woman with bagfuls of money to flaunt. All these activities take a toll on your concentration and energy.

To become successful, it is better if you do not indulge in these silly activities which every other woman is doing in the society. Instead, involve yourself in some creative and purposeful activities, like reading books which can boost your moral, besides giving you knowledge and confidence. You can also learn painting or photography which may not have

a direct bearing on your success but would certainly give you a new vista of information.

Success comes your way when your preparation meets the opportunity. If you can ingrain three essential things in your attitude, your chances of succeeding would certainly increase. These are: *hard work, training* and *self-discipline*. A secret of success is consistency of the purpose. It is often the matter of hanging on longer, when others have quit or given up. If you can come out with better ways of doing a thing, you will see that success is yours. This search is important and has got a direct relationship with your intelligence and creativity.

Stating aptly, the word "genius" has everything to do with your intelligence and creativity. For a person lacking these qualities, using this word is futile. Every one has got the talent (potential) but what is uncommon is the courage, which can lead you to the desired heights. *Success is often the matter of focusing upon important things and making yourself amenable to improvements*. Reaching out to the minutest details of the task ahead, collecting as much information as possible about the job on hand gives you undoubtedly better grip on the matter.

Success comes when you make right decisions, when you learn how to make best use of your time and how to interact with the people in a positive way. **Planning Strategically** may not be a sureshot formula for success, but it does help you cope with unexpected contingencies, unseen pitfalls and their consequences. Otherwise, you may find yourself in a blind alley with no way to come out. Plans should never be considered as iron cast frames or markings on stones which should not change or cannot be changed. In fact they must be changed, upgraded, improved as per the changing needs and new business practices.

If you are leading a team, try to develop a team vision instead of imposing your individual thinking on others. The "action plan flow charts" are important documents for any corporate planning team. Give a casual glance to them, and you know successive steps and conditions required to reach your destination.

Goals setting can be likened to a long car drive, where you need a map, a budget, a direction, a destination and a schedule; and, at the end you need to know that you have arrived. Deciding for your goals can be a really tricky business. Sometimes, this decision alone is accountable for prospects of your success or failure. Your goals should be specific, realistic down to the earth and achievable too.

You can surely change your entire lifestyle by choosing worthwhile goals and then sticking to them tenaciously. For sticking, use the most powerful adhesive, and that is commitment and the burning desire for excellence. Write down your goals in your personal diary, as it is seen that people who set out their goals in writing are more serious than those with unwritten goals. While deciding your goals, don't try to burden yourself with too many of them at one go. Remember, those who begin with too many things often finish with achieving very few of them (and sometimes none of them).

If you take up too many small things also along with your main target then chances are that you will not get near to great successes. For, your interest in too many small things takes away your competency to act swiftly with required concentration in one single direction. By pushing in one direction, you will reach your goal faster.

***"Opportunities**, as a rule, don't knock a door twice. And, most often, they come in a disguised form."* Generally, people blame circumstances for their failures, but seldom themselves. Look for the circumstances you want, if you don't get them, create them. Never be afraid of challenges and problems.

Instead like wise men, take them as opportunities. Unfortunately, only a small percentage of people have such vision to take problems as opportunities.

Three things in your life you can never retrieve—spoken words, lost time and a missed opportunity. Success lies in your ability to grab the opportunity without delay when it comes your way. But here is a catch, if you wait for the good luck to strike then probably opportunities will never come your way. Because, if you wait for the waves to subside, then you will never be able to swim in a sea. In fact, there is nothing like good luck or bad luck. What matters most is your capacity to hard work along with the ability to grab opportunity and make most of it.

You may find persons ready with all sorts of explanations and excuses for not reaching to the top. Actually, the persons who trot out silly excuses know very well in their heart that how incompetent they are. But, somehow, to justify their failure they resort to excuses. Any intelligent person can judge an incompetent person because it is written on his face in bold letters. If you have failed, no problem. Accept it boldly. It is not the end of the world. Get up again, but more alert this time. Nothing valuable can you achieve without efforts.

Satisfaction will be your reward once you reach your goal. It is indeed a great fun at the end when you have achieved your goal, which other people thought impossible to achieve in the beginning. It is one of the greatest pleasures because all the great achievements were also once considered impossible. Try repeatedly if you don't get success in one go.

How do the winners differ from the losers in their mental make-up. *"The winners constantly have in their minds what they can do and what they should do next. On the contrary, losers bog their mind with what they cannot do and what they should not have done."*

Jana Navotana, 1998 wimbeldon woman's singles title holder, said immediately after the match, "Yes, I did not play my best, I was a bit nervous, but I was very determined this time about my commitment to win." (Navotana has won the wimbeldon title in her third attempt.)

If you live in the past then future holds no promise for you. You are a gone case. Look towards our matinee idol Devanand. Despite his failures and setbacks, he has not stopped making films. And, that is what, says he, has kept him going at this ripe age of seventy-five. Even the age has not succeeded in dampening his **enthusiasm** and **interest in his work.** In the words of Devanand, "It is not enough that you aim perfectly, you must hit your target too, if needed repeatedly."

"A quitter never wins and a winner never quits". *Actually, people fail only when they give up, not before that. It is seen that a person with unlimited enthusiasm can get the most wrongs right, which he comes across. What we term as competence is often the right mix of knowledge, skill and courage. It just cannot be taught by anyone. You have to acquire it yourself. All the great achievements are more the result of courage than that of the wisdom. As I have said earlier, courage is uncommon whereas we are endowed with wisdom (skills, talents), though in varying degrees. An idea, even a great one, is of no value if you don't have energy and courage to implement it.'*

Intensity of your desire to reach your goal often decides the speed of your success. It is said, "Life is like a mixture of soap, all froth and bubbles with only two solid things—one, your determination to succeed, and the other, its intensity." Nothing ventured, nothing gained. Determination can also be called as your ability of perseverance. Your skill for solving a problem is of no use if it is not supported by a strong will. *'Nothing in this world can substitute the power of perseverance and determination for a cause, because these two can still*

work when everything else has failed'. Be sure that if you lose them then chances are that you lose every chance of getting near to the success.

Here is a poser for you. How would you explain the success of selected few in the entrance tests for IIT and IIM, two most prestigious institutions of India. What factors play the deciding role when everything else is similar for most of the students? Barring a few who are poorest, most of the students have got easy access to the course material, and best of tutors. Then, what decides the success in these courses? The answer is, firm determination. Those who have it, pass out with flying colours while the rest prepare to try their luck again. You have to condition your mind that this is my target. Whatever may come, I will not deter myself from my goal, I will achieve it hundred per cent. If you have firmly resolved then you will see the sea-change.

With this we come to the last few pages of the book. As always, the most important question before us is, *What is the purpose of life? What do you understand by the ultimate tranquillity, peace of mind, ultimate truth of life? What drives you on?*

You will be known in this world for your achievements and accomplishments. Nothing else counts. But the point is, do you think that lakhs and crores in the bank or in the safe chest in your bedroom is your achievement? Or, do you think the big palatial mansion in which you live is your life-time achievement? Or, the gold, shares, properties which you would be leaving behind for your children to make them comfortable, was the purpose of your life?

Being a modern age typical Indian lady (educated, career woman of a metro city), you might have often felt, after all, what a lady can do, with so many restrictions? "How can she perform at her best," with the tide of current against her?

The answer is she can, provided she is firm in her determination. The woman has already proved that she can do a whole lot of things despite heavy odds pitted against her. She is able to do this because she has got better and larger capacity to adjust to and face the situations. She outshines the man in her capacity to suffer the pain and torture, and yet not deviate from her path and goal. *'Her unique ability to perform most diverse acts simultaneously (like managing her home efficiently and performing excellently at her office) has made her comparatively far more superior than the man'.*

But like her counterpart (man), she is governed by the same basic instincts like greed, anger, jealousy, hatred. And both of them, man and woman, have acquired these instincts in their most naked form from the animals. The society we live in, has tried to evolve certain norms and precedents which were aimed at controlling these animal instincts. All the great scholars in their masterpiece works of literature, and also various religious faiths also try to wean the human race away from these animal instincts. All the education, teachings and elderly guidance are also aimed at modifying these instincts.

But how much have all these efforts succeeded? Have we succeeded in containing our greeds and unchecked desires for wealth? Can we control our hatred against each other? No, we have not changed a bit since the evolution of human race. Otherwise, why all this corruption, killing, rapes, kidnapping? It means still we have powerful animal instincts in us which at times or most of the time, overpower the humane side of our psyche.

I firmly believe, whether man or woman, everyone of us is born as animals and slowly as we age, we have to evolve ourselves as human beings. But unfortunately, most of us remain for most part of our life as animals till our death. We don't change simply because we don't want to. This change involves the evolution, which is a painful procedure. For that

matter, every change is unwelcome. And, here this change calls for discipline of thought, action and behaviour.

Often we do the facesaving act. That is, in front of others we pose as if we are most humane, generous, kind and helping type, but deep in our heart we are the same old animals. This has placed us in a peculiar situation of double standards, like two sets of teeth of elephant, one for showing the people, other the real one for eating.

This double standard is at the root of all our troubles and tensions. High education, all-round progress of civilisation and materialistic gains—all these have not helped man throw away animal instincts. Until and unless you free your heart from the burden of hypocrisy of double standards, you would never be able to feel the real happiness and peace of mind.

Develop the attitude of easy-going person, who is out in this world to enjoy herself, to enjoy her being, to enjoy the gift of God— 'the womanhood' and ecstasy of nature. But all this is possible only when we succeed in shedding our greeds and other negative animal instincts.

Your all achievements, even small ones, will give you immense pleasure. You will be able to enjoy the fruits of success much more deeply if you start believing that all that matters in life is within your reach and access. Forget about heaven and hell. You can have your heaven, you build it right here on the earth the moment you develop enthusiasm, love and interest in life as a whole.

'Shape your life away from lies, hatred, jealousy but close to love, care and concern for all. And, you would feel the new rays of peace and contentment which would double your joy of success and achievements. Enjoy the present with an eye on the future. The life is an enjoyment, enjoy it. It is a mystery, enjoy this mystery. Love yourself, love the life, love the nature, love the God. And, that is the ultimate truth of life'.